The Jewish God Question

The Jewish God Question

What Jewish Thinkers Have Said about God, the Book, the People, and the Land

Andrew Pessin

Rowman & Littlefield
Lanham • Boulder • New York • London

Published by Rowman & Littlefield
An imprint of The Rowman & Littlefield Publishing Group, Inc.
4501 Forbes Boulevard, Suite 200, Lanham, Maryland 20706
www.rowman.com

Unit A, Whitacre Mews, 26-34 Stannary Street, London SE11 4AB, United Kingdom

British Library Cataloguing in Publication Information Available

Library of Congress Cataloging-in-Publication Data
Names: Pessin, Andrew, 1962– author.
Title: The Jewish God question : what Jewish thinkers have said about God, the Book, the People, and the Land / Andrew Pessin.
Description: Lanham, Maryland : Rowman & Littlefield, [2018] | Includes bibliographical references and index.
Identifiers: LCCN 2018012999 (print) | LCCN 2018013071 (ebook) | ISBN 9781538110997 (ebook) | ISBN 9781538110980 (hardcover : alk. paper)
Subjects: LCSH: Jewish philosophy—History. | God—Judaism—Philosophy. | Bible. Old Testament—Philosophy. | Judaism—Philosophy.
Classification: LCC B755 (ebook) | LCC B755 .P47 2018 (print) | DDC 296.3/11—dc23
LC record available at https://lccn.loc.gov/2018012999

∞™ The paper used in this publication meets the minimum requirements of American National Standard for Information Sciences—Permanence of Paper for Printed Library Materials, ANSI/NISO Z39.48-1992.

Printed in the United States of America

Contents

CONTENTS

PART II: MAIMONIDES–SFORNO (1138–c. 1550)

CONTENTS

CONTENTS

CONTENTS

CONTENTS

Introduction

Consider the many meanings of the word "Israel."

It starts as the name of a person. The biblical patriarch Jacob is given this new name after a night spent wrestling with an angel sent from God (Genesis 32:29). Jacob's sons and daughter subsequently become the "children of Israel," then multiply into the "tribes of Israel," who, collectively, as a people, are often simply called "Israel." The land (1) in which they first arose as a people, (2) which the Bible apportions between the tribes, (3) where they first obtained political sovereignty three millennia ago, and (4) where they primarily dwelled for the next millennium is called the "Land of Israel"—that is, the land of the people Israel, or simply "Israel." And of course the modern state founded in 1948 took as its official name the "State of Israel"—again, the state of the people Israel, or simply "Israel" for short.

And what does the word "Israel" mean in the first place? The Hebrew Bible tells us, "Your name shall no longer be Jacob, but Israel, for you have striven with beings divine" (Genesis 32:29). In Hebrew, in other words, the name essentially means "one who struggles with, contends with, prevails over the divine."

So, "Israel" refers to a person, a people, a land, and a state—and to struggling with (and maybe even prevailing over?) God, the way that Judaism, the religion of Israel, long has.

Welcome to the *Jewish* God Question.

Or, more accurately, the Jewish God Question*s*, for there are many that fall under this heading.

As long as there have been Jews, there have been Jewish thinkers—and they have been thinking about the many things referred to as "Israel" and all their connections. Who are the biblical patriarchs and matriarchs, and what is the precise nature of the people, the land? Who or what is God, and can His existence be proven? What is His relationship to the progenitors, the people, the land? What does God demand of the people, the Jews, and why? Why were they expelled from the land with the destruction of the Second Temple (70 CE)? Why have they been kept in exile, in dispersion, for so many long centuries? How should they relate to the broader communities in which they live? Does God still demand of them today what He demanded of them back on Mount Sinai, even in their condition of exile? And why *them*, of all people?

Starting in the seventeenth century, as the modern era arrives, the Jewish God Question, with all its many components, takes on new and sharper forms reflecting the surrounding Western cultures. What role should religion play in public life in general, if any? Should religion be discarded in favor of a life of reason, of enlightenment? Is it feasible to believe in God in the modern world? Can a Jew even fit into the broader society in which he or she has lived, and remain a *Jew*? Can (or should) one separate the Jewish person from the Jewish religion? Can (or should) one separate the Jewish people from the Land of Israel? Should Jews simply disappear as a collective body—convert, intermarry, assimilate, vanish? Or should they return to their ancient homeland and reestablish their long-lost political sovereignty? What does the Jewish religion say about all this? Or should we not even pay attention to it?

If one thing is clear, as suggested by all these questions, it is this: Jews have been *continuously* struggling with God, and everything that that struggle entails, ever since that fateful encounter between Jacob and the angel.

This book will introduce you to some of the things Jewish thinkers have said about these matters, and more. The goal is not to be comprehensive, because that is not possible. It is, rather, to sample some of the more interesting, counterintuitive, provocative things famous thinkers have had to say, as well as to introduce you to some thinkers you probably haven't heard of. You'll also notice that there is plenty of disagreement among the thinkers here. There's the famous expression, "Ask two Jews, get three opinions." This phenomenon is perhaps grounded in the great tradition of disagreement and debate represented by the ancient Talmud, which remains a central object of study for Orthodox (and many non-Orthodox) Jews to this day. This vast document records for posterity disputes on matters large and small, recognizing that where truth is the goal, "These and those are [both] the words of the living God" (Talmud Tractate *Eruvin* 13b). Truth can be difficult to discern, in other words, and all sides sincerely seeking it have something to contribute. No one ever said that "struggling with God" should be easy or straightforward.

The phenomenon is also grounded in another fact: The Jews are often divided among and against themselves. Jacob's sons did not always get along very well—they sold Joseph into slavery, remember—and the tribes that descended from them followed suit. The pattern continued through their long millennium dwelling in the Land of Israel, and then through the centuries of dispersion and exile. It only grew more intense in the modern era, when the possibility of seriously transforming, and even leaving, the Jewish religion became a live one; and all the more so with the rise of political Zionism, which really forced on many Jews the problem of deciding just who or what they and their Jewishness were and should be. The divisiveness remains in full force today, both inside and outside the State of Israel, as Jews within and without struggle not only with God, but also among themselves with respect to who or what they, and their collective, is and should be.

Ask two Jews any question and you'll get at least three opinions. In this book we ask seventy-two Jewish thinkers about the Jewish God Question and we get more opinions than we can easily count.

PART I

PHILO–IBN DAUD
c. 20 BCE–1180 CE

Introduction to Part I

We do *not* begin at the beginning.

We begin with Philo, who lived from about 20 BCE until about 50 CE. The Jewish people have a long, rich history that precedes him, of course: several millennia long according to the Bible, and at least one millennium long according to contemporary scholars, who date the reign of King David from about 1000 BCE. But much of the Jews' intellectual activity through the sixteen or so centuries after David was devoted to constructing the main texts of the Jewish religion: the Torah, the Bible, the Talmud, the *midrash*, and so forth. These texts are rich with ideas and insights, inferences and implications, legal and conceptual matters and disputes, but they are mostly not what we today might call philosophy: systematic reflection and argument by individual thinkers on or about fundamental philosophical questions. Although no sharp line can be drawn between "philosophy" and material found in these other texts, we begin with Philo because he is widely construed as the first major Jewish thinker explicitly influenced by classical Greek philosophy to begin grappling with the Jewish God Question (or questions).

In fact for Philo the major question is precisely how to reconcile various teachings from the Jewish scriptures *with* the principles of Greek philosophy. This question subsequently becomes a major theme of Jewish thinking from Philo all the way to the modern period, which starts with Spinoza (1632–77).

We'll see how this question plays out throughout part I. Here we see the initial exploration of whether God's existence can be proved philosophically. With that comes the question of what can be said about God's nature or attributes. The Hebrew Bible suggests many such attributes, but also proclaims God's "unity." Is that a contradiction? We see the first treatments of the question of creation, of whether God created the cosmos in a single first moment (as the Hebrew Bible suggests) or whether the cosmos has existed eternally (as philosophy seems to suggest). There are efforts to fit scriptural teachings about God, the cosmos, and humankind into the metaphysical categories of Greek philosophy (such as "form" and "matter"). There is reflection on the relationship between God and Israel (both the people and the Land), articulation of the special connection the people of Israel have to the Land of Israel, and of the controversial idea of "the chosen people." And there is also pushback against the whole project of thinking philosophically about God, with complaints that the philosophers' God (who is perfect, eternal, unchanging, etc.) bears no resemblance to the personal God of scripture.

We do not begin with the beginning—but this *is* the beginning of the very long conversation about the Jewish God Question.

1

Philo (c. 20 BCE–c. 50 CE)

On Beginning with "The Beginning"

On the Law, creation, and the cosmos

In the beginning God created the heaven and the earth . . . (Genesis 1:1)

Why, Philo wonders, does the Hebrew Bible begin "In the beginning," with the creation of the cosmos? So much of the book is about the Law, about the ethical and ritual practices that govern the observant Jew, so why not begin with (say) the famous giving of the Law on Mount Sinai (Exodus 19–20)?

The answer: because it is necessary to prepare the minds of those who are to live under the Law to receive the Law—and to be receptive, one must understand that the cosmos is in perfect harmony with the Law and the Law with the cosmos. The person who observes the religious laws thereby regulates his or her behavior by the same nature in accordance with which the cosmos as a whole is governed.

There are of course some who admire the cosmos so much that they hold it to be eternal, without beginning or end, and thus needing no maker. For them the cosmos itself seems an object worthy of worship. But Moses, divine prophet and author of the Hebrew Bible, had himself attained the summit of philosophy and therefore knew better. The active cause of the cosmos is a pure and unsullied mind that, operating on the passive part of the cosmos (itself incapable of life and motion), transformed it into the ever-changing world of the senses with which we are familiar.

The cosmos as we know it, in other words, required a maker.

Indeed you don't need the Bible to tell you this, for the cosmos itself demonstrates it. Our experience teaches us that any piece of work, any craft, involves the knowledge and skill of the craftsman. Who can look at a statue or painting without thinking at once of the sculptor or painter? When you enter a well-ordered city, what else would you infer but that the city is directed by good rulers? But then when you come to the great city that is this world, and you behold landscapes teeming with animals and plants, spring-fed rivers streaming into the sea, the yearly seasons yielding to one another in sequence, the sun and the moon ruling the day and night and the other heavenly bodies revolving in rhythmic order—can you avoid concluding that there exists a maker of all this? None of the works of human art is capable of making itself, but the work of the cosmos is far greater in scope and perfection; it too must have been brought into being by a comparably greater maker.

The many miracles in the Bible are important, but you do not need miracles to believe in God. What is really great and deserving of serious attention is the cosmos as a whole in its regular operations.

Though the whole cosmos indicates God's existence, a special role is played by the illuminated heavenly bodies. The Bible tells us these were created, on the fourth day, to separate day from night and to help us mark the time, the hours, the days, the years. But they serve another function beyond the merely practical one. You begin by admiring their visual beauty. Then you feel increased curiosity about what these entities are, and how they move, and what are the causes by which they are regulated. You then begin contemplating their origin. . . .

What begins in sensory experience, in observations of the heavens, leads you to . . . philosophy.

Related Chapters

2 Philo, 13 Ibn Ezra

2

Philo (c. 20 BCE–c. 50 CE)

The People of the Book, and the Book of (All) the People

The Torah expresses a universal philosophy for everyone

The Torah may have been given to the ancient Jews, Philo thinks, but it is literally for everyone—as it expresses universal life lessons transmitted via Moses, the consummate philosopher.

On the one hand there is the text, of course, which, understood literally, tells the story of the ancient Jews and conveys the many ethical and ritual laws that are to govern them. But at the same time the text is a sophisticated allegory that calls on *everyone* to lead the life of virtue that it describes.

Take Genesis 2:1, for example: "Thus the heaven and earth were completed." This brief statement of cosmology is also a statement about human nature. Speaking symbolically, Moses calls the mind "heaven" because the heavens can only be comprehended *by* our mind, our intellect, which grasps the nature of hidden, abstract, and nonphysical things; he calls sensations "earth" because the earthly realm, the world around us, is accessed by the senses, which grasp the physical. Thus we learn that the human being is a two-part entity, composed of both mind and body—a crucial insight for determining the sort of life we should lead.

Similar points are taught throughout Genesis. God formed man by breathing the soul of life—a spirit, a mind—into the physical body (2:7). We are made in the image of God (1:27) only insofar as we have minds, for God is surely nonphysical. The Garden of Eden symbolizes a model life, where the rivers surrounding Eden (2:10) represent specific virtues and life as a whole is one in which all parts of the soul are in harmony. In particular, the better part of the human being—the intellect, the mind—must dominate those parts grounded in the physical body, devoted to passions and desires. For what life can be better, ultimately, than that devoted to reflection and speculation, which elevates us from the beasts driven by their bodies' passions and desires?

Such a life isn't merely a good life. It is the *ultimate* human life. It is one in which our nonphysical mind approaches or makes contact with the divine mind that is its source and maker. It is a kind of divine ascent—which, when successful, may permit individuals direct experience of the divine voice.

We may now understand the story of Abraham, the patriarch of the Jews and founder of the Jewish religion. God says to Abraham, "Go for yourself from your land, and from your relatives, and from your father's house to the land that I will show you" (Genesis 12:1). Land, relatives, and one's father house symbolize the physical world that we all must separate ourselves from. We must no longer be so focused on our body and its needs, sensations, desires.

Indeed, the story of the ancient Jews is really the story of all individuals. The very name "Hebrew"—*ivrit*, one who passes over—indicates that the Jew is that person who separates himself from the physical world and ascends to the world of the intellect, the divine. The famous exodus from Egypt represents the emancipation all human beings must undertake to free ourselves from our enslavement to our bodies.

In time, then, all the peoples of the world will come around to obeying the laws first bequeathed to the ancient Jews, because the call to that life of virtue is a call to everyone—and because everyone who heeds that call is, in effect, a Jew.

Related Chapters

1 Philo, 4 Saadia Ben Joseph Gaon, 7 Ibn Paquda, 13 Ibn Ezra, 14 Ibn Daud, 15 Ibn Daud, 17 Maimonides, 24 Albalag, 27 Ibn Kaspi, 28 Gersonides, 30 Ben Elijah, 39 Del Medigo, 57 Salanter, 64 Cohen, 74 Levinas, 79 Leibowitz

3

Saadia Ben Joseph Gaon (882–942)

What a Long Strange Trip It *Hasn't* Been

The cosmos must have had a first moment of creation

Where exactly did this whole cosmos come from? Has it just always been here, forever, or was it created at some point in time, from absolutely nothing? No amount of sensory observation could determine an answer, Saadia Ben Joseph Gaon argues, since observation supports neither option: we never witness anything created from literally nothing, and we obviously cannot have observed anything having existed forever. Scripture of course suggests that God created the cosmos from nothing. But can reasoning, too, confirm this assertion?

Think about the nature of time. Those who believe that the cosmos always has been, and was not created, believe that it had no starting point: as far back in time as you can imagine the cosmos was there, and then even further back still. They believe, in other words, that the past stretches on infinitely behind us.

But now consider this: It is clearly impossible ever to complete an infinite journey. If you were to start traveling right now, no matter when you checked how far you had come it would always be just a finite distance. You can never arrive at infinity, which literally *means* "without end." The same is also true of a journey through time. No matter how long you have traveled, it's always a finite amount of time that will have elapsed from your starting time. Yet those who maintain that the cosmos has no beginning in time believe that the past stretches on infinitely behind us.

They therefore believe that we *have* traversed an infinite amount of time in order to reach the present moment.

But it is precisely that which is impossible! The cosmos must therefore have had some first moment, some finite amount of time ago. In short, it must have been created.

But now we must determine the cause of this creation. Could the cosmos create itself or was it created by something external to it?

Here again the nature of time provides an answer. Any act of creating must occur at some particular time, as must the event of something coming into being. So the act of creating must occur either before, after, or at the same instant as the coming into being. Could the cosmos have created itself before it came into being? Nonsense: before it came into being it wasn't there to do anything! Could it have created itself *after* it came into being? Nonsense: if it already existed, it didn't need to create itself. Could it have created itself in the very instant at which it came into being? Nonsense: an "instant" is just a point of time that has absolutely no duration. But no action can occur within a single instant, since actions always require some interval of time. So the act of creating could not take place within any instant.

The cosmos could not have created itself, therefore, and so must have had an external creator.

And finally this creation must have been "from nothing." For if it weren't, then something would have existed prior to the cosmos from which the cosmos was made. But whatever exists just *is* part of the cosmos, so that's equivalent to saying that the cosmos existed before itself, which is absurd.

It follows, then, that the cosmos has not always existed but was instead created, from nothing, by some creator distinct from the cosmos—exactly as scripture informs us.

Reason and faith happily converge.

Related Chapters

4 Saadia Ben Joseph Gaon, 7 Ibn Paquda, 9 Ibn Tzaddik, 14 Ibn Daud, 33 Crescas, 38 Abravanel, 49 Steinheim

4

Saadia Ben Joseph Gaon (882–942)

Two Ways of Being One

There is just one God, who is "one," all the way through

Scripture says much—maybe too much—from a philosopher's point of view, since many passages seem to contradict either each other or the dictates of reason. But of course scripture can never *really* conflict with reason, according to Saadia Ben Joseph Gaon, so when this occurs, something has to give. In his view, it's the strictly literal sense of the text.

To take one example, the Bible sometimes suggests that there is more than one supreme being (speaking sometimes of *Adonai* and other times of *Elohim*) and sometimes asserts that there is but one God. Reasoning teaches us the latter and so, therefore, the former passages must not be taken literally. But why, then, does the Bible speak that way? Because using different names suggests not literally that there are different gods, but instead indicates figuratively that the single divinity has multiple distinct properties or *attributes*. When God is being merciful (for example), the text uses one name; when He is displaying His divine justice, it uses another.

Fine, except now another problem arises. So scripture suggests that God has many attributes. He is merciful and just. From the fact that He created all things He obviously has great *power*; and indeed only a being who is *alive* could exercise such power, and only one who has *wisdom* could do so in the impressive manner reflected by the cosmos. Scripture also speaks of God and His *Spirit*, His *voice*, His *emotions*, and so on. Yet at the same time other passages affirm the utter, simple unity of God—that God has no parts or components or divisions within Him. But now how could a simple, undivided, unified being possess at the same time many distinct attributes?

Once again, the literal sense of some of these passages must yield. God is indeed a simple, undivided unity. But our conceptual and linguistic limits require us to use multiple words to describe Him. Consider God's "power," and "wisdom," and being "alive." That God is creator itself instantaneously includes the facts that He is powerful and wise and alive; in God these are all just one thing. But we can only reason these attributes out sequentially, over time, as illustrated in the previous paragraph, giving us the *illusion* of their distinctness. Moreover, our language lacks any single word to capture those distinct aspects so we use three words instead. As a result we can't help but think of as three distinct attributes what, in God, are all the same thing. If taken strictly literally, these words in scripture would wrongly lead us to treat as many what are, in fact, one.

Some philosophers actually *embrace* a multiplicity in God: they insist that distinctions within God make Him a trinity rather than a unity. But this view is based on a false comparison between God and human beings. We can distinguish a human being's life from his essence because we sometimes see people alive and other times not alive; we can distinguish a person's knowledge from his essence because his knowledge can change while he remains the same person. But God is not like this; God does not change, He does not take on or lose features over time. Consequently we cannot distinguish *any* of His attributes from His essence. There is not God *plus* His being alive plus His being wise; there is no multiplicity. There is just God, who is a perfect unity, a oneness, all the way through.

In short there is just the one God—who *is* One.

Related Chapters

3 Saadia Ben Joseph Gaon, 7 Ibn Paquda, 17 Maimonides, 39 Del Medigo, 87 Lebens

5

Isaac Israeli (c. 855–955)

The Descent, and Ascent, of Man

Cosmology and psychology
illuminate the way to eternal bliss

"Philosophy" means "love of wisdom." But it may also be described, according to Isaac Israeli, as the "assimilation to the Works of the Creator" and as a human being's "knowledge of himself." To see how these are all equivalent, consider the basic metaphysical structure of the cosmos.

To start, there is a hierarchy of being, of existing things. At the top is the eternal, unchanging, unique One, God. From this One descends the cosmos, in all its diversity, itself a hierarchy of beings. These include the human soul—whose ultimate goal is to return to the source of all souls, whence it came.

Some philosophers hold that the cosmos is uncreated and eternal, having always existed. Others hold that God created the cosmos out of necessity, meaning that God's very nature is such that the cosmos emanates automatically from His being. But the Hebrew Bible teaches that both are wrong, that God created the cosmos at some point in time and from a free act of will.

What God creates with His will, from nothing, is First Matter and First Form, which combine to produce Intellect. Intellect we may understand as the purely nonphysical set or source of all the different kinds of beings that are possible, as the *ideas* of all possible things, as it were. From Intellect then instantly emanates, in that necessary way described above, a series of purely spiritual substances or souls: the rational soul is the capacity for thought, the animal soul is the capacity for motion, and the vegetative soul is the capacity for mere growth. Below these is the sphere of the heavens, which, even further removed from the original spiritual light, now contains a physical aspect. Call this "nature," for it is from the motion of the heavens, ultimately, that the four basic elements (fire, air, water, and earth) are produced. It is then from these that all the objects of the world around us are produced, generate, grow, decay, and dissipate—including our own physical bodies.

So God produces by an act of will the purely spiritual Intellect, which instantly emanates the spiritual world down to nature, which subsequently produces the ever-changing physical world around us.

What, then, is a human being?

The human being has both a body and a soul, the latter divided into the rational, the animal, and the vegetative as above. When we allow our rational soul to govern us, when we steer away from animal dispositions (such as eating, drinking, sexual pursuits), when we instead incline toward ethical behavior—toward worship, purity, and sanctity; toward wisdom and understanding—then we make our rational soul more noble; we elevate it. Such pursuits raise our soul up to and beyond the sphere of the heavens, to make contact with the divine Intellect. Our soul, not being physical, is immortal at any rate, but its eternal fate depends on our behaviors when our soul is affiliated with our body. The soul purified through intellectual pursuits passes above the sphere and remains in the blissful presence of the souls above; the soul weighed down by sinful pursuits cannot penetrate the sphere and remains burning in the fires beneath it.

"Love of wisdom," then, manifests itself in knowing ourselves, the nature of our soul, and the nature of the cosmos—so that we may by our intellectual pursuits elevate our soul to "assimilate to the Works of the Creator," and so make contact with the divine Intellect for an eternity of bliss.

Related Chapters

6 Ibn Gabirol, 8 Bar Chiyya, 21 Ben Samuel, 23 Abulafia, 36 Alemanno, 40 Ebreo, 41 Almosnino, 43 Spinoza

6

Solomon Ibn Gabirol (1021–58)

On the Matter of the Soul

All objects, physical or spiritual, are a combination of matter and form, and that is the secret to blessedness

According to the "wisdom poetry" of Ibn Gabirol, the goal of human life is to transcend our temporary bodily existence and to purify our soul from the pollution of the physical world. To do this requires dedicating our life to the pursuit of knowledge, to knowledge of the divine being in particular, insofar as that is possible. And to do *that* we must seek knowledge of the divine will that extends through all creation. In other words, acquiring the right knowledge of the cosmos is a key step toward ultimately escaping the confines of our physical bodies.

Now, many thinkers follow Aristotle in analyzing the cosmos in terms of "matter and form." They understand physical objects to be some combination of matter and form—in the way that we can distinguish, in a statue of a man, for example, the shape (or form) of the statue from the marble of which it is composed—but hold that spiritual beings, such as angels or souls, are purely "forms" without any matter.

But this latter point is incorrect. In fact a kind of "universal matter" underlies *all* beings, whether they are physical or spiritual, so all beings are composed of both form and matter. Since the same matter underlies both physical and nonphysical beings, that matter itself must be neither physical nor nonphysical. We might say that it is "intelligible," able to be understood, to be grasped by our intellects, rather than physical or nonphysical.

The next key point is that this universal matter emanates from God. As matter emanates from God it creates a hierarchy of beings. At the top of course is God Himself, the divine essence. "Nearest" to Him are the spiritual beings of the celestial world, and furthest from Him are the physical beings of the cosmos. In the middle, between these extremes, are spiritual substances: Intelligence, Soul, and Nature understood as a general principle.

The human being, as a microcosm of the macrocosm, partakes of both the physical and spiritual worlds. Our physical bodies are governed by the same laws as the rest of the physical cosmos, but we are also possessed of souls that organize our body's functions, including growth, perception, and intellectual thought. The latter allows us to conceive, contain, and reflect on all the possible forms of existence. It is in doing this—in raising our intellect to contemplation of all possible intelligible substances, of universal matter and the various forms—that we come as close as possible to grasping the divine will, and thus approach or unite with God.

This, of course, should be the goal of our life in this world.

But to obtain it we must work through our physical bodies. Indeed, our two-fold nature is also reflected in the close relationship between our physical senses and our moral makeup. Of some twenty key moral traits, each is closely correlated to one of the five senses. The noblest of senses, the sense of sight, for example, is associated with moral qualities such as pride, meekness, modesty, and impudence. Associated with the sense of hearing are hate, love, mercy, and cruelty, and so on. Although the details require elaboration, the point is that if we are to attain the highest state of our soul, our state of blessedness, we must obtain knowledge as described above; but in order to do *that* we must also aim for moral perfection—which in turn requires developing the right relationship to our physical bodies, in which moral perfection is based.

Related Chapters

5 Israeli, 7 Ibn Paquda, 21 Ben Samuel, 23 Abulafia, 36 Alemanno, 40 Ebreo, 42 Sforno, 43 Spinoza, 57 Salanter

7

Bachya Ibn Paquda (c. 1050–1120)

Do the Right Thing—for the Right Reasons

*Duties of the limb are imperfect unless
accompanied by duties of the heart*

The prophet Isaiah lamented that people can be diligent in their religious observance (performing rituals, observing the Sabbath, praying) while their hands are yet "full of blood" (Isaiah 1:11ff.). For Ibn Paquda, such a scriptural text proves that external, visible, "duties of the limbs" cannot be properly performed without observance of the even more important inner, invisible "duties of the heart." You must develop genuine sincerity and devotion in your religious actions.

But doing this requires intellectual activity, for there can be no relationship to God without the appropriate knowledge of God.

The most essential knowledge is of the existence and unity of God. But since God cannot be directly understood by us, we come to our knowledge of Him indirectly, by examining His creation. Thus we may demonstrate God's existence by proving (for example) that the world had a creator. Nor could there have been more than one creator, for one would have had to create the other. Moreover, causes are always fewer than effects. However many individuals there are, there are always fewer species or kinds of them; and ultimately all existing things are reduced to two entities, matter and form, which in turn must have been produced by one entity, God.

That God Himself is a unity is clear. The cosmos shows an impressive unity of order, for example, with everything connected to everything in uniform ways, which suggests a single unifying principle. Moreover,

16

plurality always presupposes unity. If God Himself were composed of multiple parts there would be simpler elements out of which He is composed, in which case something other than God must have arranged those elements together to create God. But that is absurd.

Nor is the fundamental unity of God threatened by the fact that we conceive Him to have many different properties or attributes. To see this, let us distinguish "essential" attributes from "active" ones. "Essential attributes" are those God possesses eternally and unchangingly, such as existence, unity, and eternity. But in God, these are really all the same: God just *is* an eternally existing unity. We may conceive of them differently, but then we are merely applying three different ideas to the one unified single thing that God is. In fact these terms don't really pick out distinct properties in God, but rather amount to denying their opposites: in applying them to God we are merely saying that God is not nonexistent, not a multiplicity, and not finite in time. There may be one thing God is while there are many things He is not.

The "active" attributes are those we ascribe with reference to God's works in creation, which suggest (as scripture often does) that God has a physical form and performs physical behaviors (the "hand" or "mouth" of God, God "smote," etc.). But these modes of speech are only designed to make the concept of God a little more accessible to the many people who struggle to grasp His metaphysical nature. They allow people to acquire some knowledge of God, even if imperfect, but in fact are not genuine attributes of God. Thus they introduce no multiplicity.

With these beliefs in place, we may devote ourselves to the spiritual life, committed not merely to observing the precepts but also to developing the right intentions in observing them. We aim to serve God not for fame or repute, not for personal gain, but for the sake of God Himself—in order to align our will with God's.

Duties of the limb are imperfect unless accompanied by the duties of the heart.

Related Chapters

8

Abraham Bar Chiyya (1065–1136)

And God Did *Not* Say, "Let There Be Man"

Both scripture and philosophical reasoning demonstrate the immortality of the soul

According to Bar Chiyya, careful study of the cosmos, as well as of scripture, both demonstrate not only that "the Lord is God in the heavens above, and upon the earth beneath: there is none else" (Deuteronomy 4:39), but also that the human soul is capable of immortality.

Following Aristotle we understand that all created things may be analyzed in terms of matter and form. But there exist at least three kinds of forms.

The first is pure, self-subsistent form, a kind of form that can exist independently of matter and indeed never combines with matter. This includes all the forms of the spiritual world: the angels, seraphim, souls, and so forth. Since these do not unite with matter, they can never be perceived by human eyes, for visibility requires matter.

The second kind of form does unite with matter, and does so firmly and inseparably. These are the forms of the heavenly bodies and stars. Since bodily change only occurs when some matter loses its form and acquires a different form, these heavenly bodies, whose forms are inseparable from their matter, can and do never change.

The third kind of form also unites with matter, but does so only in temporary fashion. These are the forms of the bodies on earth. These bodies are always changing, existing for a while before changing and degenerating. When a body finally decays and goes out of existence, its form does as well.

So the first kind of form cannot exist with body, while the second and third kinds of forms cannot exist without bodies. For the sake of a complete system now, reason teaches us that there must be a fourth kind of form—namely, one that can exist either with *or* without the body: a form that temporarily unites with the body but then returns to its original condition when the body goes out of existence. The only form worthy of such a description, of course, is the human soul—which must, therefore, be immortal, in that it can survive the death of the body.

These philosophical considerations are also supported by scripture.

The beginning of Genesis (for example) varies its expressions for God's acts of creation. Sometimes it says, "Let there be *x*," followed by, "And there was *x*," while other times it says only one or neither. Where "let there be" is used, the object created exists permanently and without change in this world. If it is also followed with "and there was" then the object, such as eternal light, will continue its existence even into the next world. In cases where "let there be" is followed instead by "and it was so," the object, such as the heavenly bodies, will exist permanently in this world but *not* continue into the next world. When neither expression is used but we merely read (for example), "Let the waters be gathered" (1:9) or "Let the earth produce grass" (1:11), then these are things that change their forms and have permanent existence neither in this world nor in the next.

What about human beings?

We do not find "let there be," so man has no permanence in this world. But we do find, "And the man was a living soul" (Genesis 2:9), so he shall have a permanent existence in the next world. The definite article "the" indicates that not every person lives forever in the next world, but only the good person.

Thus scripture and philosophical reasoning converge: the human being is capable of having an immortal soul.

Related Chapters

5 Israeli, 6 Ibn Gabirol, 21 Ben Samuel, 32 Crescas

9

Joseph Ibn Tzaddik (?–1149)

In the Beginning *Was* the Beginning—of Time

How to reconcile the eternal unchanging nature of God's will with His creating the cosmos

Human beings have a rational soul, Ibn Tzaddik observes, whose obvious function is to acquire knowledge. But while the rational soul is ultimately destined for the spiritual world, it finds itself for now very much in the physical world, embodied. To achieve its ultimate spiritual destination, via the acquisition of knowledge, it must work through this physical obstacle. Thus you must suppress the animal desires grounded in your physical body and, using reason as your guide, acquire knowledge first of the physical world, then, from self-reflection, of the nonphysical world, the spiritual world, and finally, of God.

But acquiring knowledge of God requires rejecting many false beliefs people have about the Creator. God is not some form of physical body, for example. But even those who understand that God is purely spiritual make various errors. Some (for example) argue that God, who is eternal, is not possessed of a will that is itself eternal, for they worry that an eternal will would be a second eternal thing distinct from God. Instead they argue that whenever God wills for something to occur, He *creates* a will at that moment for the specific purpose in mind.

But this claim is absurd.

If God cannot create something without first creating a will through which to create the thing, then how does He create that will? Either (1) by means of creating another will, or (2) simply and directly. If (1), then we must ask how He creates that *other* will. Does that require the creation of yet another will, and so on, to infinity? But if (2), if God can create something simply and directly, then why not just create the desired object in that way, without invoking some separately created will as an intermediary?

Moreover, these thinkers, in imagining God to create a will at a certain time after a period of not having that will, are introducing change into God—which cannot be, in a perfect, eternal spiritual being.

In fact there is a deep dilemma here. If God's will *is* eternal and unchanging, and He created the cosmos with His will, then the cosmos itself must be eternal, having existed forever, going back infinitely in time—which we reject, as both scripture and reason teach us. But if we say that He created the cosmos after some period of *not* creating, we seem to introduce a change in Him—which we also reject.

The solution?

We maintain the eternality of God's essence, including His will, but deny the consequence that the cosmos has existed infinitely back into time.

For time itself is something created. Time, after all, is the measure of motion, as we measure a day by the sun appearing in the same spot in the sky, or a year by the celestial bodies having the same positions in the nighttime sky. Without bodies existing and moving, time is undefined and simply does not exist. As both scripture and reason teach, there was a first moment of creation of the cosmos, at which moment, time itself began. But then, by definition, there was no time prior to that first moment.

If there was no time prior to creation, then there was no prior period of "not creating."

Thus God did not change from a state of not-willing to willing. And while His will remains eternal and unchanging, we need not say the cosmos has existed infinitely back in time—for the amount of time stretching back to that first moment of creation is perfectly finite.

Related Chapters

3 Saadia Ben Joseph Gaon, 7 Ibn Paquda, 14 Ibn Daud, 33 Crescas, 38 Abravanel, 49 Steinheim

10

Judah Halevi (c. 1075–1141)

The Philosopher's God

The God who does not hear or care is not the God of the Hebrew Bible

Although philosophy has important merits, the purely philosophical approach to religious matters is deeply inadequate, according to Halevi—for reason cannot compete with revelation and historical testimony when it comes to grasping the nature of God.

Consider, first, God as the philosopher conceives Him.

The philosopher's God, in being perfect, desires and needs nothing. In being perfect He is eternally unchanging, so He cannot initiate actions or intervene in the cosmos; in fact the cosmos itself must have existed eternally lest God Himself "change" upon willing to create it. In being unchanging, God must also be ignorant of what is going on in the world, for the world, including us and our individual lives, is always changing. This God is distant, remote, does not hear our prayers, does not respond, is not concerned. He merely exists eternally in self-contemplation, "emanating" the cosmos in a necessary manner in the way that the sun emanates light: impersonally, unintentionally, uncaringly. The philosopher's aim in life is, accordingly, only to seek philosophical knowledge of this being, believing that in so doing his individual mind in some way unites with God's mind. The philosopher thus has neither need of nor interest in religion, filled as it is with ceremonies, rituals, practices—and community.

To the contrary, *we* believe in God not on the basis of abstract reasoning but on the basis of direct experience and testimony; and the God we believe in is the God of the Hebrew Bible, a personal God, one who observes, hears, and cares, who expresses desires and who intervenes, with respect to whom we seek not merely knowledge but a *relationship*—and who did indeed initiate a particular relationship with a particular person and his descendants at a particular time.

In fact, strictly philosophical considerations, based only on general reasoning about the cosmos, cannot even meaningfully distinguish between the different religions: no cosmological reasons support choosing any religion over any other. But even a little casual reasoning shows that not all religions are created equal.

Christianity and Islam, for example, both affirm the truth of the Jews' Hebrew Bible, the Torah, even while claiming to supersede it in different ways. So if you are choosing which religion to believe you must begin with the Torah. But what the Torah relates is a miraculous revelation on Mount Sinai that occurred before more than 600,000 people, followed by forty years of ongoing miracles as the people wandered through the desert. The subsequent testimony by this immense number of firsthand witnesses, handed down for generations, is far more credible than any abstract reasoning about the cosmos. The later religions all accept this point, only adding later miracles of their own—but far less credible miracles, witnessed by far fewer people and occurring only over smaller stretches of time.

So you shouldn't merely start with the Torah, but also *end* with it.

And what is the basic content of the Torah's Mount Sinai revelation?

Do not ask the philosophers, for it is nothing that they could deduce with their reasoning. Rather, it is the specific set of commands and prohibitions, ceremonies and rituals, constituting the religion of the children of Israel, Judaism. A truly reasonable person, then, reaching conclusions on the basis of historical facts, evidence, and testimony, should believe in the God of the Torah—the personal God, the God who appeared in history—and in what this God has commanded us to do.

Related Chapters

11 Halevi, 12 Halevi, 14 Ibn Daud, 16 Maimonides, 32 Crescas, 35 Albo, 37 Bivach, 38 Abravanel, 40 Ebreo, 41 Almosnino, 43 Spinoza, 75 Heschel, 76 Berkovits, 82 Wyschogrod

11

Judah Halevi (c. 1075–1141)

The Spiritual Lighthouse

The children of Israel were chosen for the mission of spreading the divine light

Once we understand that Judaism is based not on philosophy but on a historical event, Halevi observes, we understand that our goal is not merely to obtain some philosophical knowledge of God but to live *with* God, in relation to God, in closeness to God. Through scripture and through historical testimony it also becomes clear that the Jewish people have a special role to play in humankind's overall journey toward sharing that goal as well.

It began with the first human being, Adam, who possessed a unique spiritual connection to God. This connection, this divine spirit, passed from Adam to his son Abel and then to Adam's third son, Seth; subsequently it was inherited by one individual in each generation down to Noah and then down to Abraham. From Abraham it passed to Isaac; from Isaac to Jacob, soon renamed "Israel"; and only then was it passed down to multiple individuals, to all the sons of Jacob, who in time bequeathed it to all the children of Israel. Of course, the divine spirit is not equally strong in everyone in the Jewish community; but even disobedient members possess it, even if they don't exhibit it clearly.

With respect to intelligence and moral qualities, to be sure, there is no difference between the children of Israel and all the other nations of the world. But this religious spirit or connection is the unique possession of the former.

24

The highest manifestation of this quality is, of course, in prophecy.

Some philosophers think that prophecy is simply a matter of someone's intellect getting into an appropriate state of contemplating God; that in reflecting on God our intellects merge with God's intellect, almost as a matter of nature, and "read His mind." But if that were so, philosophers would regularly become prophets. In fact *no* philosophers have become prophets precisely because prophecy is *not* a natural result of human reason. It is a real communication from God, one experienced not abstractly in the intellect but in a full sensory manner, providing not merely understanding but also an intimate connection to God that moves one to love, and to reverence, and to worship. It is a *super*natural event that occurs only for individuals already blessed with the divine spirit. Though all may join the Jewish religion, and God surely rewards the righteous of all nations, prophecy itself has been restricted to the children of Israel.

The epitome of prophecy was of course the revelation on Mount Sinai, when the children of Israel, collectively blessed with the divine spirit, received the divine communication. And what was communicated were all the commandments, ethical and ritual, captured in scripture and the oral tradition, available to us not by reason but only by virtue of that prophetic revelation. From all this it is clear that what God seeks from us is more than just good intentions and clever reasoning, but a specific set of religious and ethical practices whereby we live our lives in closeness to God. He seeks this from us, the children of Israel, and by extension, by the light that shines in us and through us, from all the nations of the world.

Reason may not show this, but scripture and tradition surely do—that the children of Israel were chosen for the divine mission of spreading the divine light through the world.

Related Chapters

10 Halevi, 12 Halevi, 13 Ibn Ezra, 30 Ben Elijah, 37 Bivach, 38 Abravanel, 44 Spinoza, 50 Geiger, 70 Kaplan, 82 Wyschogrod, 83 Borowitz

12

Judah Halevi (c. 1075–1141)

Home Is Where the Heart Is

The children of Israel belong in the Land of Israel

He may have been in the West, Halevi's famous poem remarks, written from his house in Spain some time before his late life journey to live in the Land of Israel—but his heart was in the East.

For if possession of the divine spirit is the special inheritance of the children of Israel and gives those so blessed the capacity to connect to God, then the Land of Israel is the place *where* that connection is most readily found. Just as the soil in one country may be better suited than others for growing certain plants, so the Land of Israel is better suited than any for that divine connection—in particular, as manifest in prophecy.

Indeed, whoever prophesied did so either in the Land of Israel itself or concerning it.

In the Cave of the Patriarchs in Hebron are buried the great prophets Abraham, Isaac, and Jacob and their spouses. Abraham's prophetic experiences are precisely what brought him *to* the Land. Jacob, also known as "Israel," ascribed his prophetic visions not to the purity of his soul, but to the place itself, the Land. The gift of prophecy was then inherited by their descendants, culminating in the collective revelation on Mount Sinai that occurred in the Land, for scripture reminds us that everything on this side of the Red Sea is part of the Land (Exodus 23:31); scripture also states that the Temple, where God's presence was most concentrated, was built on Mount Moriah in Jerusalem. The children of Israel retained the gift of prophecy as long as they remained in the Land and faithfully fulfilled the divine commandments.

But even when the children of Israel are in exile and the Temple is destroyed, the Land remains holy; as such it remains central to the soul and aspirations of every Jew. Scripture and the Talmud abound in passages testifying to this: All roads lead to the Land (they say), but none from it. It is better to dwell in the Land among heathens than abroad among Israelites. To be buried there is as if to be buried beneath the altar of the Temple, but still far better to live there than merely have your body sent there after death. He who walks four yards in the Land is assured of happiness in the world to come, and so on.

"Have mercy on Zion, on Jerusalem, for it is the source of our life": so we say each week in synagogue, after our prayer—which we perform facing the holy city from wherever we are in the world.

Tradition tells us that the Second Temple was destroyed because, after the sixth century BCE exile to Babylon, not all Israelites returned home; they preferred their comfortable material life there over their spiritual life in their Land. But the nation of Israel, in exile from the Land, is like the "dry bones" seen by the prophet Ezekiel: barely alive, being punished for our many sins. We, the children of Israel, can only achieve our perfection, our purpose, by returning to the Land and rebuilding Jerusalem . . . which can only happen, as the Psalm explains, when her children yearn for her so much that we "cherish her very stones and favor her dust" (Psalms 102:15).

But when Israel returns to its Land as it must, the divine spirit may once again be manifest on earth; and Israel shall serve as a light unto the nations, showing all the way to a life of closeness with God.

For the sake of all, then, the children of Israel belong in the Land— the Land *of* Israel.

Related Chapters

10 Halevi, 11 Halevi, 19 Nachmanides, 23 Abulafia, 30 Ben Elijah, 44 Spinoza, 50 Geiger, 51 Holdheim, 52 Sofer, 58 Kalischer, 59 Pinsker, 60 Herzl, 61 Ahad Ha'am, 63 Schneersohn, 65 Cohen, 66 Rosenzweig, 68 Bialik, 69 Kook, 78 Fackenheim, 79 Leibowitz

13

Abraham Ibn Ezra (1089–1164)

The History over the Mystery

*Why God prefaces the Ten Commandments
with a history lesson*

According to Ibn Ezra, Judah Halevi once asked him why the biblical passage in which God dictates the Ten Commandments begins, "I am *Hashem** your God who took you out of the land of Egypt, from the house of slavery" (Exodus 20:2). Wouldn't it have made more sense to begin with something like, "I am *Hashem* who made the heaven and the earth, and made you"—for surely that was the more impressive feat?

Halevi provides his own answer in the *Kuzari* (I.25ff.). For one thing, God's speaking to the Israelites this way at Mount Sinai underscores the source of the Jews' belief in God: it is based in direct personal experience. No one was around to experience the initial creation of the "heaven and earth," obviously, but the Jewish people directly experienced their emancipation from Egypt at God's hands, with all the miracles on their behalf. God also spoke this way to emphasize the special obligations the Israelites had to God as a consequence of God's special relationship to them. Had the commandments subsequently communicated by God been binding only because God created the cosmos in general, they would have been equally binding on all people. Other peoples are welcome to join the

---

*The biblical text uses the proper name of God here, but it is traditional *not* to use it when quoting the text. Instead, we substitute "*Hashem*," or "the Name," in place of the actual name.

Jewish religion, of course, but the Israelites were *particularly* chosen to be subjects of the Law—and through that obligation, ultimately, to spread monotheism to the world.

But now we can elaborate on this answer. The statement actually has two parts. The first, "I am *Hashem*," is an assertion of God's existence, a proposition that can be understood by the wise of all nations. The study of the natural world, the ordered regularity both of processes on earth and in the heavenly spheres, sufficiently demonstrate the divine handiwork, at least to the astute. Though there is disagreement between the non-Jewish and Jewish philosophers over the details of creation—the former are inclined to believe the cosmos has existed eternally; the latter, that it was created at the first moment of time—all ultimately agree that there is a creator. There is not much point, then, in including this point explicitly in the scriptural passage.

But this sort of belief in the creator, which requires some knowledge of nature and the ability to reason about it, is available *only* to the astute. Thus to the expression, "I am *Hashem*," addressed to the enlightened, God added, "who brought you out of Egypt," addressed to the masses— the Jewish masses—so that they too could secure their knowledge of God, based as it was in their direct personal experience.

By reminding us of what He did specifically for us, further, we learn three more things, as scripture explains (Deuteronomy 6:20–25). First, though God created all human beings, we Jews have specific obligations to Him (as Halevi notes) as a consequence of His actions on our behalf. Second, we learn that God's commandments are not for His needs, but for our good—as His bringing us out from slavery was clearly for our good. Finally, we learn that the pursuit of the commandments is for the sake of justice and righteousness. What God did for us was just and right; in obeying His commandments, therefore, *we* will do what is just and right.

In obeying the commandments, we children of Israel, of that generation and all subsequent generations, become wise; in becoming wise our intellect, our rational soul, is empowered; and in that process we become truly free, including from the astrological influences of the heavenly bodies created by the same God who created the heaven and the earth.

Related Chapters

2 Philo, 11 Halevi, 16 Maimonides, 22 De Leon, 37 Bivach, 41 Almosnino, 42 Sforno, 49 Steinheim, 57 Salanter, 64 Cohen, 66 Rosenzweig, 70 Kaplan, 71 Soloveitchik, 76 Berkovits, 79 Leibowitz, 83 Borowitz

14

Abraham Ibn Daud (Rabad) (1110–80)

The Unmoved Mover

Philosophical principles prove the existence of the nonphysical God of Judaism

According to Ibn Daud, scripture itself tells us that Judaism has a philosophical foundation, when it says that other nations shall recognize that the divine commandments reflect wisdom and understanding (Deuteronomy 4:6). The religious principles that we received by revelation, in other words, are ultimately identical with the philosophical principles other nations arrive at only after much intellectual labor. These principles are naturally those of Aristotle, which explain the cosmos in such terms as matter and form, causation, motion, the rational, animal, and vegetative souls, and so forth—and with some philosophical work we can express Jewish ideas in these terms as well.

In fact, Aristotelian concepts can even prove the existence of God.

For consider the nature of motion. We see motion all around us, but what explains this motion?

Nothing can cause itself to move. Why? Because causes must first contain within themselves whatever they bring about in their effects: there must be heat in the flame (for example) for the flame to heat up the water. After all, if a cause *could* produce an effect that didn't already preexist in some way in the cause, then that effect would come into being literally from nothing—but creating something from nothing is incomprehensible, a miracle, that we cannot ascribe to any ordinary, created thing. In any case, scripture itself suggests that every motion must have something causing that motion (Job 38:36–37, Proverbs 30:4).

So every moving thing must be caused to move by some other moving thing. But now what causes the preceding moving thing to move? By the same reasoning, it too must have some other thing moving it, and so on, to infinity. If anything moves, then there must be an infinite series of moving things.

But any actual infinity, such as an infinite series of objects, is impossible. An infinite series would have an infinite number of members. But there is no such thing as an "infinite number." Every number is finite: the members of that series will be numbered first, or second, or third, and so on, and no matter how far you go, you never discover the infinite number. Moreover, scripture itself affirms the finiteness of everything in the cosmos (Isaiah 40:12).

If motion requires an infinite series of moving things, but such a series is impossible, then motion would be impossible—unless there exists something that could terminate that series without belonging to it, some thing that moves other things while not itself subject to motion. Since motion is clearly not impossible (we see it all around us!), there must exist such a thing: a First Mover.

This First Mover, naturally, is God.

That this being is different from everything in the created cosmos is clear enough, if only in that it can move other things without itself being moved. But we can also show that this being must be nonphysical—that is, not a body.

If the First Mover is itself immovable, then nothing limits or determines its power to move other things. To say that its power is unlimited is to say, literally, that it is infinite, without limit.

But now no *body* could have infinite power. For any physical body can be divided into parts. If these parts themselves have infinite power, then the sum of the parts would be greater than infinity, which is absurd. But if they have finite power, then the sum of the parts must be finite.

If the First Mover has infinite power, then, it cannot be a body.

Thus philosophy shows that God exists, and is nonphysical—just as Judaism teaches.

Related Chapters

3 Saadia Ben Joseph Gaon, 7 Ibn Paquda, 9 Ibn Tzaddik, 10 Halevi, 15 Ibn Daud, 27 Ibn Kaspi, 32 Crescas, 33 Crescas, 38 Abravanel, 39 Del Medigo, 41 Almosnino, 49 Steinheim

15

Abraham Ibn Daud (Rabad) (1110–80)

What God Does Not Know, Despite Knowing Everything

Although our free actions cannot be foreknown, there is no lack in God's knowledge

It is no secret that scriptural passages sometimes seem to contradict each other. But since scripture contains only truth and truth never contradicts, Ibn Daud observes, we know that when that happens, one of the passages must be interpreted in some nonliteral (metaphorical, symbolic) way.

Which one? The one that runs against the dictates of reason—that is, of philosophy.

An important such example concerns our free will.

Scripture teaches both that God rules over everything and that human beings have real choice in their actions. The former suggests that God predetermines everything that happens, for example, by establishing long sequences of causes that ultimately produce each event. All human actions, including the choices and decisions that lead to them, seem to be produced by such chains; but then if so, they would not be genuinely *free* actions, under our control.

So God's complete rule over the world seems inconsistent with human freedom.

To resolve this tension, we must understand that God created the world such that some events occur necessarily (they *must* happen), some events are impossible (they *cannot* happen), and some events are "possible": nothing in the causal chain of events leading up to them guarantees that they will occur nor guarantees that they will not. They may occur;

they may not; neither is predetermined. Free human actions naturally fall into this latter category.

But now note that this lack of predetermination does not suggest any deficiency or imperfection in God, as some might object. An all-powerful God surely *can* create a world that contains possible events, for God's power would be limited if He could not. And further, an all-good God *would* create such a world, for a world that contains events such as human free actions (and thus moral responsibility) seems overall superior in value to a world that does not.

On such a view, it is true, God does not know in advance what free actions we may undertake. God creates each person with her possible actions, and knows those actions as "possible" for her, that she may, or may not, perform them. But since it is not predetermined which of her possible actions she will actually perform, He does not know what she will freely do.

But neither is this apparent "lack" of knowledge any deficiency in God. For it is not an *actual* lack. A person lacks knowledge when there are facts that he does not know. But here there are no such facts. To say an action is possible is precisely to say there is no further fact about whether it will occur or not. Knowing that a given free action is possible *is* knowing everything there is to know about it. So there is no further fact that God does not know—and God cannot be said to lack knowledge.

Since reason and scripture both maintain that human beings act freely, we know that any passages suggesting anything different must be interpreted cautiously. So when (for example) God "hardens" Pharaoh's heart (Exodus 7:3), this cannot mean that God removed from Pharaoh the power of free choice, as some suggest. It means merely (as other considerations show) that once Pharaoh made his free choice not to allow the Israelites to leave Egypt, God enabled him to proceed in accordance with his own free will—and ultimately, of course, to justly suffer the consequences.

Related Chapters

2 Philo, 14 Ibn Daud, 16 Maimonides, 17 Maimonides, 24 Albalag, 25 Abner of Burgos, 26 Pollegar, 27 Ibn Kaspi, 28 Gersonides, 29 Gersonides, 30 Ben Elijah, 31 Ben Joshua, 34 Crescas, 39 Del Medigo, 43 Spinoza, 44 Spinoza, 49 Steinheim, 72 Strauss, 73 Strauss, 76 Berkovits, 80 Jonas

PART II

MAIMONIDES–SFORNO
1138–c. 1550

Introduction to Part II

If no sharp line can be drawn between philosophy and the material in religious texts, then neither can one be drawn between the various periods of thought about the Jewish God Question. Nevertheless, there is a natural divide between the era before Maimonides (1138–1204), and after. Before he appeared, nobody spoke of him (obviously). But after, it was not possible *not* to speak of him. Indeed a significant proportion of medieval thinking was either a defense, elaboration, criticism of, or response to Maimonides.

Maimonides himself was a complex individual. He was a preeminent rabbi, a leading authority on *halacha* (Jewish Law), a worldly individual immersed in the intellectual culture of his time as well as physician to the sultan, and a world-class philosopher. He, and his works, were in fact quite controversial in the Jewish community. As a rabbi and legal thinker he was second to none; but in his philosophy he seemed to endorse the views of the ancient Greek Aristotle and of various medieval Muslim philosophers influenced by Aristotle, which often seemed to contradict the Jewish scriptures. So while Maimonides's Jewish writings were revered, his philosophical writings were condemned and sometimes even burned!

Despite the controversy, his themes are among the dominant themes of the next five or so centuries. Thus in part II we see extensive discussion of the relationship between philosophy and religion, between reason and faith, about how to interpret the Bible, the natures of prophecy and miracles, the point and purpose of the *mitzvot* (divine commandments). There is continued grappling with the proofs of God's existence, with the many divine attributes, and with divine unity. We see the first appearance in our book of the "problem of evil," of the attempt to make sense of the existence of evil in a cosmos created by the all-powerful and good God; and while the famous problem of reconciling God's knowledge of the future with human free will first appeared in part I, it is here that it hits its stride. Almost every major thinker weighs in, producing a dizzying array of ideas, insights, and different positions. Other themes continue from part I, such as the special relationship of the children of Israel to the Land of Israel and the overall picture of the human being's place in the cosmos.

As in part I, too, we also see some pushback to the Maimonidean project. The movement of Karaism, for example, calls for a return to the written text of the Bible alone, thus undoing centuries worth of rabbinic interpretation of the Bible (and the "oral Law," as codified in the Talmud), as well as of philosophy. More important, we see the rise of the Kabbalah, the Jewish mystical movement that resists the overly intellectual approach to Jewish matters pioneered by Maimonides and his followers. What matters most isn't intellectual contemplation of God, Kabbalists insist, but *love* of God as expressed in a wide variety of spiritual activities; the Jew should aim to align not his intellect with God, through rational reflection, but his *will* with God's, through love and action.

No, not everyone agrees with Maimonides, on most issues. In fact almost everyone disagrees, on almost every issue. But almost every thinker directly *grapples* with him during this period, one way or another, when they grapple with the Jewish God Question.

16

Maimonides (1135–1204)

Not That Many Are Called

*Very few people are properly prepared to
study the philosophical truths of religion*

Religion is for everyone, Maimonides thinks, but truly understanding religious truths may not be.

That understanding comes from philosophy obviously, but not everyone is suited to philosophy; and even those who may be should not *start* their study of religion with philosophy. For a little philosophy can be dangerous. It can quickly lead to great confusion, and as you begin to glimpse apparent tensions between reason and faith it can lead to skepticism and even the rejection of faith. Just as an infant fed only meat will die—not because meat is intrinsically bad, but because the infant is unfit to digest it—so, too, philosophical truths about religion should not be offered to those who are inadequately prepared to receive them. Scripture is written in ordinary language for a reason: its goal is to guide people through life, not to express the deeper philosophical truths hidden within. Thus everyone must begin with its literal truths, and only the properly trained individual should, under the guidance of a teacher, attempt to probe more deeply.

And how patient one must be!

For no one's intellect is sufficient early on to grapple with philosophy. The intellect must be developed carefully, via preparatory studies of long duration. You must first master logic, then mathematics, and then physics before even *thinking* about philosophy. Moral conduct is also a prerequisite, for only someone whose character is pure, calm, and steadfast can attain the necessary intellectual perfection. And finally mundane concerns will frequently slow you down: we all must look after our physical necessities and care for our families, after all. Even the most skilled person cannot do philosophy properly if he is distracted by the simple maintenance of life, and so much the more so if he is distracted by all the unnecessary temptations of modern, and especially immoral, life.

For all these reasons, the philosophy of religion must be restricted to those with the proper intellectual tools, the years of intellectual and moral training, and a general freedom from mundane cares. You may have heard the idea that many are called but few are chosen; in this view, to the contrary, it's apparent that not that many are called.

But just to be clear, it's not that ordinary people should be taught *nothing* philosophical about God. There are certain truths that must be impressed upon everyone as soon as they are capable of grasping them: that God is one, that none besides Him is to be worshipped, that He is nonphysical, that He is eternal, that His existence is completely unlike the existence of any of His creatures, and so forth. Everyone must grasp at least these truths even if they cannot grasp the philosophical arguments that prove their truth. But certain other things should remain secret to those who do not meet the criteria above: the precise nature of the attributes of God (such as His will, perception, knowledge); certain questions about the creation of the cosmos and God's providence over it; questions about the nature of the language we use when speaking about God, and so forth. For no more good can come of providing the ill-equipped with these important secrets than can come of serving filet mignon to an infant.

It's best for all concerned to leave the meat to the philosophers.

Related Chapters

10 Halevi, 13 Ibn Ezra, 15 Ibn Daud, 17 Maimonides, 18 Maimonides, 30 Ben Elijah, 32 Crescas, 37 Bivach, 38 Abravanel, 39 Del Medigo, 40 Ebreo, 72 Strauss, 73 Strauss, 75 Heschel, 83 Borowitz

17

Maimonides (1138–1204)

Speaking of God . . .

On what can, and cannot, be said about God

While scripture contains only truths, Maimonides observes, just *which* truths it contains requires philosophical interpretation. Scripture tells us that God made human beings in His image, that He sees various things, that He moves about, and so on, which suggest that God is a physical being much like us. That, however, is clearly false, so we need some guidance as to just how to interpret such passages.

We need to determine, in other words, what can, and cannot, be said about God.

Begin by noting that God is so unique and superior that He literally can have *nothing* in common with any other being; whatever we can say of another cannot literally be said of Him. Further, God is also a perfect simple unity, not composed of any smaller parts or aspects. Putting these two points together generates the problem. When scripture says that God is good (for example), we know by the first point that "good" cannot mean exactly the same thing applied to God as it does applied to ordinary things; and when it says that God is also powerful, or eternal, or angry, we know by the second point that these words do not refer to distinct qualities in God—since He is a unity—even though they are distinct in us.

So what *do* they mean?

The qualities scripture ascribes to God fall into two categories. The first are *nonessential*: qualities that don't determine what *kind* of thing a given being is. For example, transient qualities such as being angry, or feeling love, are nonessential to human beings since we remain human beings even as these come and go. In contrast, *essential* qualities *define* the being. Perhaps being rational is essential to us, since anything lacking that capacity wouldn't truly be a human being. For God, such qualities as being omnipotent and wise are essential while His being at various times angry, jealous, or merciful would be nonessential.

Now God, unlike us, is not literally subject to transient nonessential qualities. So when scripture describes Him this way it must be doing something else: namely, describing His *actions*, if indirectly. It's not that God Himself is literally merciful, in other words, but that He performs merciful acts such as providing for life. Neither is God literally wrathful, but rather He does wrathful things, such as create floods.

The essential qualities are more subtle.

From above we can never say literally what God is since our words never literally apply to Him. Instead what we can do is describe what God is *not*, and that is the key. When scripture tells us that God has power it is really saying that God is not weak; when it says that God has wisdom it is saying that He does not lack intelligence, and so on. In neither case does scripture speak directly of what God Himself *is*, and so in neither case does it directly attribute any multiplicity within Him. Though He is Himself one simple thing, there can be many things He is *not*.

Now these moves may seem like little verbal tricks, but they really aren't. To say what God is not is not to say what He is. But God so completely transcends our powers of comprehension that we simply *cannot* say what He is. The only legitimate alternative to this interpretation is to hold that when scripture says that God is powerful it is simply speaking falsely.

And that is something that scripture never does.

Related Chapters

18

Maimonides (1138–1204)

And Behold, It Still *Is* Pretty Good

How the perfectly good, all-powerful God could make a world containing so much evil

And God saw all that He had made, and behold it was very good. (Genesis 1:31)

It might have been easy to agree with this verdict after day six of Creation, when God renders it. But *now*? A quick look around reveals much that does not seem very good at all: everything suffers, decays, and dies. If the perfectly good and all-powerful God is responsible for the existence of everything, then how could there be so much imperfection and evil in the world?

It's a hard question, but Maimonides thinks it can be answered.

Consider, to begin, the difference between light and darkness. Light has genuine being or existence, and wherever it does exist something actively produces it, some source of light. But darkness neither has genuine being nor must it be actively produced: it's what you get when there is nothing to produce light. Similarly, creatures who can see have a genuine property: seeing is something we do and sight is an ability we possess. But a creature who is blind does not possess some *other* ability for blindness. Not seeing is not something it *does*. Rather, blindness is what results in the absence of sight.

The natural evils of the world, then, are like darkness and blindness, with no real existence of their own. Terrible things like poverty, illness, and death are really nothing but the absence of wealth, health, and life. Once we recognize this then we see that God does not create evils after all, for these evils are not "actively produced." Everything God creates is in itself good. But goodness is a matter of degree, and when He produces things with less goodness than we might like, we call it an "evil." But in itself it is just a lesser degree of the goodness that we desire. Poverty and illness aren't themselves things, but merely states in which we have less money and health than we desire.

And indeed we often show great ignorance in our judgments about what is evil! We naturally think of our own illnesses and deaths as great evils and wish they could be avoided. But that doesn't really make much sense. We are physical beings made of matter and it's the nature of matter to decay; to wish that we didn't become ill or die would be like wishing that we physical beings were not physical beings. But that is not to wish that we were healthier; it's to wish that we didn't exist at all, since a non-physical being wouldn't be us! And nobody wishes that.

Our judgments about evil can also be remarkably self-centered. If something happens against our personal desires or interests we immediately condemn it as evil, as if everything were all about us personally. But individual people, and even all humanity, are but the tiniest components in this immensely vast cosmos—a cosmos that is not made worse because some beings enjoy less goodness than others, but rather, is made more beautiful by the tremendous variety of beings it contains. We may not like it, but the cosmos just might be better off overall, as a whole, if we personally happen to be enjoying less goodness than we might. Who are we to declare that the cosmos as a whole is only good if things go well for us in particular?

So everything God does *is* good, to various degrees, then *and* now— and we shouldn't be so quick to judge as an evil our own rank in the relative distribution of goods.

Related Chapters

16 Maimonides, 17 Maimonides, 22 De Leon, 42 Sforno, 43 Spinoza, 74 Levinas, 77 Arendt, 79 Leibowitz, 80 Jonas

19

Moses Ben Nachman
(Nachmanides, Ramban)
(1194–1270)

Though the Messiah May Tarry, We Should Not

The Torah obligates the Jew to return to the Land of Israel

Many passages in the Talmud stress the importance or even the obligation of the children of Israel to live in the Land of Israel. In one such passage, however, an apparently dissenting opinion arises. Rav Judah claims that the Torah *forbids* our returning from exile to the Land of Israel, citing "three oaths," including that we Jews (1) should not go up to the Land "like a wall" and (2) should not rebel against the nations of the world (Talmud Tractate *Ketubot* 110b–111a). Some commentators cite this passage to claim that we must wait for the messiah before returning to the Land, lest we stir up our oppressors and bring disaster upon ourselves.

Nachmanides disagrees.

First, the Land of Israel is uniquely holy. So holy, in fact, that the beloved matriarch Rachel, second wife to the patriarch Jacob (and sister to his first wife, Leah), died en route to the Land of Israel rather than entering it. Why would God allow this to occur? Because while it is permissible *outside* Israel for a man to marry two sisters, inside, the holiness of the Land forbids it. Thus even the matriarch Rachel could not enter, lest the holy soil be desecrated!

The Land of Israel is so holy that, in fact, the Torah's commandments are only truly obligatory for those Jews who live *in* the Land. Outside the Land we observe the Law out of respect for the rabbinical mandates, of course, and also so that the many individual laws will not be unfamiliar to us when we do return to the Land. But strictly speaking, they only apply within the Land.

That we are obliged to return *to* this Holy Land is actually part of the divine covenant, found in the Torah itself. When God tells Moses, "You shall possess the Land and you shall settle in it, for to you have I given the Land to possess it" (Numbers 33:53), He is speaking not merely to those children of Israel wandering in the desert but also to every generation since. Whether the Land is desolate or held by others, we who live in exile are obligated to return, to possess, to settle. And since all the laws strictly apply only to those living in the Land, the commandment to possess and settle it is essentially equal in importance to all the laws put together!

Of course the Bible also suggests that it is God who will give the Land to the Jews, as He did with the original conquest: "For not by their sword did they possess the land, nor did their own arm help them; but by Your right hand, Your arm, and the light of Your countenance, for you favored them" (Psalms 44:4). Some point to this passage, and to the "oaths" above, to suggest we must wait for the messiah and for God to return the Land to us.

But no: this passage merely reminds us that it is God who ultimately determines all outcomes. Our obligations to possess and settle the Land—or at least to *attempt* to possess and settle—remain, though whether our attempts succeed is, of course, in God's hands.

Nor need the oaths above contradict this obligation. Perhaps we may not storm the Land "like a wall," and it is clearly good advice to be cautious about stirring the nations of the world against us. But individuals surely are obligated to make their way to the Land with the permission of the nations, as much as possible—and once there, as much as possible, to possess it, to settle it, to obtain sovereignty.

Related Chapters

12 Halevi, 20 Nachmanides, 30 Ben Elijah, 44 Spinoza, 50 Geiger, 51 Holdheim, 52 Sofer, 58 Kalischer, 59 Pinsker, 60 Herzl, 61 Ahad Ha'am, 62 Berdichevsky, 63 Schneersohn, 65 Cohen, 66 Rosenzweig, 68 Bialik, 69 Kook, 78 Fackenheim, 79 Leibowitz

20

Moses Ben Nachman
(Nachmanides, Ramban)
(1194–1270)

The Messiah Still Tarries—
Contrary Opinions Notwithstanding

Contra the Christian claim, Jews do not believe the messiah has yet appeared

In the famous Disputation at Barcelona in 1263, the Christian opponents sought to prove, on the basis of Jewish texts themselves, three main points: First, that the Talmudic sages believed that the messiah had in fact already appeared in their times and could be identified with Jesus of Nazareth. Second, that the messiah foretold by the Jewish prophets was not an ordinary human being but of divine nature. Third, that, therefore, Judaism had now been superseded by Christianity, so Jews should stop observing the precepts of the Torah. Nachmanides, bravely speaking before the hostile audience, rejects all three points.

For one thing, the passages the Christians invoke to defend their points are *aggadah*—that is, nonlegal texts such as historical anecdotes, moral exhortations, folk tales, practical advice, and so forth. Such passages are in no way legally binding or obligatory on Jews in general, so they could not possibly show that Judaism is committed to the beliefs the Christians claim.

In any case, those passages do not mean what the Christians claim they mean. Could the Talmudic sages really have believed Jesus to be the messiah? The Jesus episode occurred during the period of the Second Temple, while the major sages lived many years (even centuries) after the destruction of the Temple in 70 CE. If these sages believed that Jesus was the messiah and that the religion based on him were true, then how did they remain in the Jewish faith? Why did they not convert and turn to belief in Jesus? To the contrary they remained Jews all their lives, and died as Jews—they and their children and their students.

Nor is the claim that Jewish sources believed the messiah to be divine any better founded. First, it defies all logic to accept a combination of divinity and humanity in one being. Many prophetic texts in fact show that this conception is alien to the prophets, who clearly understood the future messiah to be a man of flesh and blood; the Jewish mind simply cannot fathom the notion that the Creator implanted a divine being in the womb of a woman. Perhaps Christians who grow up hearing this idea their whole lives can accept it, but anyone hearing it for the first time, as an adult, would find it very hard to accept. And while the famous passage in Isaiah 53 might be interpreted as a description of the life and resurrection of the messiah, that is not how we *Jews* have interpreted it. Instead it speaks of the fate of the people of Israel, whom the prophets regularly refer to as God's servant.

Finally, the prophetic promises describing the messianic age have clearly not been fulfilled. Rather than enjoying a period of peace and justice, the world has been filled since the time of Jesus with violence and injustice, and, indeed, the Christians are among the most warmongering people of all. Jesus did not even usher in growth and prosperity for Rome, then the ruler of the world. After adopting Christianity as the state religion in the fourth century Rome only declined, to the point where those who believe in Islam, which arose *after* Christianity, now possess a greater dominion than Christians.

Not only does Judaism reject the belief that Jesus was the messiah then, but nothing in Judaism has been superseded—and in fact the truth of Christianity itself is very much in question.

Related Chapters

19 Nachmanides, 50 Geiger, 51 Holdheim, 52 Sofer, 79 Leibowitz

21

Hillel Ben Samuel (1220–95)

The Ultimate Meeting of the Minds

In defense of personal immortality from the challenge of the universal intellect

Great as Maimonides was, according to Ben Samuel, there is at least one matter where he goes in the wrong direction. On the nature of the human soul and the question of personal immortality, Maimonides seems to share the view of the famous Muslim philosopher, Averroes (1126–98).

And that is the problem.

For on that doctrine there is no such thing as an individual, human intellect: all human beings ultimately share a single, universal intellect. That may sound strange but there *are* many arguments in its favor. For example, what our intellects do is contemplate general, universal, abstract truths, such as those of mathematics. But the mathematics one person contemplates is identical to that of any other, and so the contents of our intellects are all identical. Further, the mathematical entities we contemplate, such as eternally existing and unchanging numbers and shapes, could not really exist within our individual bodies or minds—both of which come into existence and go out of existence and constantly change along the way. They could only exist in some single, eternal, unchanging mind, to which we somehow have access.

Nevertheless, this doctrine cannot be quite right.

After all, it would wreak havoc on the notions of immortality and reward and punishment so central to Jewish faith. It would entail that after our deaths there is nothing individual about us that remains: what endures is the single universal intellect or rational soul, but not *my* soul, or *your* soul, or anyone else's. If nothing individual remains, there is no room for our religion's teaching that some individuals merit reward after death and others merit punishment.

What the doctrine does get right is that the rational soul, our intellect, is nonphysical and therefore distinct from the body. That is easily shown since, unlike everything physical, the rational soul is neither divisible into components or parts nor subject to motion. Further, *what* the rational soul contemplates are indeed eternal, unchanging, and general *nonphysical* truths—but then as we noted, it could not be located or grounded in our bodies, which are decidedly mortal, constantly changing, and quite individual.

The doctrine also gets right the idea that in some sense, the individual human soul is related to or derived from something more universal. Indeed there is the universal soul that is God, from whom emanate, as others have spelled out, the separate intelligences governing the heavenly bodies and the "Active Intellect"—the source of and locus for the universal abstract truths our intellects contemplate. But then there is one additional stage of emanation, which produces what the doctrine has wrongly rejected: the individual, nonphysical, distinct substances that are our rational souls.

With this in place, we can now make sense of the *ultimate* reward and punishment. Though some scriptural passages suggest that these are physical in nature, these must not be taken literally: a nonphysical soul cannot be affected by physical events in the appropriate way. And in any case, if reward and punishment were really physical, then why bother placing them after death, after the soul separates from the body? One might as well give the living person eternal life, with eternal reward or punishment accordingly.

No, reward and punishment are spiritual in nature, in accordance with the nonphysical nature of the soul. The reward for those deserving is for one's soul—one's individual, personal soul—to be drawn closer to the universal soul of God from which it emanated; the punishment, to be dropped further away.

Related Chapters

22

Moses De Leon (1240–1305)*

Sex as a Mystical Experience

Jewish mysticism sees a cosmos in which God battles dark forces, and seeks our assistance

Maimonides held that sex was like transporting dung: a shameful, if necessary, activity that should be done sparingly and discreetly. Such a view reflects the overly rational approach to Judaism, suggests De Leon, an approach that peaks in the Maimonidean idea that the highest form of Jewish worship is quiet, passive, philosophical contemplation of God—something available only to those few who can pursue philosophy. In contrast, the Jewish mystical approach, known as Kabbalah, depicts a turbulent cosmos in which God continuously battles dark forces and actively demands our participation in these battles. Even human sex, it turns out, can have cosmic consequences.

To appreciate this, one must see how the Torah is filled with deeper meaning, how human beings mirror the cosmos in our structure, how our actions have supernatural consequences.

The Torah does not merely relate stories. Rather, every single letter is exalted, mysterious, containing secrets of the cosmos. Nor is it an accident that it was written in Hebrew, the divine language God used to create the cosmos. The Torah is the blueprint of creation, a spiritual roadmap; un-

---

*Moses De Leon is widely considered to be the author of the *Zohar*, the sprawling work that became a foundation of Jewish mysticism. The book presents itself (to the contrary) as the work of Rabbi Simeon bar Yochai of the second century.

raveling its mysteries reveals that map, the inner workings of God, how to travel in that landscape, the secrets and purpose of human life. Following it properly, the student shares God's powers, works with God in battling the evil forces, participates in divine undertakings. For, in the end, it's not merely that we need God.

God needs us, too.

Though the details are complex, the ancient problem of creation—of understanding how the multiplicity that is the cosmos arose from the unity that is God—may be addressed in stages. There are ten such stages, called *sefirot* (revelations, or disclosures), and in each one God reveals another aspect of His ultimately inconceivable essence. At the start is the pure, infinite, spiritual light that is God. But that spiritual light is itself a will to create, to share, to give of itself; in order to do that there must be some thing to *be* created, with which to share, to which to give. The spiritual light thus withdraws into itself, it makes "space" for lesser manifestations of itself, which in turn derive their being from the light, but their limitations from its withdrawal. This occurs multiple times, with each stage like a vessel that contains or directs a diminishing quantity of the divine light. It is only at the tenth stage that the physical cosmos, including our bodies, is created. Though we maintain through our souls our connection to the upper levels, in being embodied we are that far removed from the pure, infinite spirituality that is God.

It is the multiplicity of aspects described above—in particular the struggle or imbalance between them—that is ultimately the source of evil in the cosmos. When we come to see how our own multiplicitous nature mirrors God's and how our own proper actions may serve to decrease the imbalances within ourselves, then, filtering upward, in the cosmos at large, we shall understand how we partner with God in battling against the evil forces that continuously threaten to tear the cosmos apart.

We do this by, among other things, performing the divine commandments in the right way. And we do *that* not because, as the overly rational Maimonides suggests, they are good for *us* in various ways.

We do this because in so doing we do the cosmic work that God requires of us.

Even having sex—in the appropriate, approved circumstances of course.

Related Chapters

13 Ibn Ezra, 18 Maimonides, 23 Abulafia, 36 Alemanno, 39 Del Medigo, 40 Ebreo, 41 Almosnino, 43 Spinoza, 46 Maimon, 67 Buber, 69 Kook, 71 Soloveitchik, 75 Heschel, 87 Lebens·

23

Abraham Abulafia (1240–c. 1292)

What's in a Name? Only *Everything*

Prophetic Kabbalah leads the way to spiritual perfection and redemption

The Kabbalah inspired by Moses de Leon's *Zohar* emphasizes themes such as the activity and inner nature of God, our ability to work with and affect God and thus impact the cosmos, and the communal and ethnocentric dimensions of Judaism. Abulafia's "prophetic Kabbalah," in contrast, emphasizes the inner psychological processes of the human soul as it strives for spiritual perfection; provides practical techniques for achieving this goal, primarily for the individual in seclusion, and to this end is open to sources outside Judaism; and sees itself less as an alternative to Maimonides's rationalistic philosophy than as a *fulfillment* of it.

For it is Maimonides who teaches that spiritual perfection is mental perfection, a state in which there occurs a kind of union between the human mind and God, or God's mind. Another name for this phenomenon is *prophecy*, for it is precisely during such moments that God transmits His messages directly from His mind to the prophet's. Since God's mind contains all—including the mysteries of the Torah in accordance with which God created the cosmos—a prophet may also receive secret knowledge of the created world. This could permit the prophet (should he choose) to manipulate nature for spiritual ends, by means of magic, astrology, and similar pursuits.

Nor is prophecy a phenomenon whose time has passed. To attain this supreme state today we must first clarify the nature of the *sefirot* (revelations, or disclosures). Many Kabbalists conceive them as aspects of God or of God's essence, but that concept risks violating the essential unity of God, and doing so even more severely than the Christians, with their claims about the trinity, or the three-fold nature, of God. Instead we must understand *sefirot* as entities *created* by God, as the conduits or channels that guide God's overflow in His creation and ongoing maintenance of the cosmos. Moreover, since we human beings are microcosms of the macrocosm, *sefirot* may also be identified with our own internal psychological states. To acquire proper knowledge of them thus means acquiring self-knowledge, a process that in return requires obtaining the appropriate moral and intellectual virtues—but once complete, results in our receiving the spiritual flow from God.

In other words: prophecy.

The main obstacle to obtaining this self-knowledge is the physical body itself: our faculty of imagination, in particular, obscures our intellectual clarity by overwhelming us with sensory experiences. But fortunately we may overcome this obstacle by entering upon the "Path of the (Divine) Names." The Hebrew language has many mystical properties (its letters are the building blocks of the cosmos, after all!). Thus Hebrew may be employed, along with certain meditative and contemplative techniques, to bring us along. We may, for example, meditate on the Hebrew letters composing God's many different names; recombine those letters in different ways; examine and visualize the many permutations of those recombinations; conjoin them with certain breathing techniques, physical postures, and so on. Doing this in the right way will not only bring us new, deeper, and previously hidden interpretations of the Torah (which is composed of those letters), but will also produce comprehension of the many Divine Names, and in so doing elevate our psychological state to the desired point. These techniques free our rational soul from the bonds of the physical body, and achieve the mystical union with God.

In so doing, too, we may indeed receive redemption—understood not historically and communally, as the messiah's ingathering of the exiles, but psychologically, as freedom from the body and, thus, as intellectual immortality.

Related Chapters

5 Israeli, 6 Ibn Gabirol, 12 Halevi, 21 Ben Samuel, 22 De Leon, 36 Alemanno, 39 Del Medigo, 40 Ebreo, 43 Spinoza, 46 Maimon, 67 Buber, 69 Kook, 71 Soloveitchik, 75 Heschel, 87 Lebens

24

Isaac Albalag (late thirteenth century)

Agree to Disagree

*Sometimes both scripture and philosophy
are true—even where they disagree*

Where precisely do philosophy and Judaism agree and disagree? Albalag asks.

Happily there is indeed much agreement. For example, four major Jewish doctrines are also affirmed by philosophy: (1) the existence of reward and punishment, (2) the survival of the soul after death, (3) the existence of a master who rewards and punishes, and (4) the existence of a providence that rewards or punishes according to one's deeds. Where philosophy and religion differ here is only in their mode of presentation: the Torah teaches these through stories that can be understood by all, while philosophy teaches them through reason and proof to a select group of properly trained individuals.

These differences also reflect different goals. The Torah aims to promote the well-being of the common people. It does this by teaching them whatever truths their minds are capable of grasping, in a language they can understand. God may be represented in a physical or bodily manner; the soul's punishment, conceived by the metaphor of roasting in fire; its delights, by physical delights; and so on. Since it is just too hard to imagine the cosmos as having always existed, its origin is presented in simple ways, as the generation of its various components, and so on.

The aim of philosophy, to the contrary, is the development and well-being of the elite, the highly intelligent, the educated. Their well-being depends on their knowing *true* reality, completely and accurately. Much of this truth would be misunderstood if overheard by the common person, and would be thought even to contradict the Torah. The Torah wisely withholds these matters, either by not mentioning them or by obscuring them in figurative language. So wherever the precise truth may lie with respect to those four doctrines listed above—as demonstrated through solid logical proofs—it suffices for the well-being of the masses that they believe them just as stated, on the basis of tradition.

That the Torah might obscure true philosophical doctrines is not, of course, any deficiency in the Torah, but rather reflects a deficiency in those who hear it. Where knowledge of some philosophical truth serves the common person the Torah will state that truth quite clearly. But in other cases the philosophical truth may well be obscured—so much so that the plain meaning of scripture may even appear to contradict the philosophical truth!

How shall we proceed then?

In such cases we must let the prophetic writings guide us. While philosophical truths may be arrived at by reasoning, prophetic truths only arrive via divinely appointed prophets, and thus trump all. So where philosophy conflicts with scripture, check the prophets. If the prophets do not support the plain meaning of scripture then we must interpret scripture in some nonliteral way, such as allegorically, so that it conforms to the philosophical truth demonstrated by reason.

And where the plain meaning *is* supported by prophecy? Obviously we must accept the plain meaning. But then what about the contradicting philosophical doctrine that was supported by reason? *We must accept that doctrine too*—the former by virtue of faith in the prophets, the latter by virtue of philosophical demonstration.

They are *both* true, if in different ways or modes.

This "double truth" idea will leave certain doctrines outside our full understanding, since we cannot really make sense of accepting contradictions. But it is better to do this than to insist that, where scripture and philosophy contradict, one must go—because, over time, philosophy will likely win out and scripture will be rejected.

Related Chapters

2 Philo, 15 Ibn Daud, 17 Maimonides, 27 Ibn Kaspi, 30 Ben Elijah, 32 Crescas, 38 Abravanel, 39 Del Medigo, 41 Almosnino, 44 Spinoza, 70 Kaplan, 71 Soloveitchik, 72 Strauss, 73 Strauss

25

Abner of Burgos[*] (1270–1347)

Voluntary Actions in a Predetermined World

Human freedom can be preserved
even in a world where everything is caused

At least since Aristotle the idea that our actions are "predetermined," already determined in advance, has been seen as a threat to human freedom. And surely there are many possible predeterminers of our actions: the heavenly bodies studied by astrology, the laws of nature on earth, God's foreknowledge, and so on. To preserve our freedom, some deny the predeterminism; but this, thinks Abner of Burgos, is a mistake.

Let us define a "voluntary agent" as one who can, by his own nature, perform alternative actions: for example, he can at some given time either perform a given action or refrain from performing it. Put differently, nothing in his nature or *essence* predetermines which action he will perform, so both are equally possible for him.

But now, this does not mean that *nothing* causes his action. What determines just which alternative he eventually chooses? There is a causal chain, a series of events stretching back, where each event is caused by one preceding it; and then, stretching forward, whatever is occurring at the moment of action *causes* the subsequent relevant action. Many events contribute to this chain, along the way and at the moment of action: the current sensory stimulus, other sensory input, the imagination, thoughts, reasoning, and so forth. Call the set of all the relevant causal factors within

---

*Also known as Alfonso de Valladolid, after he converted to Christianity.

the agent his "complete will." We can then say that his actions are brought about, or caused, by his complete will.

On this picture, the agent acts "voluntarily" even though his action is predetermined: that is, nothing in his *essence* necessarily produces the relevant action, although the long causal chain, proceeding through his various psychological states, does dictate which action he performs.

Note, too, that the causal chain need not include only elements internal to the person—for surely the laws of nature governing the cosmos, from the heavenly bodies to the physical body of each individual, also contribute. There is an important sense, then, in which we do not have *ultimate* control over our actions. Events have already occurred, in the heavens and on earth, that influence our bodies and thus our complete will. In fact it is precisely because our actions are causally predetermined in this way that they are knowable in advance. God's having foreknowledge of every single detail of human behavior is possible precisely because of this predetermination.

But by the same token, this does not mean that human deliberation is pointless. To the contrary, our deliberation, our sequence of thoughts and reasoning, ultimately causes our actions as part of our complete will: the steps of deliberation are steps in the causal chain. That is the sense in which our actions are "up to us": our deliberations produce them. This is true even as the deliberations themselves are caused by earlier steps in the chain, leading back to celestial and other external causes.

In another sense, of course, our deliberations are not "up to us." They feel as if they are, but this is an illusion; it is part of God's providence that we remain ignorant of the causes that operate on us and in us—and thus of what lies ahead for us. At the moment of acting we may say that alternative choices for us are possible, but only in this sense: that as far as we can *tell*, multiple options are available to us.

But this is enough. For despite the predeterminism that makes God's foreknowledge possible, our actions remain "voluntary" in that our essence is open to alternative possibilities, and our deliberations play a key role in determining our behavior.

And that's all that matters.

Related Chapters

26

Isaac Pollegar (d. c. 1330)

It Really *Is* "Up to You"

Human freedom refutes causal predeterminism

Abner of Burgos argues that all human actions are predetermined, and thus affirms God's foreknowledge of our behavior. As a gesture toward preserving human freedom in his system, Abner offers (1) a sense in which actions can still be called "voluntary," and (2) a sense in which, though a person may choose to perform action A, it was still "possible" for him not to.

But neither of these is convincing, according to Pollegar.

For Abner's predeterminism essentially collapses the metaphysical distinction between the "necessary" and the "possible." Something is "necessary" if it cannot *not* be; an action or event is necessary if it must occur, or if its *not* occurring is *im*possible. Something is "possible" if it is neither necessary nor impossible; an action or event is possible if it is both able to occur and also able not to occur.

Now Abner asks us to distinguish between something being "necessary by its nature or essence" and something being "possible by its essence yet necessitated by its cause." To illustrate, suppose you have a lump of wax that has been shaped a particular way by a person. By its nature or essence it's possible for the wax to have many different shapes; nothing in its essence requires it to have the shape it now has. But yet its shape *is* necessitated by its cause: given that the person behaved a certain way, the wax had to have this shape and no other. This is precisely the sense in which Abner calls human agents (or their actions) "voluntary": nothing in the essence of a person necessitates that he behave a specific way at a specific time.

But yet the very existence of causes that produce the outcome in question undermines this picture. Given that the causal chain exists and stretches far back into the past, the specific behavior indeed *is* necessary: no alternative behavior is actually possible. Something that is predetermined to occur, then, is necessary, and cannot be called "possible." When we ask whether an action was necessary, we are not inquiring whether, in entirely different circumstances, a different action might have occurred. We are inquiring whether in this world, with its history, with its chain of causes, a different action could occur.

That's what wrong with (2) above, too. Abner claims that it is possible in a certain sense that a person either do, or not do, a given action, or that a person's deliberations could go one way or could go another way: it is possible "as far as she knows," because she does not know of all the factors causing her deliberations.

But this sense of "possible" is simply not relevant. What matters is not what she knows, but what is the case—and as long as a causal chain necessarily produces the deliberations and the behavior, no alternative deliberations or behavior are possible, period.

To preserve genuinely free action, then, we must reject predeterminism.

And that predeterminism, in fact, is false may be demonstrated multiple ways. Many arguments (from Maimonides, for example) refute astrological predeterminism, the view that the heavenly bodies necessitate our behaviors. More directly, it is an irrefutable fact from our own experience (Abner's claims to the contrary notwithstanding) that our deliberations, our choices, are largely up to us. For it is simply incredible to maintain that all my actions are necessarily predetermined in advance prior to or independent of my thoughts, my reflections, my deliberations, which have a real, not merely illusory, role in their production.

We do act freely, then—without predetermination.

Related Chapters

15 Ibn Daud, 25 Abner of Burgos, 27 Ibn Kaspi, 29 Gersonides, 31 Ben Joshua, 34 Crescas, 43 Spinoza, 49 Steinheim, 76 Berkovits, 80 Jonas

27

Joseph Ibn Kaspi (1279–1331)

Distance Makes the Heart Grow Harder

Reading the Bible literally and naturally is preferable

If you want to understand what the Hebrew Bible is actually saying, according to Ibn Kaspi, your emphasis should be on a literal, minimalist approach to the text.

Some passages may be read allegorically, perhaps, but this should be restricted to instances of moral education for the largely uneducated masses. When Maimonides interprets biblical references to "female" and "male" as references to Aristotle's matter and form, he is wrongly interjecting philosophy into the text where it does not belong.

To read the text for what it says, you must place it in its historical context. Much of the Bible is a historical narrative about real persons and events, composed in a manner that reflects the language, customs, and beliefs of its protagonists. The great biblical figures, important as they are, are not philosophers, so their statements and their actions cannot be interpreted as presenting philosophical truths.

When miracles are related, for example, they are presented as they were interpreted by these individuals, living in their times, with their various worldviews. But what seems miraculous to someone living in ancient times, ignorant of contemporary science, may not be truly miraculous; biblical descriptions of miracles (such as resurrection of the dead, say) need not entail that real events occurred contrary to nature.

In fact, reading "supernatural" events into the Bible can generate difficult problems. Consider the famous example of God "hardening Pharaoh's heart" (Exodus 7:3), resulting in Pharaoh's refusing to let the Israelites leave Egypt. On the supernatural reading, God overrides some natural process, which in turn raises the question of how it could possibly be just for God then to punish Pharaoh (and the Egyptians) for his obstinacy, when God himself was the cause of the obstinacy!

The solution is to recognize, first, that there is a sense in which God is the cause (or a cause) of everything: God originally created the cosmos; He endows all things with their characteristics and powers, establishes the laws of nature, and so on. We may say God is the "distant" cause of all things.

But this does not mean that God is the *immediate* cause of everything. Indeed, when God created human beings He gave them the power of free choice, including the power to choose the good or choose the bad. So when someone chooses the good, we may say that God is a cause of that choice insofar as He endowed the individual with the power to choose the good. But it is the individual himself, using his God-given power, who is the immediate cause of the choice, insofar as he exercises the power that God gave him.

The same applies to the bad choices human beings make. When Pharaoh's heart becomes hardened—when Pharaoh makes the various bad choices that constitute that story—he too is exercising the power of free choice that God gave him. Pharaoh is the immediate cause of that act of choice, and thus bears the essential responsibility for it. When the Bible refers to God's role here, it is saying nothing more than that God is the distant cause of all things—which does not mean that God is immediately responsible for the bad choice.

We need not read this episode allegorically, or figuratively, or symbolically, then—but *naturally*.

Related Chapters

2 Philo, 14 Ibn Daud, 15 Ibn Daud, 17 Maimonides, 24 Albalag, 25 Abner of Burgos, 26 Pollegar, 27 Ibn Kaspi, 28 Gersonides, 29 Gersonides, 30 Ben Elijah, 31 Ben Joshua, 34 Crescas, 39 Del Medigo, 43 Spinoza, 44 Spinoza, 49 Steinheim, 76 Berkovits, 80 Jonas

28

Levi Ben Gerson (Gersonides)
(1288–1344)

What We Talk about When We Talk about God

Our ordinary language does apply to God despite the great gap between God and ordinary things

According to Maimonides, when we speak about God—when we ascribe to Him goodness, or power, or knowledge, and so forth—we are not actually speaking about what He is; we are indirectly stating what He is *not*. This theory does acknowledge the profound difference between God and the rest of creation, Gersonides concedes. It also solves some philosophical problems: for example, it preserves God's unity by denying that the many different things we do say about Him involve any multiplicity in His nature.

Nevertheless, the theory must be rejected.

If there truly were *no* commonality or analogy between the language we apply to the cosmos and that we apply to God, then we couldn't meaningfully speak of God at all. We would simply have no idea at all what we mean when we speak about God! Nor would we have any idea at all what the Hebrew Bible is talking about when it mentions God. When we (or the Bible) say God is powerful, or has knowledge, those words must have *some* relationship, however imperfect, to what they mean when applied to ordinary objects—otherwise we could just as well say that God is yellow, or round, along with the caveat that those words don't mean what they mean in ordinary use.

Nor does Maimonides help by allowing "negative" statements, as if we can at least meaningfully say what God is *not*. We cannot say God is "good" because of the language problem, he says, but we *can* say, "God is not evil." But for that latter sentence to be relevant we must assume that "evil" there means something like what it ordinarily means, for example, when we say "Abraham is not evil." But if words can resemble each other in meaning in the "negative" case, then why cannot they resemble each other in the affirmative case, too, when we say "God is good"?

And indeed the word being used negatively *must* have a similar meaning applied to God and to ordinary things, otherwise we would have no idea just which negations to make. Why do we say, "God is not a physical body"? Because physical bodies are subject to various imperfections (divisibility, destruction, etc.), and we do not wish to attribute imperfections to God. But if "physical body" does not have the same meaning applied to God as applied to the cosmos, then why would applying it to God involve ascribing Him any imperfection? We could just as well say that "God is not a *spiritual* being," too—if "spiritual" applied to God does not imply the same *perfections* that it implies in the cosmos.

To the contrary, our ordinary words *must* have some applicability to God. When we say God is powerful or has knowledge, we must mean something like what we mean when we apply those words to ordinary things. Of course we also recognize that God is very unlike us, superior to us in every way. Goodness in Him may not be exactly like goodness in us, not least in being far superior in quality and quantity to ours. We might say that the various perfections all exist in God in some superior way to the way they exist in us, and in that way God is both a model for us and we are created in His image.

But saying *that* presupposes we at least know what we are talking about, when we talk about God.

Related Chapters

2 Philo, 7 Ibn Paquda, 15 Ibn Daud, 17 Maimonides, 24 Albalag, 27 Ibn Kaspi, 29 Gersonides, 30 Ben Elijah, 31 Ben Joshua, 34 Crescas, 39 Del Medigo, 44 Spinoza

29

Levi Ben Gerson (Gersonides) (1288–1344)

If God Only Knew

Divine foreknowledge really is incompatible with human freedom, and so must be rejected

We have seen how causal predeterminism challenges human free will: if there are long causal chains producing our actions, then our actions are not ultimately up to us. But now God's omniscience also raises this problem. For if God knows everything then He knows in advance what you are going to do at any given moment; but if He *knows* that you will do it, and if, in His perfection, He is incapable of being mistaken, then it follows that you *must* do it. You have no alternatives. But then your action isn't free.

Maimonides applies his theory of language to this problem, Gersonides notes. On that theory, God's "knowledge" is utterly different in nature than ours. And surely it is: unlike for us, God's knowledge ranges over the infinite; it is eternal and immutable (though it covers non-eternal and changing things); it encompasses many things without introducing a multiplicity into God, and so forth. So, too, Maimonides holds, God's knowledge of our future free actions does not take away the freedom of those actions.

But this is no response at all. To say God has "knowledge" must mean *something* similar to what we mean when we say *we* have knowledge, and as far as we can grasp, having knowledge does raise all the problems mentioned above: change, multiplicity, and human freedom. For Maimonides to say that God's foreknowledge does not rule out human freedom without any explanation for just *how* it doesn't is not to say anything at all! It amounts to insisting that God knows our future free actions without in fact reconciling the foreknowledge and the freedom.

The problem runs deep.

For what do we mean when we say that God knows a future free action? If this means that God believes the given action will *probably* occur, we call this, in us, a mere opinion. If this means that God believes the given action will occur and yet it could turn out that it doesn't, we call this, in us, an error. Or if this means only that the given action may or may not occur without indicating which, then we call this, in us, uncertainty. Maimonides may insist that "knowledge" in God doesn't mean the same as "knowledge" in us, but in the end this amounts to ascribing to God either opinion, error, or uncertainty, and merely insisting that we *call* it "knowledge."

No.

If knowledge means anything like what we think it means, then God's knowing in advance what you will do means that you are not free to do otherwise, and you lose your freedom of action, period. To preserve our freedom of action, then, we must admit that *not even God knows our future free actions*. And preserve our freedom we must—for the Torah is filled with commandments and a system of rewards and punishment that only makes sense, is only just and fair, on the assumption that we are free to choose whether or not, and when and how, we obey.

Does this mean we are ascribing some sort of deficiency or imperfection to God? True, God would be imperfect were there any facts about the cosmos that He did not know. But there are no such facts about our future free actions. It simply is not yet determined what actions a free person will perform.

So while God may not know our future free actions, there is nothing knowable that God does not know.

Related Chapters

30

Aaron Ben Elijah of Nicomedia (c. 1328–69)

You Should Get That in Writing

On privileging the written Law over the oral Law

While Maimonides was the leading figure for those who granted religious authority to the Talmudic rabbis, Aaron Ben Elijah aims to be the same for the Karaites—a sect that repudiated the rabbinic "oral Law" in favor of the plainest meanings of the written Torah. Thus in his writings Ben Elijah often targets Maimonides.

Philosophical methods may have their merits, Ben Elijah grants, but Maimonides often takes them too far. He chooses to prove God's existence, for example, on the assumption that the cosmos has existed eternally. Such a strategy would be more powerful, he claims, since it's *harder* to prove God's existence on that assumption. But that is dangerous, because it could easily mislead people into believing that the cosmos is indeed eternal, in direct opposition to the Torah in Genesis.

Maimonides's theory of language is no better. He claims that we cannot speak meaningfully of what God is, only of what He is not. But there is no real difference between positive and negative speech. If we say something is "not mineral" and "not plant," then we are clearly claiming it is "animal." When we say God is "not ignorant," we immediately understand that "God has knowledge." In any case, the Torah readily speaks of God's positive attributes, so why shouldn't we?

Some object, saying that admitting positive attributes amounts to wrongly claiming that we know God's essence. Others object that admitting positive attributes amounts to introducing multiplicity in God's essence, in the distinguishable attributes of power, knowledge, goodness, and so forth.

But in ascribing attributes to God we do not claim to know His essence. All we know is God's existence, and that we learn from His effects in the cosmos. Indeed it is really His existence we are characterizing with these attributes, not His essence. Nor are we ascribing any multiplicity to Him. Yes, in us, these attributes are distinguishable: our power is different from our knowledge, for example. But these exist in God in a different manner, for in God they are one and the same. God's single, indivisible essence, in other words, has many different effects in the world—on the basis of which we characterize Him with the positive attributes.

And while Maimonides gets things mostly right with respect to prophecy, he fails to draw the proper ultimate conclusion. Yes, becoming a prophet requires intellectual and ethical perfection; the imagination plays an important role; and Moses was the greatest prophet. But *why* was Moses the greatest? Because other prophets received divine inspiration in visions or dreams, while he received his while awake. Because others received theirs through the imagination and so spoke in allegories and parables, while Moses received his intellectually, hence spoke in plain language. Others were left exhausted by their prophetic experiences, while Moses could withstand even speaking "face to face" with God. And most important, while other prophets needed to convince the people of their authority, the authority of Moses was made plain to all the people directly and openly, with perfect authentication, on Mount Sinai.

That is why we accept *his* Law, because we know it is *God's* Law—the Law that states of itself, "You shall not add to it, nor diminish it" (Deuteronomy 13:1).

And that is why we must reject the oral Law—because of the many rabbinic additions to, and subtractions from, the written Law of the Torah delivered directly from God to His people, by means of His greatest prophet.

Related Chapters

2 Philo, 11 Halevi, 12 Halevi, 15 Ibn Daud, 16 Maimonides, 17 Maimonides, 24 Albalag, 27 Ibn Kaspi, 28 Gersonides, 39 Del Medigo, 44 Spinoza

31

Moses Ben Joshua of Narbonne (Narboni) (d. c. 1362)

Don't Do Everything Possible

God knows the cosmos by knowing Himself, and thus makes room for human freedom

Ben Joshua offers his own contributions to the debate about the relationship between causal predeterminism, God's foreknowledge, and human free actions.

First, empirical observation reveals that while there are many causal factors in the cosmos, not many do their causing with *necessity*. Much in nature occurs with some combination of the "necessary" and the "possible" (that is, non-necessary). The heavenly bodies studied by astrology, for example, affect what happens on earth, influencing our choices, but they do not *compel* our actions. Many natural events occur one way without interference, but a different way with interference: for example, every living thing will necessarily die, but whether it dies "naturally," or by illness, or by some fatal accident, depends on many external factors not built into its nature.

Simply put, not all causes are necessary. There is plenty of chance in nature, and there is human voluntary activity, which is not necessitated.

What, then, about foreknowledge? Does God's knowing in advance what you are going to do mean that you are not free not to do it?

To protect our freedom some philosophers deny God's foreknowledge, for example, by arguing that God does not know all the particular details of the cosmos. What He knows are the general rules and laws, the "universals," the unchanging and eternal aspects of the cosmos, not the ever-changing, minute details. But then, on this view, He doesn't know what particular actions human beings perform, so His knowledge wouldn't preclude those actions from being free.

What is correct here is the recognition that God's knowledge is very different in kind from ours—but that doesn't quite mean it does not encompass particulars.

God is eternal and unchanging, true. He is of course "one," an indivisible unity. But God is also fundamentally active, not passive. Put these together and God *cannot* know the cosmos the way we do, by being causally affected by it, for that would make Him both passive and, because the cosmos is always changing, changeable. He must not know what occurs *because* it occurs, then, but the contrary: what occurs in the cosmos occurs *because He knows it.*

God therefore knows the cosmos insofar as He knows *Himself,* His own single, unchanging essence. Since all things ultimately derive from Him, all things are contained within His essence, in some exalted manner, in some unified, unchanging way. If the unified unchanging God is in no way passive, then His thinking of His own essence must ultimately be causally responsible for everything that occurs. And since everything—both the particular details and the general laws—exists in Him as a unity, His knowledge cannot be classified as being about either.

Rather, it transcends both; yet it also *encompasses* both, insofar as both are consequences of His ongoing causal activity.

And just what is it that the cosmos (and God's knowledge) contains? Yes, it contains all the particulars in the world, including even the actions of human beings. But insofar as your actions are truly voluntary, there are, in addition to the actual acts you choose, the alternative possible actions that you chose not to perform. God's self-reflection, His self-knowledge, includes and brings about all of your actions as well as *all the alternative possible actions that do not get chosen.* And insofar as you genuinely have alternative possibilities when you act, insofar as alternative possibilities exist, your actions remain free.

The fact that you *will* act a certain way, then, does not remove the possibility that you won't—or, consequently, your freedom.

Related Chapters

15 Ibn Daud, 17 Maimonides, 25 Abner of Burgos, 26 Pollegar, 27 Ibn Kaspi, 28 Gersonides, 29 Gersonides, 34 Crescas, 43 Spinoza, 49 Steinheim, 76 Berkovits, 80 Jonas

32

Chasdai Ben Judah Crescas (c. 1340–1410/11)

Love of God over Love of Wisdom

Contra the philosophers, it is not knowledge of but love of God that confers immortality

Philosophy has great virtues, according to Crescas, as do the great philosophers such as Maimonides and Gersonides—but in the end the essence of Judaism is not so much theoretical as it is spiritual and emotional. It is less about knowledge of God than about love and worship of God, through observing the commandments.

For what is the purpose of the Law? The Hebrew Bible leads us to acquire true beliefs; it teaches us how to perfect our morals; and it promises, by means of these, happiness of body and of soul. But since the latter would be the best and most worthy, the former must be understood as a means toward that end. Moral perfection and bodily happiness are part of the process of purifying the soul. As for the acquisition of true beliefs— that is, of *knowledge*—some philosophers think that it is specifically this that bestows immortality on us, by allowing our immaterial soul to transcend the limits of the body.

But that is incorrect, both according to scripture and to philosophy. Rather, eternal life and immortality are obtained by careful observance of the divine commandments.

Not that the others reject the commandments, of course, but they see observing them as being in the service of knowledge, as making possible the life of intellectual contemplation and thus spiritual immortality. But it is not at all clear how that works. What relationship could our intellectual souls ever have to our physical bodies, if our souls are truly spiritual and nonphysical? And how exactly does intellectual contemplation of eternal truths confer immortality on the intellect contemplating them? Would merely thinking about some mathematical theorem (for example) confer immortality? Would someone thinking about several mathematical theorems somehow become more immortal? And anyway, why should anyone bother with Torah if they could obtain immortality merely by studying a little mathematics?

One might object that not just any knowledge will do, that although philosophers are fond of invoking mathematics—since it concerns eternal, necessary beings (like numbers and shapes) and eternal, necessary truths—perhaps it is only knowledge of God that confers immortality. But that introduces a new problem. Our knowledge of God is very limited. Almost everyone agrees that we can have no substantial knowledge of God's essence. Maimonides himself, the arch representative of the intellectual school, says in his account of language that we cannot even have *limited* knowledge of God—so there should be no immortality!

Clearly the whole strategy is wrong.

Theoretical knowledge does not lead to immortality in the manner described. What leads to eternal happiness, rather, is the love and fear of God. Scripture, and the Talmud, are filled with passages testifying to this. But philosophy teaches it, too. The soul is, after all, some form of spiritual substance; since it is not physical and not subject to decay, it is capable of separating from the body and existing by itself forever, whether it has intellectual knowledge or not. Moreover many thinkers speak of the intellectual soul somehow becoming united to God. But what is the cause of unity, in nature, and elsewhere, if not love? The perfected soul, then, is one that is capable of the greatest love of, and thus unity with, God; and it is in unity with God that our greatest human happiness lies.

Philosophy has its virtues—but developing the genuine love of God may not be among them.

Related Chapters

8 Bar Chiyya, 10 Halevi, 14 Ibn Daud, 16 Maimonides, 24 Albalag, 33 Crescas, 34 Crescas, 37 Bivach, 40 Ebreo, 41 Almosnino, 42 Sforno, 75 Heschel, 76 Berkovits, 79 Leibowitz, 82 Wyschogrod

33

Chasdai Ben Judah Crescas
(c. 1340–1410/11)

Keep On Keeping On

*Even an eternal cosmos requires God
to create it—and to keep it in existence*

Can the cosmos itself prove God's existence? Crescas asks.

Maimonides gives it a go, but too much under the influence of Aristotle. He accepts Aristotle's claim that there are no actually existing, infinite magnitudes, then follows him in rejecting the possibility of an infinite series of "movers," thus leading to the existence of an "unmoved mover." But the problem is that Aristotle's key premise, against infinite magnitudes, is simply false. For there is an infinite fullness or void surrounding our cosmos, and so there's no reason to reject the infinite series of movers—and we lose the proof of God's existence.

Instead, let us distinguish between a "necessary" being and a "possible" being. The former is anything that *must* exist, something whose nature or essence is such that it is impossible for it *not* to exist. The latter is something whose nature permits it to exist but also permits it not to exist.

Now any "possible" event clearly requires some earlier cause in order to come into existence: since its own nature doesn't guarantee its existence, something else must bring it into being. But now suppose the causal event is *itself* a "possible" one. Then it too must require an earlier event to explain why it exists, since its own nature does not, and so on.

But the cosmos could not consist entirely of a series of possible events like this.

Why not? Because if all causal events were possible as described, then the entire series would itself be possible—able to exist, but also able not to exist—and then we would have no explanation for why the series as a whole exists rather than not. This is true even if the series goes back to infinity, for even an infinite series of possible events is still itself merely "possible"—so even the infinite series, as a whole, requires a cause.

To make sense of the cosmos, then, there must exist at least one cause that is not itself an effect of some other cause, that is in itself a necessary being: obviously, God.

As far as the origin of the cosmos goes, Maimonides thinks that the debate over whether the cosmos has existed eternally (Aristotle) or, as scripture suggests, was created *ex nihilo* (out of nothing) by God is irresolvable philosophically. He merely points out that belief in an eternal cosmos would upset Judaism by leading people to give up belief in God the creator, would make miracles impossible, and so forth.

But he is wrong here, too.

An eternal cosmos need not upset Judaism, even if the series of events goes infinitely back in time—for as we just saw, even such a series would itself be a "possible" thing, and thus still requires God's causal activity in order to exist. If the cosmos has existed eternally then that merely means that God has been bringing it into existence since eternity, not that it exists independently of God.

Indeed this is what it really means to say that God creates *ex nihilo*, out of nothing: not that there was originally nothing followed by some first moment of creation, as many think, but that all created things are such that without God's causal activity they would not exist. In fact we should not even think of creation as a one-time thing, long ago. For if God creates *ex nihilo*, then His creative activity must be ongoing. Since nothing can exist on its own, the moment God's activity were to cease, the cosmos would go out of existence.

God's creative activity, in other words, continues to this day.

Related Chapters

34

Chasdai Ben Judah Crescas
(c. 1340–1410/11)

Determined to Be Free

*There is foreknowledge and causal predeterminism—
and freedom and moral responsibility*

Both Gersonides and Maimonides weigh in on God's foreknowledge, causal predeterminism, and human free will. And both, according to Crescas, fail to deliver.

Gersonides accepts that God's foreknowledge of our actions would preclude our freedom, because His knowing what you will do means you are not free *not* to do it. So to preserve our freedom, he denies that God has any knowledge of particular events at all, including of our particular actions.

But this move is unacceptable. It makes God ignorant of nearly everything. God would not know of the patriarchs, or the Israelites, or of entire courses of events, of history. Nor, in His ignorance, would He have been able to intervene, speak to the patriarchs, deliver the revelation at Mount Sinai, and so on. This is not the God of scripture, of Judaism.

But at least Gersonides tries. Maimonides merely insists that God's foreknowledge does not rule out our freedom, without being able to explain other than to say that "knowledge" in God means something different than it does in us.

We can do better.

Suppose someone performs a free action in front of you: he waves at you, being perfectly free not to. At that moment you know perfectly well that his action occurred, but your knowing that in no way takes away the freedom of his action.

But now God, unlike us, is not a temporal being. He exists outside time altogether. That means, however, that His knowledge of the future may be compared to our knowledge of the present: from outside time, He simply "sees" your friend freely wave his hand in the future in the way that you see it while it is occurring. And just as your seeing (and thus knowing) that your friend is waving does not take away his freedom in so doing, so God's seeing (and thus knowing) the event does not itself take away its freedom.

It's not the knowledge that's the problem, in other words, but something else: the causal predeterminism. For we must admit that all our actions are the products ultimately of long causal chains of events that do, indeed, necessitate our actions.

But this predeterminism does not mean that we have *no* control over our actions. For our deliberations still retain their role in producing our actions. Indeed our deliberations are part of the causal chain, and for those actions we call "voluntary," we do them precisely because our deliberations lead us to do them; had we deliberated otherwise we would have acted differently. When our actions flow from our deliberations in this way, when they are not compelled by anything external to us, they are perfectly free, even if they are the product of a causal chain.

Commandments, rewards, and punishments all make perfectly good sense in this system as well. They contribute to the causal chain that produces our actions and help guide our behavior in the appropriate ways.

It's true that we must not disseminate this view widely, to the masses. Some might consider it a license to do evil: anything I do, someone might say, I was compelled to do by the long causal chain and I am not responsible for it. But that fails to appreciate how our actions flow through us, are part of us, as products of our deliberations, and that we are therefore responsible for them—and justly rewarded and punished when we behave well and poorly respectively.

So God does foreknow all our actions and there is a causal predeterminism, but everything that matters about our freedom and moral responsibility is preserved.

Related Chapters

15 Ibn Daud, 17 Maimonides, 25 Abner of Burgos, 26 Pollegar, 27 Ibn Kaspi, 28 Gersonides, 29 Gersonides, 31 Ben Joshua, 32 Crescas, 33 Crescas, 43 Spinoza, 49 Steinheim, 76 Berkovits, 80 Jonas

35

Joseph Albo (1380–1444)

Back to Basics

*There are just three basic principles to Judaism,
which also has the surest claim to divine origin*

Judaism is complicated, so some try to simplify it by summarizing what they take to be its most basic principles. Maimonides generates thirteen "principles of faith" while others argue for as many as twenty-six, but according to Albo, there are just three: the existence of God, the system of reward and punishment, and revelation. All the rest of the debates—about God's nature, the creation of the cosmos, prophecy, free choice, and so forth—are either of secondary importance or inessential to the religion.

To appreciate this, first note that since human beings are social animals, we must have laws that provide communal order: "natural law" refers to rules such as prohibiting violence, robbery, and so on, and will thus be found within any social or political grouping.

But natural law alone is insufficient to meet our social needs. To this must be added, therefore, "conventional law," the laws made by political rulers to govern commercial and social relations. While natural law is the same for all communities, conventional law may vary across persons, needs, times, and places. Natural law is what is minimally necessary for humans to survive in groups; conventional law aims to help them thrive.

Then there is "divine law," instituted by God, aiming not merely for our thriving but for our *perfection*, our truest happiness. Communicated to us via the prophet, divine law is superior to conventional law in many ways. In addition to ordering human conduct it perfects theoretical speculation and knowledge. Unlike conventional law it is not limited by uncertainty or error. Conventional law is subject to change in a way divine law is not, and conventional law cannot always fairly and accurately mete out rewards and punishments, while divine law is immutable and always (ultimately) fair and accurate, and so on.

What is essential for something to be a "divine law"? Clearly, the divine being must exist and communicate the law to us. Further, that law must have a goal, one superior to what conventional law can accomplish. Thus we have the three essential principles of divine law, of Judaism: the existence of God, revelation, and the system of reward and punishment including eternal life.

Ultimately, divine law is known to us empirically, via the revelation on Sinai and the prophecy of Moses, testified to by the long chain of tradition. To determine whether a religion truly is of divine origin, you must first affirm that it endorses the three principles just stated and then evaluate whether the promulgator of the religion is a genuine messenger of God. The best evidence for that is the revelation on Mount Sinai, for the entire people witnessed firsthand that Moses was directly addressed by God. Other religions, such as Christianity and Islam, have a far weaker claim in this regard.

Indeed you must not fear to compare your religion against others. It's true that if we allow people to question their religions, then some people, beset by uncertainties, might never settle on any religion at all. But preventing people from questioning leads to greater problems. Either we would have to say that all religions equally lead to human perfection and happiness—which seems absurd, given how profoundly religions disagree with each other—or else God would seem very unjust, in leaving many people trapped into false religions.

And when you do compare the different religions, you'll note, first, that Judaism is indeed a divine law as presented above—and then, that it also has the surest claim to having a divine source.

Related Chapters

10 Halevi, 37 Bivach, 38 Abravanel, 75 Heschel, 76 Berkovits

36

Yochanan Alemanno (c. 1435–1504)

It's in the Stars—and in the Torah

On astrology and the Hebrew Bible

A man very much of his time, Alemanno accepts the scientific validity of astrology along with its metaphysics, and goes on to create a fusion of astrology, biblical interpretation, and Kabbalah. This makes sense: if the Hebrew Bible is necessarily true and astrology is a true science, after all, then they must be compatible! Also making sense, then, are some of the many themes that emerge among the various contemporary Jewish thinkers sharing the same worldview: the Mount Sinai revelation occurred in accordance with astrological calculations; biblical events reflect the influences of the stars; great biblical figures and later rabbis were expert astrologers; a superior intellect can conjoin with God's intellect, in so doing grasping all the forces and laws of nature; such an individual can then override the forces of astrological causality, even performing miracles; the various *mitzvot* serve as tools to manipulate astrological forces, for example, by drawing spiritual energy from the higher cosmological bodies into the earthly realm; and so, therefore, one who performs *mitzvot* can remove himself from the causal predeterminism of the cosmological forces, and so on.

Jewish texts, then, contain not only spiritual lessons and metaphysics but also practical methods for influencing events on earth. To that end, a person should become well versed not only in Bible, Talmud, philosophy, science, and Kabbalah but also alchemy, astrology, dream interpretation, and the "magical" use of talismans, amulets, and incantations.

In this view of the cosmos there is no meaningful distinction between that which is alive and that which is inanimate. All beings are endowed with a spirit that moves them and is affected by other beings; all beings influence each other through natural attractions and repulsions. That which we think of as "spiritual" permeates everything we think of as "physical." Or more precisely, perhaps, the spiritual energy or force that permeates all things can assume physical forms.

In fact the spirit of God itself trickles down into and throughout creation, in the forms of the various *sefirot* that serve as instruments of God's activity in the worlds below Him. One who properly grasps the spiritual structure of the cosmos can thereby tap into that energy and direct it or redirect it in various ways—for example, as the astrologers do as described above.

One particularly important method for doing this relies on the nature of language. While the words in human languages signify objects as mediated by human concepts, words in the divine language, Hebrew, directly express the real essences of objects. As such they possess an innate creative power: one who masters the divine language masters the essences of all objects and is thus empowered to create them. Techniques for contemplating and manipulating the letters of Hebrew serve, in fact, to unite one's intellect with God's.

So united, you are afforded both a grasp of the laws of nature as well as the power to direct the flow of nature. The adept philosopher-magician can thus control natural substances, predict future events, heal those suffering from physical or mental afflictions, and more—including enjoying a temporary union with God in this life and the bliss of immortality in the afterlife.

Such an individual—such as the great King Solomon, whose *Song of Songs* reflects this hidden wisdom—is the perfect human being, serving as a true intermediary between the physical and spiritual levels of reality.

Related Chapters

5 Israeli, 6 Ibn Gabirol, 21 Ben Samuel, 22 De Leon, 23 Abulafia, 39 Del Medigo, 40 Ebreo, 43 Spinoza, 46 Maimon, 67 Buber, 69 Kook, 71 Soloveitchik, 75 Heschel, 87 Lebens

37

Abraham Bivach (Bibago) (mid-fifteenth century)

It's Reasonable to Believe on Faith

Knowledge based on faith is superior to rational knowledge

According to Maimonides, one of the divine commandments is to believe that God exists. But does such a command even make sense? Crescas, for example, argues that Jews cannot be commanded to believe *anything* because belief is not "volitional"—that is, not up to our choice or will. Any reward and punishment that go along with observing (or not) the commandments would therefore be utterly unjust if applied to belief.

To resolve this dispute, according to Bibago, we must first distinguish between beliefs acquired through rational operations and those acquired via faith.

Sentences or propositions may come to be believed either on the basis of (1) rational inquiry, such as investigation, argument, and proof, or (2) traditional authority. The manner of achieving this knowledge is independent of its specific content, so two people can accept the exact same proposition but do so by these different means. The former we may call "rational knowledge," while the latter we may call "knowledge on faith."

The latter, in fact, is superior to the former in several ways.

For one thing, not everyone is capable of serious rational inquiry, while faith is accessible to nearly everyone. There's thus no need to limit the knowledge of important truths—ones important to human blessedness—to the elite philosophers and intellectuals. For another, many philosophical doctrines engender endless debate and bitter disputes that never reach any resolution, and our efforts at reasoning are not merely laborious but prone to distortion, fallacy, and error. In contrast, the important Jewish doctrines are all based on a reliable tradition that stretches back centuries, to Moses. So faith provides a more *reliable* access to knowledge than does rational inquiry.

There is of course another, deeper difference between the two. Rational knowledge is indeed not volitional, as discussed above. It is not up to us what beliefs we accept during rational inquiry. Once we understand an argument we find ourselves either compelled to accept its conclusion, or unpersuaded. And surely we deserve no credit or discredit, neither reward nor punishment, for believing whatever our intellect compels us to believe!

But faith, to the contrary, is acquired through choice and will, as confirmed in scripture: "I have chosen the way of faith" (Psalms 119:30). And since the key propositions we believe on faith are neither provable nor disprovable by reason, we are not compelled either to accept or reject them—and thus we do so by our freedom of choice.

In fact there is a very close relationship between faith and the many commandments. Some of the commandments we share with the Gentiles: we are all forbidden from stealing, for example. But the force and purpose of this commandment is quite different in the two cases. We all prohibit theft for the sake of the general welfare, or forbid bad actions in general so that individuals will not acquire bad habits in their souls. But we Jews go further. We are commanded as we are in order to know that there is a God who *is* the commander. It is in obeying the commandments that we come to have that unshakable faith in the existence of the Creator.

So it is not on the basis of rational demonstration that we acquire the knowledge necessary for human blessedness. It is through performance of the commandments, which is under our will, that we come to grasp those truths—truths that we choose to believe, with utter conviction.

Thus it is that voluntary faith is deserving of that ultimate reward.

Related Chapters

10 Halevi, 11 Halevi, 13 Ibn Ezra, 16 Maimonides, 32 Crescas, 35 Albo, 40 Ebreo, 41 Almosnino, 70 Kaplan, 75 Heschel, 83 Borowitz

38

Isaac Abravanel (1437–1508)

All or None

Every commandment, large or small, and every word of scripture is equally important

In their hyper-rationalism the philosophers try to distill Judaism into a few basic principles: Maimonides provides thirteen, others as many as twenty-six, Albo as few as three. According to Abravanel, however, the whole project is a mistake.

It starts with the beginning. That the children of Israel are the "chosen" people does *not* mean that God picked us for a special task, nor that we possess some special propensity to relate to God, but simply this: that we have ourselves chosen to commit ourselves to God. But this means a full-scale commitment not just to some few basic principles, *but to the entire package.*

The Talmudic rabbis make clear that every Israelite is obliged to accept every single part of the Torah, the small as well as the great (Talmud Tractate *Sanhedrin* 99a). There is no difference between denying the whole thing (for example, by saying it is not of divine origin) and denying any part of it, any verse, any word. Even Maimonides acknowledges that the entire Torah is from the mouth of the Almighty. But then it follows that we must not postulate some beliefs as "first principles" that every believer must accept, while others are secondary or even dispensable.

The same applies to the commandments: all of them are equally obligatory, equally valuable, equally important.

The same hyper-rationalism also leads philosophers toward "naturalistic" approaches to the miracles in scripture, toward seeing them as

89

perfectly natural phenomena. A purely ordered, miracle-less world seems more rational to them, and thus more fitting for a very rational God. Thus Gersonides claims (for example) that the sun only *seemed* to stand still to allow the Israelites victory in battle (Joshua 10:13). And where there are miracles, he develops a complicated theory in which not God Himself, but a separate entity—the "Agent Intellect"—is responsible for them: since the rational God Himself can admit of no change, His causal activity cannot change. Gersonides even ultimately rejects God's creation of the cosmos, holding instead that matter has existed eternally!

To the contrary, we hold that it is God who created the cosmos from nothing by his infinite power, and God Himself who brings about the many miracles in scripture.

For it is God who created natural things, and He can change their function if He wills. And that God creates miracles no more disturbs His unchanging causal activity than does His initial creation: for God unchangingly wills what is best, whether that is the continued operation of the natural order or its occasional interruption. Thus *all* activity in the world, natural and miraculous, comes ultimately from God, by means of His unchanging will.

To be sure, miracles come in different types. Some are very similar to natural phenomena, such as the plague of locusts upon Egypt (Exodus 10:12–15); though in this instance it was a miracle, such phenomena can occur naturally. Other miracles go beyond nature, such as the great flood or the matriarch Sarah's pregnancy at age ninety: while rain and pregnancy occur naturally, they do not occur in such quantity or at that age. And finally some miracles contradict nature, such as the splitting of the Red Sea, inasmuch as by their natures alone such phenomena simply could not happen.

But what all these share is this: they are performed by God, by His will, when doing so will accomplish divine ends. That is the belief to which we must commit ourselves fully, completely, entirely, in accordance with the plain word of scripture.

Related Chapters

3 Saadia Ben Joseph Gaon, 9 Ibn Tzaddik, 10 Halevi, 11 Halevi, 14 Ibn Daud, 16 Maimonides, 17 Maimonides, 24 Albalag, 33 Crescas, 35 Albo, 44 Spinoza, 50 Geiger, 70 Kaplan, 82 Wyschogrod, 83 Borowitz

39

Elijah Del Medigo (1458–93)

Disagree to Disagree

There's only one truth, and scripture always has it—except when it doesn't

Religion and philosophy often seem to conflict. Scripture suggests that God created the cosmos in a first moment while philosophy suggests the cosmos is eternal; scripture speaks of prophecy, miracles, divine reward and punishment, resurrection, while philosophy challenges these; and while scripture endorses a personal, individual soul, philosophers sometimes deny individual immortality, arguing that after death our intellects live on only as merged with some universal intellect.

To deal with these conflicts, Del Medigo suggests, we must delineate the proper domains and goals of scripture and philosophy.

Some thinkers defend a "double truth" theory: religion and philosophy are entirely distinct domains, so something may be true in one while its opposite is true in the other. On this view, it may be "true philosophically" that the cosmos is eternal while it is "true religiously" that the cosmos was created.

But this move is unacceptable. To accept it amounts to accepting a contradiction, that it is both true and false that the cosmos is created. But the divine Law does not and would not oblige us to believe contradictions. We would sooner reject our religion than accept something so directly opposed to clear reason! Nor would God punish us for so doing, since it is He who bestowed on us the very intellects that cannot accept the contradictory. And so we justifiably reject any doctrine that involves contradictions: Christian ones like the virgin birth, the incarnation, transubstantiation; Kabbalistic ones about the *sefirot* (which contradict divine unity); and of course the idea of "double truth."

In fact the differences between philosophy and religion are not about which propositions are true (for on this they must ultimately agree) but about methods of demonstration and their intended audiences. The goal of scripture is to instruct us in human affairs, to guide our behavior, to promote our welfare—and to do this properly it must be able to speak to the masses. Philosophical speculation, to the contrary, is only for the select few with the ability and the leisure to undertake it.

Fortunately, on many matters the two already concur: the existence, unity, and nonphysical nature of God, for example, are both taught by scripture and provable by reason. And as for the disagreements above, even there, nothing in scripture is strictly contrary to reason: there is nothing actually contradictory in the ideas of creation, prophecy, and miracles performed by an all-powerful God, even if reason cannot prove their truth.

So what shall we do with the disagreements?

Where scripture and philosophy appear to disagree we must go with the former, for it is more likely that our reasoning has gone astray than that scripture has. Further, we must appreciate the dangers of introducing philosophical speculation, designed for the few, into discussions with the masses. For should we demand philosophical proof of (for example) some basic truth in scripture, then any difficulties we encounter will risk bringing those truths into question and doubt, with harmful consequences. Most important, we must recognize that the purpose of scripture is actually best served by keeping the philosophizing to the philosophers. What matters is that most people behave properly, follow the rules, are good people. Should the masses prefer to believe in individual resurrection while the philosophers deny individual immortality, or the former prefer creation while the latter prefer eternity, then as long as both behave, both will be rewarded.

In some of these cases, the philosophical doctrine is perhaps even the correct one. But even so—it is better for the philosophers to keep that among themselves than to let that information out.

Related Chapters

2 Philo, 14 Ibn Daud, 15 Ibn Daud, 16 Maimonides, 17 Maimonides, 21 Ben Samuel, 22 De Leon, 23 Abulafia, 24 Albalag, 27 Ibn Kaspi, 28 Gersonides, 30 Ben Elijah, 36 Alemanno, 40 Ebreo, 41 Almosnino, 44 Spinoza, 70 Kaplan, 72 Strauss, 73 Strauss

40

Leone Ebreo (Judah Abravanel) (c. 1460–after 1523)

All You Need Is Love

Love is all you need

Truth is one, according to Ebreo—which means that different traditions may each reflect, to different extents and in different ways, the very same truth. Thus there is much we can still learn from the ancient Greek thinkers and from the rich medieval tradition of philosophy, even if revealed Judaism, including the ancient Kabbalah (which he thinks influenced Plato), is the most perfect expression of the divine truths.

Plato in particular has much to teach us, especially about the value of beauty and love in understanding the cosmos and our purpose within it.

To properly grasp the cosmos is to grasp the hierarchy, and circle, of love.

The cosmos comes into being as a descent of love. God creates it out of love—the self-love of the more perfect being producing reflections of itself, of diminishing perfection. Love originates from Him and is successively imparted, like the gift of a father to his child, from the greater to the lesser, so that His perfection and beauty may be diffused as broadly as possible. Thus, first created are the angelic natures, then the heavenly bodies from high above down to the moon, and then the earthly bodies, down to lowly matter.

That is the lowest point of the circle, but then the ascent, the return, begins.

For lowly matter naturally desires the elemental forms as beautiful and more perfect than itself, and these forms in turn desire to become part of the compound objects and the vegetative bodies, those living bodies capable of maintaining themselves in existence. Living things naturally gravitate toward becoming "sensitive," able to sense and perceive, and then develop sensuous love for the intellect and desire to become beings with intellectual capacity, or reason: human beings. Human beings, with our intellects, pass, with intellectual love, from grasping less beautiful things to more beautiful things; sensuous love of lower things leads us to higher love of higher things, and as we find ourselves drawn to beautiful things we come to grasp, desire to unite with, beauty in general. Contemplating that, we are naturally drawn to the highest beauty, the most perfect beauty—that of the divinity—as we grasp and love the highest being.

In this way the circle of love closes: the cosmos created from love descending from the divinity returns *to* the divinity, insofar as it produces intellectual beings who devote themselves to grasping the highest beauty.

Maimonides holds that knowledge of God amounts to or produces love of God, and that a life devoted to that end is the highest life. True enough, except that his overemphasis on intellect restricts the good life to the elite few. Moreover he wrongly devalues the imagination and figurative speech. For him the imagination conflicts with the intellect, the latter being clear and pure while the former is obscure and distorted. For him, Moses was in fact a great philosopher unsullied by emotions and imagination, and only spoke figuratively to reach the masses. The philosopher must then strip away all the obscurity to get at the real (philosophical) truths.

To the contrary, the human imagination is not a hindrance to truth but the very thing that enables us to grasp it—by allowing us to recognize the beautiful and create beautiful things that imitate or participate in the beautiful. Beautiful speech doesn't merely "stir the emotions" but stirs the process by which we come to love that which is beautiful—and in so doing come truly to imitate God, who creates out of love, and thus come to return to God, in love.

Related Chapters

5 Israeli, 6 Ibn Gabirol, 10 Halevi, 16 Maimonides, 17 Maimonides, 21 Ben Samuel, 22 De Leon, 23 Abulafia, 32 Crescas, 36 Alemanno, 37 Bivach, 39 Del Medigo, 41 Almosnino, 66 Rosenzweig, 67 Buber, 75 Heschel, 76 Berkovits

41

Moses Ben Baruch Almosnino
(c. 1515–c. 1580)

Where There's a Will There's a Way

The goal is to align not our intellect with God's but our will

If Maimonides demythologizes Judaism by interpreting it rationally and diminishing its supernatural elements, then Almosnino, in sync with the trends of his era, helps remythologize it.

Jewish souls are not merely distinct from the body but are literally divine: they are part of God's essence, carved from God (as it were) and infused into the human body. As such, the soul preexists the body, is holy and eternal; prior to infusion it exists in a special "world of souls," to which it may return after the body's death if it has perfected itself on earth. While in the body the soul serves a moral purpose: in directing the body to perform good deeds and obtain knowledge, it both elevates the body and purifies itself of its bodily attachments. The degree to which it succeeds determines its reward in the next world.

While pursuing the "path of reason" has its benefits for a soul, philosophical wisdom leads at best to earthly happiness. Jewish souls who pursue the "path of faith," of Torah and *mitzvot*, to the contrary, have access both to earthly perfection *and* the suprarational and supernatural knowledge required for eternal happiness. This is no easy task, as the soul is immersed in its body, tempted by it. The soul must gain control over the body, "spiritualize" it by acquiring the various virtues, and direct it toward not mere knowledge of, but *love* of God.

The superiority of love over knowledge is reflected in the fact that the human will is higher than the intellect. The will is entirely free, as the intellect cannot compel any particular behavior. Indeed it is the will that directs the intellect to obtain knowledge in the first place. It is the will that we most deeply share with God, whose divine will is expressed in the Torah and in the world. To study Torah is to study the will of God; the goal is to align our wills with that will. The Torah is thus the intermediary through which we align our wills with God's, and thus attain that union with God that is our ultimate goal.

Why do we observe the commandments, perform *mitzvot*, then? Not merely (as Maimonides says) because they help us attain the self-control necessary for pursuing philosophical knowledge of God, but also because they have intrinsic value as expressions of God's will. In aligning our will with God's as we perform *mitzvot*, we directly experience and express, again, not our knowledge of God but our *love* of God.

This basic idea is also found in the Jewish yearning for the messiah, for redemption—understood not merely politically, as a great leader gathering the exiles into the Land of Israel, but also spiritually or psychologically, as the individual soul freeing itself from its exile in the body. This is the true freedom for which Jews yearn—to be earned by devotion to God and Torah even during our ongoing political exile. Indeed when the messiah does come, it is this freedom he will bring: all Jews will see the *Shechina*, the divine presence, even during their lifetime as their bodies become purely spiritualized.

And that is *all* Jews, for while the woman's intellect has traditionally been thought inferior to the man's, this blessed state of immortality depends on faith, the perfection of the will, and the performance of *mitzvot*, at all of which women can excel as well as men.

Related Chapters

10 Halevi, 13 Ibn Ezra, 14 Ibn Daud, 17 Maimonides, 22 De Leon, 24 Albalag, 32 Crescas, 37 Bivach, 39 Del Medigo, 40 Ebreo, 42 Sforno, 66 Rosenzweig, 71 Soloveitchik, 75 Heschel, 76 Berkovits, 79 Leibowitz

42

Obadiah Sforno (c. 1470–c. 1550)

Do the Right Thing
(Which Requires Knowing What That Is)

Moral perfection is an aspect of intellectual perfection,
so both are required for the good Jewish life

Intellect or will? Knowledge or morality? Rationality or love? Some follow Maimonides in stressing the former of each pair, holding that the
best Jewish life is one spent acquiring knowledge of God. Others, such as
Crescas and Almosnino, stress the latter, emphasizing not knowledge of
but love of God—a love expressed or produced by a life of *mitzvot* and
moral excellence.

Sforno finds a middle ground.

To be sure, practice is superior to theory. Mere intellectual perfection
is not sufficient for felicity, blessedness, or the immortality of the soul.
Nor does intellectual knowledge of God somehow unite the human intellect with God, or God's intellect, or with the semidivine "Active Intellect"
(a murky entity, whose existence should be rejected in any case). Rather,
the blessed life and immortality are achieved via the voluntary performance of God's will, as revealed in the divine law—by means of *mitzvot*
and morality, in acts of loving-kindness and justice.

Nevertheless, this does not mean we should *reject* the intellectual approach to God, nor belittle the importance of intellectual perfection in the
blessed life, as some are inclined to do. The key is to recognize just how
closely related moral and intellectual perfection are.

For moral perfection is in fact a part or aspect of intellectual perfection.

For one thing, the intellectual soul that also performs moral actions is clearly superior to the one that does not. The former is even more like God Himself, who is perfect both intellectually and morally, than is the latter. The pursuit of morality therefore increases the perfection of the intellect.

Moral excellence also directly involves intellectual excellence. The moral excellence through which one aims at good deeds is a matter of considering general moral principles with correct judgment, an intellectual act. You can't pursue moral actions unless you understand what constitutes morality!

Moreover, it is precisely by virtue of understanding that God wishes us to perform good actions that we desire to perform them—since we desire to fulfill God's will. We assimilate ourselves to God *by* endeavoring to fulfill His wishes, which requires intellectually grasping what those wishes are. In doing this we seek to perform good actions not for our own sake (for a reward or from fear of punishment), but for *their* own sake, because we love God's goodness and wish to be like Him.

It may be true that some moral actions are not in themselves relevant to the perfection of the intellect. The latter is primarily a contemplative activity, after all, while the former is a matter of behavior and practice. And yet insofar as our moral actions reflect the desire to fulfill the will of the Creator, and it is through our intellect that we grasp that will, then this very desire is intellectual in nature. The key is to recognize that our knowledge of God's will precedes our performance of good works.

And so some err in the overwhelming emphasis on the intellect. Others err in the overwhelming emphasis on practice and morality. For the blessed life is one in which our moral perfection is itself an aspect of our intellectual perfection.

Related Chapters

PART III

SPINOZA–PINSKER
1632–1891

Introduction to Part III

No, no sharp lines between historical periods are ever really possible. But if part II nevertheless amounts to the Maimonides period, then part III belongs to Spinoza.

Like Maimonides, Baruch Spinoza (1632–77) was a controversial figure in the Jewish community. But while Maimonides also garnered great respect due to his preeminence in and devotion to *halacha*, Spinoza, to the contrary, got himself excommunicated. That was fine with him, apparently, at least intellectually. For his work succeeded as much as any other thinker's in removing the rational foundations of religious belief in general. Start with his rejection of a supernatural God; add to it his rejection of free will; add his claim that the Hebrew Bible is not a product of divine revelation but the unclear, sloppily assembled work of very fallible people, and take it from there.

So while Maimonides attempted to reconcile religious belief with rationality, Spinoza essentially argued that rationality should simply supersede religious belief. Indeed the Western world as a whole was entering the "Enlightenment," its practitioners conceiving themselves as emerging from the medieval darkness of religious superstition. In such a world, reason holds sway, and human rights are guaranteed not by arbitrary ancient dictates of a perhaps imaginary God, but by the well-ordered societies constructed by rational leaders.

In such a context the Jewish God Question began to take on striking new forms. Less pressing was the need to reconcile Jewish beliefs with Western philosophy, or to provide reasonable accounts of religious doctrines (including the existence and nature of God). Much more pressing was the problem of reconciling Judaism, and the Jewish people, with the modern age. The dominant questions, as we saw in the preface, included these: Is it feasible to believe in God in the modern world? Should Judaism be discarded altogether in favor of reason, enlightenment? Should a Jew attempt to fit into his surrounding society or distance himself from it? Can a Jew even fit into that society and remain a *Jew*? What changes must be made to Judaism to reconcile it with that society? Can (or should) one separate the Jewish person from the Jewish religion? Can (or should) one separate the Jewish people from the Land of Israel? Should Jews simply disappear as a collective body, convert, intermarry, assimilate, vanish? Or should they return to their ancient homeland and reestablish their long-lost political sovereignty? What does the Jewish religion say about all this? Or should we not even pay attention to it?

It is in this period that Jews really begin grappling with Jewish identity. That is because for the first time Jewish identity was becoming a matter of choice, something it was actually possible to modify and/or give up. Much of this conversation occurs among nineteenth-century German Jews, who seem desperate to fit into the society that was for the first time starting to open its doors to them—or at least seeming to. In light of the subsequent horrors of the twentieth-century Holocaust perpetrated by the German Nazis, it is difficult to read these discussions without a retrospective lump in the throat.

As in all periods, there is some pushback to the dominant themes as well. A modern Orthodoxy also arises in this period, as an effort to affirm traditional Jewish identity in response to its erosion at the hands of enlightenment and emancipation. And we see the first risings of the modern nationalist movement of the Jews, known as political Zionism.

But discussion of that will have to wait for part IV.

43

Baruch Spinoza (1632–77)

One with God—Literally

Everything is God; and neither we, nor God, acts freely

Many philosophers accept the idea that everything that exists is either a "substance" or a feature or aspect *of* some substance. Spinoza agrees—but then draws some astonishing implications from this idea.

What is a *substance*? Something capable of existing independently of other things. The color of a particular fruit (say, the red of an apple) is *not* a substance because the apple's redness cannot exist independently of the apple; it is rather a feature or aspect of the apple. But the apple can exist without that particular color, for example as it grows and ripens. So the apple would seem to be a substance, an individual, physical substance.

Except that this isn't quite right. Because an apple cannot really exist independently of other things. In fact *nothing* in the physical cosmos can exist independently, nor can even the cosmos as a whole do so. Why not? Because anyone who believes in God agrees that the cosmos and its contents were created by God and depend on God not only for their initial creation but for remaining in existence since. God continuously sustains the cosmos at every moment at which it exists—and so neither the cosmos as a whole nor anything in it counts as a substance.

If a "substance" can exist independently then, strictly speaking, there is only one substance: God Himself, who depends on nothing and on whom all other things depend.

But then what is the cosmos, if it isn't a substance? There is only one other option: it must be a feature or aspect *of* some substance. But what substance? There is only one option here, too, so the answer is unavoidable: God.

So everything that exists—you, that apple, the heavens—is really just a feature or aspect of God.

But that isn't all.

People think of God as being very like a person. In particular they imagine that He freely chooses to do most, and maybe everything, that He does—as we do. Well, they're right about the parallel, but they're wrong in all the details.

Let's first note that God both exists necessarily and is the cause of His own existence.

It may sound strange to speak of something causing itself, but it shouldn't. A cause is a logical explanation of or reason for some effect, much as we'd say that the reason a given figure is a square is that it has four sides. When we say that, we don't mean that first it has four sides and then it comes to be a square; we mean that its four sides *explain* its being a square. As such, causes need not exist before their effects but may be simultaneous with them. To say that God causes Himself is then merely to say that His very nature or essence, as an infinite or unlimited being, explains why He exists. Or to put it differently, the very idea of God includes the fact that He exists: it's part of *what* He is, *that* He is. It's therefore impossible for God not to exist, and so God exists necessarily.

But now, in a valid logical argument, the premises necessitate the conclusion: it's impossible for the premises to be true without the conclusion's being true. Since causes just are logical explanations, they too will necessitate their effects: it's impossible for the cause to exist without the effect also existing. Since God necessarily exists and causes (that is, necessitates) Himself, with all His features and aspects, then every feature or aspect of God must also necessarily exist. By His own nature, then, God is necessitated to do everything He does. Which means that He could not act in any way other than He does.

But the cosmos just is a feature or aspect of God. So in necessarily causing Himself to exist God necessitates the entire *cosmos* to exist and everything that occurs therein—in the precise sequence and manner that it does, according to the laws of nature.

This of course includes us: whatever we do we are necessitated to do by the laws of nature, which are necessitated by God. It's therefore impossible for us ever to act otherwise than we do.

So we do not act freely.

And neither does God.

So God is very much like us after all.

Related Chapters

10 Halevi, 15 Ibn Daud, 18 Maimonides, 21 Ben Samuel, 22 De Leon, 23 Abulafia, 25 Abner of Burgos, 26 Pollegar, 27 Ibn Kaspi, 29 Gersonides, 31 Ben Joshua, 34 Crescas, 36 Alemanno, 44 Spinoza, 46 Maimon, 49 Steinheim, 67 Buber, 71 Soloveitchik, 76 Berkovits, 80 Jonas

44

Baruch Spinoza (1632–77)

Gazing at Eternity with Fresh Eyes

The modern age requires a rethinking of the nature of the Bible, starting with a rejection of the supernatural

The highest goal of human life, says Spinoza, is to acquire a love of God through correct knowledge of God, an intellectual love, as it were. Only with that knowledge do we acquire genuine freedom, the freedom from being governed by our emotions; for once we grasp the true nature of God and the cosmos, once we see that how things are is how they *must* be, once we see all from the perspective of eternity, then and only then can we truly *accept* the cosmos. To live by reason, and to love by reason, is human blessedness, and it is that for which we aim.

Organized religions preach blessedness of course, but we must approach them with the same careful reason that we apply to the natural world. We must separate religion from the politics that sometimes intrudes; we must get at the true core messages before human institutions corrupt them. We must also separate the political structures of the modern state from the religious institutions with which they have become entangled. In so doing we advance political and religious peace—as consensus on universal truths, undistorted by particularist perspectives and agendas, should only promote such peace.

To do this requires reading the Hebrew Bible with fresh eyes, the eyes of a scientist, to understand what it really teaches. We must not import into the text what is not there, such as our own prejudices and preferences, and avoid exporting from the text only what we wish. Even the great

Maimonides is guilty of these sins, forcing the biblical text into a synthesis with an archaic philosophy that it just cannot sustain.

Such fresh eyes reveal that while the Bible does sketch a political structure, it is one limited to its time: a theocracy with no distinction between divine and civil law, between religion and state. There were advantages to this at the time, for the Israelites who were newly liberated from slavery and living in the Land of Israel. But now that that kingdom is long gone, Mosaic Law is simply obsolete, and Jews are no longer bound to follow even its ceremonies and rituals. Theocracy may have been useful once, but it is out of place in the modern era.

Fresh eyes in fact challenge *many* of the theses long endorsed by traditional Judaism.

Prophecy is nothing supernatural, and teaches nothing philosophical or scientific; it is only a matter of moral advising. The Jewish people were not "chosen" in any sense other than that, for a time, they were a flourishing sovereign nation; that is of course no longer true. The divine Law is nothing other than the laws of nature; all the ceremonies and rituals of Judaism have at best only political or social usefulness, not divine sanction. Miracles are not possible, for miracles violate nature; and since God is nothing more than nature, admitting them would be to deny God. The Torah (the first five books of the Bible) was likely not written by Moses himself but had other authors; and indeed the Bible as a whole, like any other historical, human-authored text, may not have always existed in the form we have it today. And so on.

In short: God is everything, so God is nature, so there is nothing supernatural—not in the cosmos, and not in this ancient text, once read properly.

In the enlightened modern world we must forge a modern religion, one preaching universal morality and true blessedness, freed from the shackles of emotion and historical and institutional darkness.

Related Chapters

11 Halevi, 12 Halevi, 15 Ibn Daud, 17 Maimonides, 24 Albalag, 27 Ibn Kaspi, 28 Gersonides, 30 Ben Elijah, 38 Abravanel, 39 Del Medigo, 45 Mendelssohn, 47 Ascher, 50 Geiger, 51 Holdheim, 65 Cohen, 72 Strauss, 73 Strauss

45

Moses Mendelssohn (1729–86)

Have Your Kosher Cake (and Eat It, Too)

*An observant Jew can also be a full citizen
of the nation in which s/he lives*

Can Jews, with their separate ways and laws, be successfully incorporated into the larger modern society? Yes, argues Mendelssohn—once it's understood that traditional Judaism is perfectly rational, and that it is a personal, voluntary commitment consistent with broader citizenship.

First, in general, there must be a sharp separation between the state and religion. A state should be an association of human beings who agree to work together to support their temporal welfare and security, its powers regulating only behaviors relevant to that end. A state has no business regulating any individual's internal sentiments or beliefs, or conceptions of eternal welfare. While a state may legitimately coerce individuals to obey its legitimate laws, religion may not do so, but merely educate and persuade.

Next, nothing in Judaism is "against reason," for Judaism is not a religion of doctrines or dogmas, of principles necessary for salvation, so there is nothing in it that *could* contradict reason. The great voice on Mount Sinai did not proclaim and demand consent to otherwise inaccessible propositions such as, "I am the Eternal God, the necessarily existent being, omnipotent and omniscient," and so on. That God exists and has these attributes may well be true, but these truths are not unique to Judaism; indeed there are *no* eternal truths other than those entirely comprehensible to human reason and demonstrable by rational means.

What was revealed at Sinai was not a set of doctrines, but *legislation*: laws, commandments, rules of life promoting both temporal and eternal blessedness. The Jewish religion demands of Jews not particular beliefs but particular actions, not "You shall believe" but "You shall do." Faith is demanded not in the sense of "irrational belief in the truth of a proposition" but in the sense of trust, reliance, and confidence in God and in these rules. Maimonides may have formulated "principles of faith," triggering many debates, but none of the disputants ever accuses the others of being *heretics*. That's because what really matters is practice, not belief.

In ancient times these laws were a constitution for the Jewish state, where state and religion were one. Those who broke the religious laws were rightfully subject to state punishment, because only the state is authorized to punish. But with the destruction of the Second Temple in 70 CE the political bonds of the nation were dissolved, and religious offenses were no longer crimes against the state. The religion, as a religion, can allow no punishment other than the one the remorseful sinner *voluntarily* imposes on himself.

This doesn't mean that Jews should reject these laws. To the contrary these laws remain binding on Jews, on all Jews, as a matter of conscience, unless clear and compelling reasons demonstrate otherwise. For example, laws that presuppose Jewish sovereignty over the Land of Israel (Temple sacrifices, priestly purification, agriculture, etc.) are obviously no longer applicable, given the exile. But all other rules, personal duties, must be observed, not as a matter of coercion but of individual conscience. Neither the state nor the Jewish community has the power to coerce with respect to such matters.

And so the individual Jew should adapt himself to the morals and constitution of the land in which he resides as far as possible, while retaining the religion of his forefathers—no matter how cumbersome that may be. As long as Judaism remains a rational, personal, voluntary practice and requires public allegiance to none other than the state authorities, nothing in it contradicts life as a full, if Jewish, member of civil society.

Related Chapters

17 Maimonides, 35 Albo, 38 Abravanel, 44 Spinoza, 46 Maimon, 47 Ascher, 48 Zunz, 49 Steinheim, 50 Geiger, 51 Holdheim, 52 Sofer, 53 Frankel, 54 Krochmal, 55 Hirsch, 64 Cohen, 72 Strauss, 73 Strauss

46

Solomon Maimon (1753–1800)

Don't Belong to Any Club That Has You for a Member

Spinoza is not an atheist, and Mendelssohn wrongly thinks you can reject Jewish Law yet remain part of the Jewish community

The great philosopher Immanuel Kant (1724–1804) said that none of his critics understood him as well as Maimon, for few had Maimon's acumen. Yet despite his brilliance, Maimon did not "fit in": as a Jew he was excluded from the Gentile philosophical community, and with his sympathies for the excommunicated Spinoza and his critique of Mendelssohn, he was not embraced by the Jews either.

Spinoza indeed is a problem for many Jews, for his identification of God and nature is read by many as a form of atheism. If God is nothing other than nature, after all, then nothing exists beyond nature, nothing "super-natural."

But this reading fails to appreciate how Spinoza's philosophy actually resembles the Kabbalah. Spinoza argues that the physical cosmos and all the things therein are really just finite "aspects" of the infinite substance, the infinite being. All things, in other words, are just different kinds of limitations of the infinite being. But this is just a version of the Kabbalistic idea of *tzimtzum*, divine self-contraction. God, whose infinite being is unlimited, "contracts" Himself in order to make "space" for other, limited and finite beings. These "new" beings are not created out of materials independent of God, for nothing is independent of God. Rather they are simply different ways in which God may contract or limit Himself into finite forms.

"God is nature," then, means nothing more than that nature is a limited form of God. Spinoza's system is not atheism, but *acosmism*—for it denies that the cosmos is in any way independent of, has an independent status from, God.

Spinoza gets another thing right: there is no real distinction between the Jewish religion and the Jewish political community. Jewish Law, *halacha*, is really just the laws of the Jewish state. Anyone who considers himself a member of the Jewish community must therefore follow those laws. For Spinoza, all of that expired when the Jewish political community was destroyed with the Second Temple (70 CE). But the essential point still applies: to be part of the Jewish community, to enjoy whatever rights and privileges that membership confers, obligates you to obey those laws. The difference is that in the modern era we believe that individuals should have freedom of choice about which community to join, and should not be coerced in religious matters. If someone should choose to remove himself from the Jewish community and free himself from those laws, that is his right.

Here is where Mendelssohn gets mixed up. In his zeal to affirm freedom of conscience he argues that the Jewish community should *not* have the right to excommunicate someone. But he also argues that anyone born a Jew should live and die according to Jewish Law. But now what is the Jewish community but the contemporary Jewish political community? And what is a state that does not itself have certain rights? Excommunication is merely the expression of a basic right that all political institutions have: if you oppose the laws of the community, then you also forego whatever rights and privileges obtain from that membership therein—and must therefore be excluded from it.

You can certainly choose to exclude yourself from a community, and perhaps in this enlightened age, now is the time to remove yourself from ancient Jewish Law. But you cannot demand the benefits of belonging while rejecting that Law.

Related Chapters

47

Saul Ascher (1767–1822)

To Everything There Is a Season—
Including Traditional Judaism

*Modern times require a reformulation of Judaism,
from a religion of law to one of belief*

According to Ascher, Mendelssohn's insistence that Jews should continue observing Jewish Law even while attempting integration into broader civil society is profoundly flawed.

First, Mendelssohn argues that what God revealed on Sinai was neither doctrines nor dogmas nor "eternal truths" (about God's existence and nature), but only legislation, the Law. But what then is the purpose of the Law, particularly when human reason can now demonstrate the relevant eternal truths on its own? If its purpose is to establish a Mosaic constitution, as Mendelssohn seems to suggest, then the Law must cease the moment this constitution no longer exists (as it did with the destruction of the Second Temple in 70 CE). Or if its purpose is merely to teach people the historical truths about the Jewish people and their relationship to God, then its work is done: now that people already know these truths, they can forego the Law.

If anything, the broader civil integration that Mendelssohn seeks for Jews is only *hampered* by our ongoing commitment to the Law, which maintains us as a distinct population within the community. True integration thus requires a thorough reform, a *reformulation* of Judaism. Rather than see it as essentially legislation—one whose purpose is now fulfilled and that keeps us segregated—we must establish a new constitution, one that will maintain the religious faith of our ancestors, reflect the true essence of

Judaism, and guide us toward becoming good persons and good citizens of our surrounding communities. The rabbinic authorities may not approve, for they treat any changes in or to the Law as an absolute abandonment of Judaism. But it is precisely their ancient authority that must now be over-ridden in modern times.

So which essential features of Judaism should be preserved, and thus shape this reformulation of the faith? That Judaism aims at making people happy; that it contains an original revelation requiring faith in a set of beliefs about the nature and existence of God; that obedience to the Law was only a means to an end; that the Law was relevant only to maintaining the society over time and preserving certain memories. But the Law is not itself the *essence* of the religion, hence it may be transformed (and even overturned) when the goal of human happiness may be obtained by other means. On these principles we need not reject (for example) the observance of the Sabbath altogether; we may still consider it "sacred," and maintain its essence, while changing all its details—so that observing it need not exclude us from participating in wider society.

And change those details we must, for our maintaining the ancient Law makes us subject to the ridicule of other citizens, who call out, "Your religion is no longer good for our time! Deny it and become full human beings!" What we must show is that the essence of our religion—not the Law, but our beliefs—indeed does make us as full human beings and full citizens as those surrounding us who believe in the Christian religion.

What do we believe? In God, the God who revealed Himself to our ancestors, who gave them laws that were sacred to them and maintained them on the same path that we are on today—a path we now follow not by means of Law, but through our faith in God and His prophets.

The Law, and rabbinic authority, had their appropriate times and places. But the rational, enlightened world is neither.

Related Chapters

44 Spinoza, 45 Mendelssohn, 46 Maimon, 48 Zunz, 49 Steinheim, 50 Geiger, 51 Holdheim, 52 Sofer, 53 Frankel, 70 Kaplan, 83 Borowitz

48

Leopold Zunz (1794–1886)

Those Who Can, Do;
Those Who Cannot, Study

*Modern scholarship (or "science") is essential
for Jews to become full members of society*

The situation for Jews in the early nineteenth century was not very good, but Zunz has a proposal for how to repair it. In a word, *Wissenschaft*; in an English word, "science"; in a phrase, the "Society for the Culture and Scientific Study of the Jews."

Despite the early blossoming of the ideals of emancipation, we Jews are in an impoverished and vulnerable state, politically, economically, spiritually, and psychologically. Long lacking civil rights, we now find ourselves sorely in need of correction and improvement, both internally and externally. The long list of internal flaws includes our inclination toward superstition and avarice; our outdated, meaningless customs and ceremonial laws; a contempt of secular and practical education; ignorance and even immorality among the students of the *yeshiva* (religious school); and objectionable attitudes toward the female sex. Nor is our external situation among the Christians much better, as we are excluded from commerce, crafts, and agriculture, and are stereotyped by our fellow citizens as lazy; unsophisticated; coarse in speech, comportment, and manners; and disinterested in integrating into broader society. All this culminated in the dreadful riots against us that broke out throughout Germany in 1819, known as the "Hep! Hep!" riots, named after the medieval Crusaders' terrifying call to murder Jews.

It is time to break free of this impoverishment and vulnerability, and to do so via *Wissenschaft*, or "science." In place of the shackles of traditional religious Judaism we must now devote ourselves to the study *of* our religion, our history, and our culture.

The goal of the "Society for the Culture and Scientific Study of the Jews" is to promote and produce a scholarly overview of "rabbinic literature"—that is, the history of Jewish writing and culture. Previously such work has been neglected. Traditional religious Jews scorn modern secular scholarship as sacrilegious, while secular Jews see no value in studying ancient rabbinic writings; and when Christian scholars have done such work it has only been to distort classical Jewish sources and validate their own religion. It is time now for modern Jews to apply scholarly methods to these ancient texts, to produce histories, philosophical studies, theologies, legal texts, linguistic and philological texts, studies of the natural sciences and medicine in these texts, studies of poetry, and so on. In so doing we shall extract the living spirit or essence of the Judaism that has, over time, become ossified. We shall extract the good and the beautiful from centuries of Jewish writings in order to keep Jewishness alive, in respectable modern forms, into the era of the liberal nation-state.

This task is necessary not merely for the internal welfare of our people. The "Science of Judaism," by bestowing upon Judaism the respect this long tradition deserves, will also facilitate our obtaining our deserved rights and liberty as full members of German society. While developing this science will require the development of many schools, seminaries, and synagogues, it is also essential that we do not segregate Jewish scholarship into Jewish institutions. We must not ghettoize Jewish scholarship; instead it must become incorporated into the well-established and flourishing organs of the modern German universities. As Jewish scholarship gains academic legitimacy in this manner, it can help remove barriers to the civil integration of Jews.

Indeed, scholarship, the spread of careful reason, emphasis on (in a word) *science*, can only help dissolve the irrational prejudices that grip so many. Thus it is that modern Jews can in their fatherland ultimately become brothers, and achieve an equal footing, with all other German citizens.

Related Chapters

45 Mendelssohn, 47 Ascher, 50 Geiger, 51 Holdheim, 52 Sofer, 53 Frankel, 54 Krochmal, 55 Hirsch, 56 Hirsch, 65 Cohen, 70 Kaplan, 83 Borowitz

49

Solomon Steinheim (1789–1866)

Ya Gotta Believe!

The metaphysical doctrine of creation ex nihilo *is part of Judaism's essence*

Those who seek progress, who attempt to reconcile Judaism with the modern age, Steinheim argues, have misunderstood not merely the external aspects of the religion (such as its rituals) but also its most basic ideas.

Mendelssohn and his disciples, for example, admirably aim to purge Judaism of its superstitious elements. But they do so by shaping it into a form pleasing to the shallow rationalism of their day—namely, by denying to Judaism any metaphysical or cosmological doctrines, any "eternal truths," affirming only its modes of worship, the laws, the rituals. This capitulation to the reigning ideal leaves little of Judaism except periwig and beard, and these ephemeral fashions themselves soon made way for the more modern pomade and powder. It is no surprise that Mendelssohn's own descendants soon converted to Christianity!

Judaism is far more than its worship and laws. For its *metaphysical truths* are its vital nerve, its essential heart, its inner flame; and it is this spiritual heart, passed down through generations with the mother's milk, that has retained our collective identity, as if spiritually sealed, through the centuries of exile and dispersion.

The metaphysical essence of Judaism is in fact as simple as it is profound. It is not available to us by the ordinary methods of acquiring knowledge of the cosmos, via sensory experience, innate ideas, and reason. It is—it was—given to us only in revelation: that the cosmos was created, by God, *ex nihilo*, out of nothing.

The old maxim of philosophy, the purely rational approach to the cosmos, holds the opposite instead, that nothing comes from nothing. On that maxim everything that occurs in the cosmos must have a cause, a cause that generates its effect, compels it to occur. When we discover the cause of something we find ourselves able to explain or understand the phenomenon. The whole idea of the cosmos being intelligible, able to be understood and explained, is thus based on that maxim.

Fair enough, but there is also a serious downside to the maxim. The cosmos governed by it, in which everything has a cause, is also one in which there can be no human freedom. For human beings are components of the natural world; our bodies are among the physical bodies governed by laws of nature. If everything has a cause, then so, too, do all our bodily actions; and with the chain of causation stretching far back in time, to events out of our control, we cannot avoid the conclusion that nothing we do, we ever do freely.

Without freedom on the highest level, in the creation and operations of the cosmos, then, there can be no human freedom—as well as no possibility of the morality that requires such freedom.

And that is why revelation is so profound. Scripture teaches us that the philosophical maxim is false, that God Himself created the world out of nothing, that something *can* come from nothing. The maxim, shattered, now makes it possible that, just as the divinity did with creation, so too we may do in our own conduct: act from or out of nothing, and create our behavior. The revealed doctrine of creation at the heart of our religion thus shifts its implications from metaphysical knowledge to the realm of action—and brings forth the moral human being whose actions are freely generated.

It is the metaphysical content of Judaism, not its rituals, laws, and worship, that wins the fight of freedom against necessity, of morality against sensuality, of theology against idolatry.

Related Chapters

3 Saadia Ben Joseph Gaon, 7 Ibn Paquda, 9 Ibn Tzaddik, 13 Ibn Ezra, 14 Ibn Daud, 15 Ibn Daud, 25 Abner of Burgos, 26 Pollegar, 27 Ibn Kaspi, 29 Gersonides, 31 Ben Joshua, 33 Crescas, 34 Crescas, 43 Spinoza, 45 Mendelssohn, 47 Ascher, 76 Berkovits, 80 Jonas

50

Abraham Geiger (1810–74)

The More Things Change, the More They Stay the Same

The unchanging essence of Judaism itself dictates Judaism's modern reform

As the "Science of Judaism" shows, according to Geiger, Judaism has always changed and evolved over time, even while maintaining its essential character. Now that the modern era opens the possibility of Jews becoming full and integrated members of their societies, it is time for it to evolve again, time to reform Judaism. No longer should Jews be seen as a separate people or nation. No longer should we demand collective political rights, nor entertain messianic hopes of national redemption and a return from "exile" to the Land of Israel. Rather, Judaism must become, not the constitution of the Jewish state (as once it was), but a religion that an individual can choose privately to adopt. Just as a person could be a German of the Protestant faith, so one could be a German of the Jewish faith.

But this is not to *reject* Judaism—for the study of Jewish history shows that change is the norm, and even offers guidance on how to proceed.

We may discern four major periods of Jewish history.

Judaism began within the context of a full national life, with both a national language and a history. Its first period, which we may label "Revelation," begins in the earliest prehistory of the children of Israel and extends to the close of the biblical period (roughly fifth century BCE). In this era Jewish people were vigorously creative as they incorporated religious and ethical truths into the biblical texts they were composing.

121

The second period, "Tradition," extends until the close of the Talmud in the sixth century CE. During this period the biblical material was processed, molded, and adapted for living conditions in constantly changing times and places. Notably, the children of Israel underwent expulsions and dispersal, and the Jewish religion adapted even as it began to transcend national boundaries.

Then began the long period of "Rigid Legalism," lasting until the present day, in which the rabbis engaged in their toilsome preoccupation with *halacha*, the laws. Their increasingly rigid codification of and allegiance to the Law was perhaps necessary as Jews endured centuries under dark, medieval oppression. But that period, thankfully, has ended with modern European emancipation.

And now we have entered the age of "Liberation"—liberation from the ancient customs and from the shackles of the Law, as we now guide ourselves by reason. But our goal, again, is not entirely to sever the bond with the past, but rather to learn from it as we revitalize Judaism for the modern era. We seek to maintain its essence, the fixed character that has ever remained the same even as our religion adapted itself to changing historical circumstances.

That essence?

To bear witness, for the sake of all humanity, to the existence of the one and only God—grasp of which in turn teaches us, in a rational manner, of universal moral truths, of the unity of mankind, the equality of all before the law, the equality of all citizens with respect to duties and rights from the state, as well as the complete freedom of the individual in his religious convictions.

The modern age indeed liberates us—from the Law, from ceremonies and rituals that long ago lost point and purpose, from outdated authorities, even from the use of the archaic Hebrew language in the contemporary prayer service. But while the modern age severs us from the external trappings of our past, it is not only *not* a severing from the actual essence of Judaism, but rather the natural next stage in its ongoing evolution.

Related Chapters

11 Halevi, 12 Halevi, 20 Nachmanides, 38 Abravanel, 44 Spinoza, 45 Mendelssohn, 46 Maimon, 47 Ascher, 48 Zunz, 51 Holdheim, 52 Sofer, 53 Frankel, 54 Krochmal, 55 Hirsch, 56 Hirsch, 70 Kaplan, 83 Borowitz

51

Samuel Holdheim (1806–60)

Love Your Compatriot as You Love Yourself

The spiritual mission of Judaism
is best served by its radical reform

The true mission of Judaism, according to Holdheim, is not particular, but universal: it seeks not to restore the ancient theocracy in the Land of Israel but to merge Jewry into the political and national frameworks of the current day.

Careful study of the Talmud, for example, reveals that much of the original ceremonial law, the rituals and *mitzvot*, existed because the Jews had to be kept separate from other peoples, as holiness expresses itself by means of separation. That many ancient peoples were pagan made this concern more pressing. Had the Jews been the only people in the world, there would have been no need for laws to *keep* them apart.

Since those days, of course, much of humankind has come to the monotheism at the heart of Judaism. But if the laws are unnecessary when the Jews are physically alone in the world, they are also unnecessary now— when the Jews are no longer *spiritually* alone in their religious beliefs.

For this was our mission: to spread belief in the one God, along with the universal morality that accompanies it (in the form, for example, of the seven "Noachide Laws"). That was our *messianic* task, to make these the common possession of all. And we have indeed come a long way toward completing this task, in our millennia-long history. All those innumerable peoples and nations that once were pagan were converted to our universal monotheism, largely because we have been dispersed throughout them.

Contemporary Judaism must now be reformed to reflect the new conditions.

The messianic era must not therefore be conceived as a return to the ancient political theocracy, a backwards step that removes us from the societies in which we are at home. Indeed those who today hope for a national restoration contradict our feelings for the fatherland; further, they distance us in the eyes of our compatriots from our essential task of merging ourselves and our religion. Moreover, those with this hope fail to understand the necessary distinction between religion and nationality. Being Jewish by religion, which we affirm, must not be mistaken for the idea of being Jewish by "nationality," which we reject.

Some who wish to return to the Land of Israel to create a political state do so because they wish to aid their oppressed coreligionists. But their wish, and their work, should aim instead toward terminating the oppression itself. And in any case their goal is misconceived, for the messianic hope of our religion is for *spiritual* redemption and liberation. This in no way depends on the establishment of a Jewish state, but rather on our successful integration into the political and national structures of today.

To that end, there are many reforms to be made to our faith. The commandment to love one's brother, formerly understood to refer to the love only of a fellow Israelite, must also oblige us with regard to our compatriots, our fellow Germans. Indeed compatriots first, we say, and coreligionists second! Moreover we must reject circumcision, and reform the traditional laws of marriage and divorce to better match our culture's norms. For the same reason, we should move the Sabbath from Saturday to Sunday.

It is in this way that we can better become Germans, Germans of the Jewish faith—and thus maintain the long-term preservation of Judaism among the nations without diminishing the sense of unity we share with all people.

We shall nourish our love for Judaism without diminishing our love of humankind.

Related Chapters

12 Halevi, 20 Nachmanides, 44 Spinoza, 45 Mendelssohn, 46 Maimon, 47 Ascher, 48 Zunz, 50 Geiger, 52 Sofer, 53 Frankel, 54 Krochmal, 55 Hirsch, 56 Hirsch, 57 Salanter, 64 Cohen, 70 Kaplan, 74 Levinas, 83 Borowitz

52

Moses Sofer (Hatam Sofer)
(1762–1839)

Same as It Ever Was

Contra "Reform," one should change nothing in Judaism unless absolutely necessary

The movement to "reform" Judaism was underway, and Sofer, a traditionalist, is not happy with what he sees.

People who do not submit to the yoke of heaven have lately appeared, seeking to nullify the divine covenant through various schemes. Their synagogues are closed all week, opening only for the Sabbath. But even there they alter the texts of prayers dating back to the Men of the Great Assembly (sixth century BCE). They add and they subtract, remove benedictions mandated by the Talmud—even the benedictions for the messiah and for the rebuilding of Jerusalem! They appoint a non-Jew to play a musical instrument on the holy Sabbath, desecrating it, wishing to be like their non-Jewish compatriots who have music in their religious services. Not surprisingly most of their prayers are in German, as well.

They call this a "reform" of Judaism, but this is not the Jewish religion as it has been known since ancient times, since the prophets, since the Second Temple. This is not the Jewish religion in the Mishna, in the Talmud, the centuries of commentaries. For nearly two thousand years the basic ideas of our religion have been established, and no one has protested. But now insignificant foxes breach the walls, change the prayers and benedictions, alter the hours and times that have been appointed for them.

This is no reform of Judaism, but a rejection of it.

They say that prayers for the messiah and the restoration of the Holy Temple in Jerusalem are now moot, since we are dwelling in peace and tranquility among the nations. But this is not so. Even when we had sovereignty in our Holy Land we prayed for the messiah, so that all humanity could experience the goodness of the Lord. We do not need the fruits of the easy and tranquil life among the nations. We do not pour our hearts out daily in hope of illusory material tranquility. Our eternal hope is to dwell in the presence of God in the Land of Israel, the place designated for His service and the observance of Torah.

Indeed we are as prisoners of the war of the destruction of the Second Temple. We dwell among the nations temporarily, and we are grateful to those who have extended us great kindnesses. We do not disregard tranquility, where we find it. But our place is not where we are, but there, in the Land of Israel, and when that time comes for our return, God will repay handsomely those of the nations who treated us with kindness.

The "reformers" do not even pray in the sacred tongue of Hebrew! The common people do not understand that tongue, they say. But then the answer is to have each person learn the meaning of the prayers and recite them in Hebrew, which is far better than reciting them in another language. One does not act in such a way before a human king. He who speaks with the king must speak the language of the king. All the more so with the King of Kings.

It is forbidden to pray from vernacular prayer books. It is forbidden to play a musical instrument in the synagogue on the Sabbath. One should change *nothing* unless absolutely necessary—not the reader's stand, the arrangement of the services, the ways we do things in service to God—for we trace our prayers all the way back to the ancient days, when the eternal God so commanded us.

And still commands us to this day.

Related Chapters

12 Halevi, 20 Nachmanides, 45 Mendelssohn, 47 Ascher, 48 Zunz, 50 Geiger, 51 Holdheim, 53 Frankel, 54 Krochmal, 55 Hirsch, 56 Hirsch, 70 Kaplan, 83 Borowitz

53

Zacharias Frankel (1801–75)

Goldilocks Judaism

Reform jettisons too much, Orthodoxy jettisons too little; the middle ground is just right

At the 1845 Reform Rabbinical Conference in Frankfurt, leaders argued that Hebrew should be replaced in the liturgy with German. Frankel, though sympathetic to the need to reform Judaism, walked out in protest.

The Reformers have gone too far, he thinks, not only in language and liturgy, but also in essentially rejecting the Talmud, the Sabbath, and any conception of messianic hope. Capitulating to the spirit of the times—as ephemeral and fickle as that can be—they are actually creating a *new* religion to appeal to some highly assimilated German Jews, but one estranged from the needs and wishes of the Jewish people as a whole.

What we need is something that better conserves tradition.

One response is that of the Orthodox, for whom the performance of *mitzvot* as handed down from posterity is inseparable from Judaism. Their position may be clear, but it goes to the opposite extreme of Reform: it is too far *out* of touch with the times. Orthodoxy treats Judaism ahistorically, as if historical context and change did not exist. The result is empty and mechanical observance of obsolete traditions. Unable to grow with the times, it is destined not to survive.

In fact, as the Science of Judaism has shown, traditional Judaism *has* changed over time. The Reformers cite a study, for example, that claims that already in the third-century Mishna, the rabbis were inventing new laws that they then read back into the Bible through fanciful interpretations.

Though other studies suggest that many of those laws date as far back as the sixth century BCE, the point remains: the rabbis often generated novel rulings and halachic changes.

So Judaism can and does change, and indeed must. But not the way the Reformers do it. To them Jewish history has been entirely passive, with religious changes arising only in order to adapt to always dominant, external forces. As such, Reformers feel authorized to change Judaism as they see fit, in accordance with contemporary times, and to do so in large, sudden strokes.

What they fail to understand is that the Jewish religion is the product of creative Jewish activity, generated by its own *internal* principles—principles that do allow it to change over time—but organically, by internal mechanisms.

What we need, then, is a "positive-historical" approach to Judaism.

The "positive" recognizes the creative force; the "historical," that the force is *internal* to Judaism. Judaism changes when the will of the people, as a whole, dictates it. Certain practices fall into disuse, cease to exist; other practices arise, in various historical contexts and times, and become popular. But this always takes place in the context of the history of the people and of the religion. *Halacha* itself does not have normative force in the abstract, does not command obedience; only the will of the people does, the will informed by its own history.

True, the Jews are a divided and divisive bunch, and Judaism no longer has priests. But we do have sages and scholars who are immersed in our history while also sensitive to the character of the times. The task is on them to help Judaism grow and evolve, in a *patient* manner—by disseminating their work on the history of our faith, with emphasis on conserving the tradition where possible, and by persuading the people that any proposed changes will not lead to the disappearance of our faith.

Reform jettisons nearly everything. Orthodoxy preserves nearly everything. The positive-historical approach seeks the middle ground.

Related Chapters

45 Mendelssohn, 47 Ascher, 48 Zunz, 50 Geiger, 51 Holdheim, 52 Sofer, 54 Krochmal, 55 Hirsch, 56 Hirsch, 70 Kaplan, 83 Borowitz, 85 Ross

54

Nachman Krochmal (1785–1840)

The Light unto the Nations

The Jews are a nation, with a spirit and history, but one with a special spirit and history

Maimonides wrote his *Guide for the Perplexed* for those who were perplexed then, about how to reconcile Judaism with Aristotle's philosophy. But modern times bring new perplexities, such as whether Judaism has any place at all in the modern world. Krochmal's *Guide for the Perplexed of Our Time* says it does.

The Reform movement sees Judaism and the Jews as "supranational": Jews are not a nation and Judaism is just a religion, so a Jewish person can be a full citizen wherever he lives while privately practicing his religion. The Orthodox see both as "ahistorical": Judaism is the religion of the Jewish people as a nation, and continues today in the same form as given by God on Sinai.

But both are wrong—as becomes clear once you grasp the true nature of the history of nations, as found in the work of such illustrious thinkers as G. W. F. Hegel (1770–1831) and others.

All nations manifest a certain "spirit" that reflects their national essence. The evolution of nations over time, the way certain nations attain historical preeminence and then decay, in fact amounts to the gradual evolution of, the making explicit of, the Absolute Spirit of God. So understood, the progression of history becomes meaningful: it is the march of human progress as the Divine Spirit increasingly becomes manifest in increasingly enlightened societies.

Along the way nations typically pass through three stages. The first is that of germination and growth, when a people coalesces into a distinct entity. The second is that of power and achievement, when the nation, moved by its spirit, actualizes its spirit fully, corresponding to that period when the nation peaks in political power and influence. Then, after having contributed its particular spiritual element to humanity in general, the nation declines, fades away, disappears from history. Empirical study shows how typical this progression is, and how Absolute Spirit becomes increasingly explicit in the sequence of nations.

The Jewish nation is different, however.

While it too has undergone cycles such as those above, at the end of each cycle it *regenerates*, in an ongoing renewal of its national spirit. We see it repeatedly: after the exile to Babylon, the destruction of the Temple, the expulsions in medieval Europe, the great expulsion from Spain, and so on.

This is no accident, for the Jewish people have, since their origin, been a repository of the Divine Spirit that never can die. The Jewish nation will continually renew, eternally renew, because it so fully manifests the eternal spirit. This is what the Bible means in so many places, when it notes that God dwells among them, that the divine presence rests in Israel, when God says to them "I am with you."

Such passages do not merely emphasize the special particularity of the Jewish people. Rather, Jewish particularity is unique precisely in that it simultaneously expresses the universal; or better, it *dissolves* the traditional distinctions between particularity and universality, between transcendence and immanence, between religion and politics. Israel, the children of Israel, expresses in its particularity the universal Divine Spirit. Unlike ancient nations who expressed their particular spirits and their particular "gods," Israel expresses the one universal God, the God who, despite His transcendence, manifests Himself or His Spirit in the course of history. Its religion is the one that most fully brings God directly into the political order.

So the Jews (like all nations) and Judaism (like all religions) have a history—but unlike others theirs is one of the eternal renewal of Absolute Spirit, as a light unto the nations.

Related Chapters

45 Mendelssohn, 46 Maimon, 47 Ascher, 48 Zunz, 50 Geiger, 51 Hold-heim, 52 Sofer, 53 Frankel, 55 Hirsch, 56 Hirsch, 66 Rosenzweig, 70 Kaplan, 83 Borowitz

55

Samson Raphael Hirsch (1808–88)

When Progress Amounts to Regress

The movement to "reform" Judaism amounts to the rejection of Judaism

"Religion allied to progress." That is the bold slogan of the German Reform movement that lures "progressive" youth, with their frock coats and evening dresses, to reject their ancient religion. Judaism obstructs progress, they claim, and so it must "reform"—or, what they *really* mean, according to Hirsch, disappear.

For "allying religion to progress" amounts to this: religion can exist as long as it does not hinder progress. "Progress," then, is that to which all other ideals must submit. But the subordination of religion to any other principle simply means the denial of religion, for if the Torah is the Law of God, how could you place *anything* above it? Only those for whom religion is *not* the word of God, who believe not in revelation given to human beings but in revelation created *by* human beings, feel entitled to lay down conditions on religion. They worship "progress" over eternal truth—by which they mean whatever cultural and intellectual fancies rule the current day.

In so doing they dance on the graves of their forefathers, mock them for being crude and uncivilized, and admit no God except themselves and their own whims.

This does not mean that Jews cannot learn from the modern world, engage with it, contribute to it. But the difference is this: the reformers seek to subordinate religion to progress, while we subordinate progress to religion.

For them, Judaism is merely a "religion" like other religions, something private and personal that an individual may pursue when he feels like it. If you like, you can take that attitude toward any human creation, but that is not Judaism. For Judaism is not a religion in that sense, not a mere appendage, but comprises all of life. You are a Jew not just in private but in the synagogue and kitchen, in the field and the warehouse, in the office; as parent, as servant and master, as individual and as citizen; in word and in deed. A Jew is one whose whole life is supported by the divine idea and lived in accordance with the divine will. A Jew is one who adapts to what God demands of him, and does not expect God to adapt to what *he* demands of God.

There is room for progress allied to religion: the modern Jew can and should assimilate to his surrounding culture, while continuing to observe *halacha*. The error is in those who take the surrounding culture as the guide and goal of the Jewish life, rather than the reverse. Great Jewish thinkers have also made this error: Maimonides, in forcing Judaism to speak the language of Aristotle, or Mendelssohn, who made Judaism private to appease the surrounding Christians. But while both thinkers personally remained committed to *halacha*, it is no surprise that their legacy does not. For once you set something above the Torah—philosophy, or society—then there isn't much point to the Torah. If the purpose of *mitzvot* is to help produce knowledge of God, then once you get some knowledge of God, you don't need the *mitzvot*; if the purpose of the Sabbath is merely to rest as the Christians do on Sundays, then the entire Talmud tractate on the Sabbath becomes nothing but petty, pedantic hairsplitting that is useful only for the dust and the moths.

"Religion allied to progress," then, dictates the rejection of God's word, and so amounts to little more than "progress alone"—without religion.

Related Chapters

56

Samson Raphael Hirsch (1808–88)

Positively Inauthentic

*The "positive-historical" school is no more
authentic Judaism than is the Reform school*

It isn't merely the German Reform movement that is rejecting authentic Judaism, according to Hirsch. The "positive-historical" school, with its dedication to the "Science of Judaism," isn't much better, as can be seen in the works of Zacharias Frankel (1801–75) and Heinrich Graetz (1817–91).

According to Frankel's well-known "scientific" book, *The Ways of the Mishna*, the oral Law is traditionally *mis*labeled as the *halacha* given to Moses from Sinai. The laws in question were not given orally by God to Moses; rather, they are of such antiquity that it is as *if* they were so given. But in fact they were the creation of later generations, and elements of the oral Law have evolved over time. Graetz, in his own work of "science," the *History of the Jews*, similarly argues that the rabbis of the Talmud were the creators, not merely the communicators, of the Law.

But this, simply, is heresy. It is a false account of Judaism that profoundly undermines traditional Jewish belief, according to which the oral Law was given to Moses along with the written Law. The oral Law isn't merely simultaneous with the written Law but *unified* with it, inseparable in practice, and eternally valid, so much so that there can be no significant distinction between the "moral" laws and the "ceremonial" laws: all are equally significant, equally divine. To undermine its authenticity is to attack the very heart of Judaism.

It is also to miss the point.

Those who pursue the Science of Judaism consider themselves deeply connected to the Jewish tradition. They adore Jewish antiquity so much that they spend hours in libraries to ascertain the names of the authors of the great texts, their dates of birth and death, the locations of their tombstones. They work hard so that, as Judaism itself descends into the grave of modernity (in their opinion), its memory might be kept alive in scholarship. They study the rites and rituals, the fasting, the prayer, the lamentations of the Jewish day of mourning, Tisha B'Av. And while some may perhaps actually observe and perform these rites you would not know it from the detachment of their scholarship.

To the contrary, the authentic Jew, the Orthodox Jew, our simple-minded fathers, did not believe in the death of these great authors at all. There in our fathers' hearts, these authors—their lamentations, their prayers—continued to live on. While forgotten tombstones crumbled somewhere, Jewish hearts maintained the only kind of immortality they ever desired. What these great authors thought and felt and sung became and is the living property of the entire people, while its origin, the mortal individuals, fades into irrelevant obscurity.

For what is more important in the end, and what would have been more important to these great authors: that we modern Jews know their names and birth dates while leaving their prayers in the dustbin of history, or that we pray their prayers whether or not we remember their names?

The Orthodox Jew must repudiate this "science" as heresy if it is raised as the standard against which religion is to be judged. Nor does it matter if the thinkers themselves may personally continue to observe the *halacha*. If they reject the foundational belief in the authenticity and eternal status of the oral Law, then they have no place in authentic Judaism. No such individuals can be appointed to leadership positions in the Orthodox Jewish community, then, unless they repudiate such beliefs.

Related Chapters

45 Mendelssohn, 46 Maimon, 47 Ascher, 48 Zunz, 50 Geiger, 51 Holdheim, 52 Sofer, 53 Frankel, 54 Krochmal, 55 Hirsch, 70 Kaplan, 83 Borowitz, 86 Rosenberg

57

Israel Salanter (1810–83)

The Only Thing I Can't Resist Is Temptation

*The righteous life requires methods of moral instruction
and correction, based in Torah and psychology*

The nineteenth century saw many competitors for the attention of young Jews: the attractions of secularization and assimilation, the rigorous study of the *yeshiva*, the mystical ecstasy of the Chassidim—and the *mussar* movement of Salanter. The term is from the Bible: Moses refers to God's reproach or reproof (*mussar*) of those who fail to follow God's laws (Deuteronomy 11:1–2). What is central to the proper Jewish life, in other words, is moral instruction, correction, and reproof.

Rigorous Torah and Talmud study is essential, of course. But such study should not be merely for its own sake. Rather it should have a practical focus, pursued with a deeper awareness of human psychology. Self-scrutiny reveals that human beings have multiple forces or powers battling within us, and so we must learn how to tame and harness these powers—even to change our natures by means of certain techniques.

In fact we possess two major competing inclinations, an evil one and a good one. The former is itself driven by bodily lust and spiritual uncleanness; the latter, both by a drive toward the good (the force of "sanctity") and by careful, commonsense thinking (the force of "right thinking") that, when applied, slows our tendency toward immediate gratification as we ponder the longer-term consequences of our actions. A key goal of worship and of study is to strengthen the good inclination in order to subdue the evil inclination.

Key to that goal, in turn, is to develop both personal humility and the appropriate fear of God. Both are reinforced when we meditate upon the fact that God is the ultimate judge who will mete out our due in accordance with our deeds. More particularly, as our self-scrutiny reveals which sins we are personally most prone to—slander, haughtiness, illicit sexual relations, dishonest business dealings, and so on—we must pursue extended study of the *halachot* concerning those sins. Torah study helps keep us from transgressing in general, of course, but focused study on specific *halachot* engrains in us not merely the severity of the transgressions but also the divine punishments we earn in committing them. That in turn strengthens the good inclination, the careful weighing of pros and cons in our behavioral choices, to resist the transgression.

It is easy enough (happily!) for many Jews to observe the "major" laws, such as the dietary laws. Many Jews feel outright revulsion at the idea of eating pork, for example, so refraining from pork is easy and natural. What extended and focused Torah study can do is imbue us with the appreciation that *all* the laws of the Torah, large and small, are equally important. We should come to feel toward slander and dishonest business dealings the same revulsion we feel toward eating pork!

The secular emphasis on rationality will not do what we require; nor the *yeshiva* movement with its emphasis on intellectual study, which is appropriate only for the elite; nor Hirsch's and others' "modern Orthodox" movement, which, with its openness to certain areas of secular knowledge, only weakens Torah knowledge in the community, despite its protestations to the contrary. What is necessary to lead us on the path of righteousness is diligent attention to Torah study in addition to *mussar*, which can instill in all—the *yeshiva* scholar and the ordinary Jew in his home—the required humility and fear of God.

Related Chapters

2 Philo, 7 Ibn Paquda, 13 Ibn Ezra, 42 Sforno, 51 Holdheim, 62 Berdichevsky, 64 Cohen, 70 Kaplan, 74 Levinas, 76 Berkovits, 83 Borowitz

58

Zvi Hirsch Kalischer (1795–1874)

Not by Miracles, but by Sweat

The ingathering of the exiles, through our own efforts, is the first phase of redemption

Jewish passivism toward national redemption has deep roots. Various biblical and Talmudic texts suggest that Jews will return from the dispersion of exile to the Land of Israel only when God sends, via miraculous supernatural acts, the prophesied messiah to lead the way. Until then: lay low and wait it out, however dreadful things get.

But Kalischer reads the key texts differently—and urges action.

The redemption will come gradually, slowly, by degrees. The return to Zion, the redemption of the Jewish people and ultimately the whole world, will at least *begin* through natural causes, by human efforts to gather the scattered children of Israel back into the Holy Land.

It will start by awakening support among the people of means and by gaining the consent of the nations to permit it. As the prophet Isaiah expresses it, "In the days to come shall Jacob take root . . . . [Y]e shall be gathered one by one, O ye children of Israel" (Isaiah 27:6, 12–13). Those who come first will be the roots, planted there in order to later produce sprigs. "And it shall come to pass . . . that the Lord will set His hand again the second time to recover the remnant of his people" (Isaiah 11:11). *Two* distinct ingatherings, two distinct phases: the first will pioneer the land, after which the people of Israel will blossom once again.

Why should God proceed in this way, rather than simply send the messiah in an obvious miracle? Perhaps because God has always tested

His people: in the Garden of Eden (with temptation), in the exodus from Egypt (with hunger and thirst), with the severe restrictions of kosher food. Throughout the exile we have suffered martyrdom in God's name, been dragged from land to land for His Torah. Only a natural beginning of the redemption is a true test for those who initiate it. To concentrate all one's energy on this holy work and to renounce home and fortune for the sake of living in Zion, desolate as it currently is—there is no greater trial, or merit, than this.

Some argue that the redemption will not come before the Jewish people repent of their sins—that is, perform *teshuva*. Perhaps, but the *beginning* of the process does not require *teshuva*; only *shuva*, return. The dawn of redemption will come when Israel acts with courage—and adopts the aims and promises of the holy prophets.

There are many practical details to be worked out: the purchase of land, the encouragement of immigration, the training of agricultural workers and other laborers. But this *can* be worked out, and so much rides on our doing so. The Talmud teaches that one who lives outside the Land of Israel is like one who has no God (Talmud Tractate *Ketubot* 110b). Many *mitzvot* can only be performed in the Holy Land, so living there is not only a commandment in itself but necessary for performing many other *mitzvot*. Our salvation as a people depends on our fulfilling these holy tasks.

But not just *our* salvation. Heaven and earth do not belong only to us. The righteous of all faiths have a share in the world to come, and all monotheistic religions recognize that our faith is the mother of them all—because we accepted the Torah at Sinai and thus brought universal, ethical monotheism into the world.

It isn't only we Jews who will be redeemed through return to our land, but, through this very means, the entire world.

Related Chapters

12 Halevi, 19 Nachmanides, 44 Spinoza, 50 Geiger, 51 Holdheim, 52 Sofer, 59 Pinsker, 60 Herzl, 61 Ahad Ha'am, 63 Schneersohn, 65 Cohen, 66 Rosenzweig, 68 Bialik, 69 Kook, 78 Fackenheim, 79 Leibowitz

59

Leon Pinsker (1821–91)

We'll Do It Our Way

Jews must emancipate themselves in order to end the scourge of Judeophobia

"If I am not for myself, who will be for me? And if not now, when?" So goes the famous quote from the ancient sage Hillel, and so begins Pinsker as he responds both to the vicious 1881 Russian pogroms and to the more general problem of the Jews in Europe.

The heart of the problem is the lack of a homeland; and the solution is, or should be, in the hands of the Jews themselves. We must not and cannot rely on others but must emancipate ourselves, or "auto-emancipate."

For too long we have been passive. The belief in a messiah, that some miraculous power would bring about political resurrection, that exile and dispersion are justly deserved divine punishment for ancient sins—these have caused us to give up on our unity as a people and our independence. Over the long centuries we gave up every thought of our homeland; we, the people without a homeland, simply forgot our homeland.

With no center of gravity, no government of our own, we are everywhere a guest and nowhere at home.

In being religious so long we have also forgotten that we are not *just* a religion, as the reformers would have us believe. But while we have forgotten, the other nations of the world have not and will not forget, that we Jews are also a people, a nation. As Moses Hess (1812–75) puts it so sharply in his *Rome and Jerusalem*, try as the reformers might, Jewish noses cannot be reformed, and our black, wavy hair cannot turn blond by conversion or be straightened out by relentless combing.

We are a people. But without a home, we are less a living people than a dead people. The nations in which we live see us as aliens, vagrants. For their rich, we seem as beggars; for their poor, we seem as millionaires. For all their classes, we are rivals.

And for their patriots, we do not belong.

Thus has arisen the disease of *Judeophobia*. The fear and hatred of Jews has become rooted in society, disseminated among all peoples. It has become hereditary, transmitted through the generations for centuries, incurable. We indeed have become the chosen people, chosen for universal hatred: the endless accusations that we are Christ-killers, that we poisoned the medieval wells, that we use their children's blood in our Passover matzah. These ludicrous claims can only take hold in diseased minds predisposed to accept them. No matter how much we protest, no matter how we prove them false, nothing dislodges them from the Judeophobic mind.

In this environment no legal emancipation decreed from government on high can produce social emancipation. As long as we remain a homeless nation we will remain aliens.

There is only one solution.

We must emancipate ourselves—and establish a homeland.

Some insist this must be our ancient homeland, in Palestine. The Jewish religion hasn't merely produced our passivity but has also kept us fixated on that particular strip of land. Even Hess subscribes to the idea, arguing that the universalistic message of Judaism—that it calls for the messianic redemption of all humanity in the end—requires the reestablishment of Jewish national life back in the Holy Land.

To the contrary, really, more or less *any* large piece of land will do, as long as it remains *ours*, subject to no foreign masters. For *that* is what is necessary for us to regain not merely our self-respect, but also the respect of the other nations—and finally put an end to the scourge of Judeophobia.

Related Chapters

12 Halevi, 19 Nachmanides, 44 Spinoza, 50 Geiger, 51 Holdheim, 52 Sofer, 58 Kalischer, 60 Herzl, 61 Ahad Ha'am, 63 Schneersohn, 65 Cohen, 66 Rosenzweig, 68 Bialik, 69 Kook, 78 Fackenheim, 79 Leibowitz

PART IV

HERZL–LEBENS
1860–

Introduction to Part IV

One of the significant themes of part III concerned the question of the character of Judaism: is it a product of, and shaped by, ever-changing historical forces or is it essentially ahistorical, a set of unchanging eternal truths and practices tracing back to the revelation on Mount Sinai and immune to the forces of history? Atheists and reformers alike endorsed the former, while traditionalists (such as the "Orthodox") endorsed the latter. Well, wherever you stand on that question, it's hard to deny that in the twentieth century, historical events made a dramatic impact on Judaism and on Jews.

The century begins with perhaps the most significant event for Jews, Jewish identity, and Judaism since the destruction of the Second Temple two millennia earlier. In 1896 Theodor Herzl founded modern political Zionism with his short book, *The Jewish State*, initiating the process that a mere fifty years later would produce the modern State of Israel. The complex consequences for the Jewish God Question began immediately, in myriad forms and matters. Are Jews a people, or is Judaism merely a religion? Should Jews return to their ancient homeland, or remain in their current countries, attempting to assimilate or fit in? What precise form should Zionism take (political, cultural, spiritual)? What attitude should specifically *Orthodox* Jews take toward the new project? Were Jews obligated to wait passively for the messiah to end the exile, or was it permissible, or desirable, or even obligatory to take the initial steps themselves?

History also made sure that the path from Herzl to the State of Israel was not a smooth one. Zionism's title as the most significant Jewish event since 70 CE was a short-lived one. The Nazi-perpetrated Holocaust eclipses it, by orders of magnitude. Judaism may well be ahistorical in some sense, but Jewish thinkers could not escape the effort to make sense of this event and its implications. Could it be construed as divine punishment? If so, for what sin, exactly? Is it proof that the traditional notion of God, as all-powerful or perfectly good, needs revising? Or is it conclusive evidence against the existence of God altogether, the latest, and most monumental, instance of the traditional problem of evil? And, most pressing of all perhaps: how ought Jews move forward from this event, if they could, as Jews?

A third event initially pales in significance against the first two, to be sure. In the long run, however, it may well prove to have major implications for the Jewish God Question.

I refer to the rise of contemporary Western liberal society in general, and to the development of feminism, or egalitarianism, in particular. Judaism and the Jewish people were born in ancient times and subsequently shaped by long centuries of social practices. That they have been deeply patriarchal and male oriented is no surprise, and nothing to apologize for. But the times have changed in the Western world, and the day of reckoning drawn nigh. Can Judaism accommodate itself to the contemporary mores of egalitarianism? Can it do so without changing its (perhaps ahistorical) essence? Can Orthodoxy do this in a way satisfactory to the needs and values of women? Or must Judaism splinter into ever more and distinct forms, continuing the processes triggered by the modernization and "reform" begun (as we saw in part III) in the Enlightenment?

And finally, while Judaism and the Jewish people grapple with these historical phenomena, the ahistorical questions themselves continue to command attention. Should the Jewish relationship to God manifest itself primarily in dogma and doctrine, or ritual observance, or in ethical practice? What role does and should religious *experience* play in the life of a Jew? What is the point and purpose of observing *mitzvot* for the individual observing them, the cosmos as a whole, and God? Can religion meet the modern challenges of rationality, provide for its practitioners what rationality cannot?

And we close with a glimpse (perhaps) of the future. The young Jewish thinker Samuel Lebens, trained both in traditional texts and contemporary philosophical techniques, shows how new discoveries in philosophy can elaborate on and maybe even solve some ancient Jewish questions: in this case, how to make sense of some mysteries in the Kabbalah. Whether you agree with him or not, such work reveals the exquisite balance that Jewish thinking seeks between the historical and the ahistorical—for the same ancient questions continue to take on new forms, and new possible answers, perpetually revealing themselves in fresh ways over the slow, patient passing of historical time.

So, no, we may not be fortunate to achieve resolution and answers that achieve consensus. But it is clear that the Jewish God Question itself will continue to be relevant for a long time to come.

60

Theodor Herzl (1860–1904)

If You Will It, It Is No Dream

The only solution to European antisemitism is the establishment of a Jewish state

The notorious 1894 Dreyfus trial in Paris proved to Herzl once and for all that the integration of Jews into modern European society simply was impossible. If there, in modern, civilized France, ground zero of enlightenment, emancipation, and human rights, the mobs can shout "Death to the Jews!" then Jews can have no proper home anywhere in Europe.

What he saw there made him a Zionist.

For there is nothing the Jews can do about the antisemitism rising everywhere in Europe, east and west. Attacked in parliaments, in the press, in the pulpit, in the street; in Russia, special taxes are levied on Jewish villages, between pogroms; in Austria, political antisemites terrorize all public life; in Paris, Jews are barred from social clubs; in Berlin, they cry, "*Juden 'raus!*" (Out with the Jews!).

The causes of this antisemitism are many, but dominant now are the political and economic. Through legal emancipation we Jews have found ourselves thrust into the middle class, where we suddenly present economic competition and thus fuel tremendous hostility. Nor does it help to insist that we are just citizens like any other, who happen to go to synagogues instead of churches, for it is clear that we are a people, a distinct people. No solution to the problem of antisemitism will be found, then, except a national one. As long as we remain in Europe as a distinct and resented community, antisemitism is inevitable.

"*Juden 'raus!*" indeed.

In fact the large-scale movement of Jews out of Europe would benefit all. Merchants would lose their competitors, rulers would enjoy greater domestic stability, and antisemitism would decline; Jews would be able to lead honorable and industrious lives, free from prejudice and oppression. Eastern European Jews will likely jump at the opportunity, especially those under the Russian czar. Western European Jews will initially resist, preferring to continue their ill-fated attempts at assimilation. Yet once they begin to see the truth of this analysis, almost all will make the move. Then those very few who remain behind will, given their small numbers, likely be able to integrate as they desire via conversion, intermarriage, assimilation—and disappear.

Indeed the departure of Jews is the only way actually to realize the enlightenment and emancipation ideals—though not in Europe. Jews will join the modern world not as citizens in other nations, as individuals, but as a nation among other nations. The new Jewish state will embody the best liberal ideals: freedom of religion, tolerance of diversity, progressive social policies including a seven-hour workday, a symbol for which should even go on the flag of the new state! There will be great stress on education, on technological advances, with prosperity for all, under the leadership of only the most talented and worthy individuals. No, Hebrew should not be the official language of the new state; it has a rich biblical pedigree but it is a dead tongue in which one cannot even ask for a train ticket! The new state should perhaps be like Switzerland, with several European national languages. The new Jew, freed from the ghetto, freed from prejudice and oppression, freed if he chooses from religious superstition and the authority of priests and rabbis, from the spiritual and intellectual weakness that invites religious belief, would stand proud and tall and free.

The Jewish state—a state of Jews, for the Jews, though open and free to others, in which all would be free to prosper.

If you will it, it is no dream.

Related Chapters

61

Ahad Ha'am (Asher Ginsberg) (1856–1927)

More Than the Jews Have Kept the Sabbath, the Sabbath Has Kept the Jews

Political Zionism seeks to solve the problem of the Jews, but what's needed is to solve the problem of Jewishness

Where Western European Jews have been emancipated, Ahad Ha'am argues, they have also assimilated, losing their Jewish identity as they rush to blend in with their neighbors. Such Jews may be externally free, but in their souls, in being motivated by external norms, they are enslaved. The Jews of Eastern Europe, though oppressed, at least remain firm in their identities and thus ultimately free.

But while Herzl's political Zionism offers one response to the problems here—move the Jews into their own state—that movement too fails to get at the deeper issues.

Herzl's state would be a state of Jews, but it wouldn't be *Jewish* so much as just another modern state. He is opposed to Hebrew and Yiddish, for example, is no fan of the Jewish religion, and even the Land of Israel is only incidental for him. Such a state would not solve the real problem, which is not (or isn't only) the external problem of antisemitism, but the internal psychological problem of the spirit: it's not about the fate of the Jews, in other words, but the fate of *Jewishness*.

This problem cannot be solved politically. That move merely creates just another state embroiled both in world conflicts and internal conflicts with the peoples currently living there, with neither purpose nor mission. Nor can the problem be solved by the Jewish religion itself.

Modern science has made it untenable to believe in the literal truth of the Bible, or even in the belief in a supernatural God.

So how can we find and preserve our Jewishness, the Jewish spirit of our people? By establishing a community in the Land of Israel, yes; but, more important, by renewed attention to our history. We must remind ourselves of the prophets, whose spiritual perfection guided us toward truth and justice; and of the Pharisees, those forerunners to the rabbis, who grasped that our spiritual mission is just as important as our material prosperity. When Rome destroyed the Second Temple, the Zealots died attempting to show material strength; but it was the Pharisees, in the person of Rabbi Johanan Ben Zakkai, whose spiritual strength let him yield Jerusalem to the Romans while escaping with the Torah to Yavneh.

Two millennia later we see that, more than Jews have kept the Torah's Sabbath, it is the Sabbath that has kept the Jews—*as* a people, perhaps now poised to resume some form of material existence in the Land of Israel.

What we seek is a spiritual rebirth. Not a religious one, for the modern era has moved on, but a rebirth of our spiritual devotion to truth and justice and the development of Jewish culture—one informed by our religion, our texts, our past, but moving forward. The return of Hebrew as a spoken language; a reformulation of religious concepts into secular and humanist ones (such as Shabbat reconceived in a non-halachic manner); continuation of those traditional practices that still work, but now embued with modern meanings; production of new Jewish literature and art, a resurrection of the Jewish heart. A gradually growing Jewish collective in the Land of Israel, living in harmony with the local population, can cultivate the Jewish culture that then will feed the Diaspora, breathe new life into diasporic communities—and once it has attained the proper level of development, may perhaps lead to a state that will be not merely one filled with Jews, but *Jewish*.

Not a political Zionism, then, but a *cultural* one.

Related Chapters

12 Halevi, 19 Nachmanides, 44 Spinoza, 50 Geiger, 51 Holdheim, 52 Sofer, 58 Kalischer, 59 Pinsker, 60 Herzl, 62 Berdichevsky, 63 Schneersohn, 65 Cohen, 66 Rosenzweig, 68 Bialik, 69 Kook, 78 Fackenheim, 79 Leibowitz

62

Micah Joseph Berdichevsky (1865–1921)

Not the Last Jew, but the First Hebrew

On the transvaluation of Jewish values, from the power of love to the love of power

Ahad Ha'am calls for a cultural Zionism, but what exactly, Berdichevsky asks, is Jewish culture? After two millennia in which the Jewish religion has dominated our consciousness, the Jewish people have become secondary to Judaism. It's now time for the Jews to come before the Judaism, before the Torah.

Jewish culture will be *whatever* it is that Jewish people create.

Ahad Ha'am says that we should be guided in the creation of our culture not by religion but by the values in our prophetic traditions: the chosenness, the commitment to truth and justice, the spiritual strength that is bound with physical passivity and weakness, the scholarly town of Yavneh over the military Zealots and the fortress of Masada, and so on.

There is some virtue in acknowledging our religious past—but the past must not stifle us.

Yet what Ahad Ha'am finds in our past is only that which stifles us: an absolute morality that constrains us, that we Jews are obligated to obey and transmit. But as great thinkers such as Friedrich Nietzsche (1844–1900) have taught us, morality is not absolute, but always relative to circumstances. Our Jewish morals have varied over time, just like others' moralities. Ahad Ha'am stresses prophetic morality, but the Bible is itself, in fact, a long and often bloody epic of power struggles and injustice. The patriarchs and matriarchs do many questionable things; rulers fight viciously to obtain power, make and break deals, advance their interests and oppress the humble. The Torah often accepts outright human indecency, sometimes rejecting behaviors such as revenge but other times endorsing it.

Nor does our tradition truly praise the passivity and weakness that Ahad Ha'am emphasizes. There is no shortage of heroes—Avimelech, Saul, Samson—who fought or died for their noble causes. And then there is the inspiring tale of Masada and of the Zealots' heroic defense of Jerusalem against the Romans.

True, after the defeat, when the Jews went into exile and were no longer normal people living in their own land, the rabbis inverted the story, criticizing the Zealots and praising Johanan Ben Zakkai for sneaking away in favor of the spirit over physical strength. But that is just the point. Since that time of our destruction we have lived in what we might call the age of Hillel, in which excessive spirituality suppresses our real life; but we must not forget that our past *also* includes another period, an age of vitality and strength, the age of Shammai. This was when we lived on our own land, did not hesitate to fight, to shed blood, our own and others', in defense of our land; when we were as attached to nature as to God, to power as to love; when we advanced our own interests and weren't much concerned what other nations thought.

The age of Hillel has dominated for two millennia, the age of life under the Law and within the scrolls, of Diaspora and exile, of passive bookishness surrounded by and always answering to alien cultures. But it is now time for a transvaluation of our exilic values (to borrow Nietzsche's phrase)—to return to our *other* past, the more distant past when we were a normal people living in our own land—when our religion worked for us rather than we for our religion. A past even before our religion, before we became the eternal guardians of a dusty parchment.

We must now become not the last Jew, but the first Hebrew.

Related Chapters

63

Shalom Dov Baer Schneersohn (1860–1920)

(Don't Be) Another Brick in the Wall

Redemption will not come by the Zionists but by the messiah, when the time is ripe

The modern Zionist movement must be rejected, according to Schneersohn, on religious grounds.

The Zionists seek to change the condition of the Jewish people through a national reawakening and return to the Land of Israel. But this represents a purely human effort to realize what are and must be messianic ambitions, for the teachings are clear: the ingathering of the exiles and the liberation of our people from external oppression will only be fulfilled by the miraculous interventions of the messiah, may he not tarry.

Moreover, the Zionists' efforts clearly violate the traditional oaths the Jewish people are asked to swear: not to take our own initiative or "force the end." In particular, (1) we should not go up to the Land "like a wall," and (2) we should not rebel against the nations of the world (Talmud Tractate *Ketubot* 110b–111a). These indicate that we must not return to the Land of Israel in any large numbers, however holy that Land is—in fact *because* of how holy that Land is. We, in our degenerate state, are not worthy of that Land. It is for similar reasons that past returns from exile (for example, before the building of the Second Temple) were only partial, and all failed. In our present state we can only hope for redemption and salvation at the hands of the Holy One Himself, not by human flesh and blood.

This would remain true even if the Jewish people were collectively to repent, abandon modern secularism, and return to religion. This would remain true even if the nations of the world were suddenly to become amenable to the idea of allowing us to return to our Holy Land. We are not even permitted to hasten the end by reciting too many prayers for it! All the more so are we forbidden to hasten it by means of physical action, such as returning by force.

And all the *more* so when these other conditions are not met. The nations of the world are *not* amenable to our return, and the Talmudic oath above forbids us from rebelling against them. (And we know all too well what happens when we stir the wrath of the powerful against us!) Moreover, the Zionists themselves actually aim to do away with our religion. In rejecting the basic tenet of messianic redemption, they reject the entire enterprise of the Jewish religion. They do this by infusing our people with the idea of being a "nation," of stressing nationhood over Torah, knowing that once one favors the former, there is not much left of the latter. They proclaim the virtue of action and decry what they consider the vice of passivity—which is in effect to reject the central message of the Torah.

For the Torah teaches that we *are* to be passive with respect to the exile, because it teaches us the *meaning* of exile. The Land vomits out those unworthy to inhabit it, and that is the fate of the Jewish people who, since ancient times, have rejected their God and His divine ways in pursuit of whatever values reign at the time. The yoke of the exile is heavy, as we have learned through centuries of persecution and oppression. But at the same time we of faith know full well that in the fullness of time, when perhaps we are worthy once more, the final redemption will come—at the hands of the Holy One and His messiah, and when the time is ripe, and not one moment sooner.

Related Chapters

12 Halevi, 19 Nachmanides, 44 Spinoza, 50 Geiger, 51 Holdheim, 52 Sofer, 58 Kalischer, 59 Pinsker, 60 Herzl, 61 Ahad Ha'am, 62 Berdichevsky, 65 Cohen, 66 Rosenzweig, 68 Bialik, 69 Kook, 78 Fackenheim, 79 Leibowitz

64

Hermann Cohen (1842–1918)

Be Reasonable

Judaism is a religion of reason

Although the great philosopher Immanuel Kant (1724–1804) is no fan of Judaism, much in his thought fits well with Jewish ideas. Kant argues that we cannot know the world as it is "in itself," its ultimate nature; so, too, Judaism is not very concerned with metaphysical speculation. Nor can we prove God's existence via facts about the cosmos, but only as a necessary condition for morality; so, too, Judaism emphasizes God as a moral being, who rewards and punishes. And just as the moral law is "engraved upon the heart" of every rational human being, so too the Divine Law is near to all of us, in our heart (Deuteronomy 30:14).

Enter Cohen now to *explicitly* analyze Judaism in Kantian terms.

For Kant the essence of religion is morality: beneath all the dogmas, rituals, and statutes there is a universal morality, one that is intrinsically rational or accessible to reason—or at least this is the *ideal*. While Kant thinks that Christianity best expresses this ideal, it may be reconstructed from Jewish sources as well.

For what Judaism teaches, first, is universal monotheism, that there is one creator of all. Moreover, this creator is the source of the single, universal moral law that binds every human being. There is one law for the foreigner and the native citizen (Leviticus 24:22); this idea permeates the Torah and rabbinic literature, is found in the idea of the "Noachide Covenant," a pact God makes with all humanity (Genesis 9:11–16), in the idea that the righteous of *every* nation will share in salvation, and so on. The idea of a universal humanity itself arose in the Hebrew Bible and its prophets.

As for the revelation on Mount Sinai, well, that represents or symbolizes the discovery, by humankind, of a universal rationality. The historical details don't matter as much as the call to moral obligation engraved on the heart of every rational person. What revelation reveals—what reason universally dictates—is the fundamental moral law that every rational agent must be treated not as a means or an instrument, but as an end in himself or herself. Whatever may have occurred historically, this law has the status of a divine, universally authoritative moral commandment—as well as being a universal principle of rationality.

As such, revelation is not a one-time affair. It is the ongoing call of moral duty, one we strive to fulfill in each new situation, in each day. The texts make this clear. Deuteronomy literally means "second law," meaning a repetition of the Law originally given in Exodus. In Deuteronomy Moses tells us that the covenant is not only with those who were on Mount Sinai, but also with all future generations (5:3). Throughout the book Moses reminds us that God enters the covenant "this day"—that is, each and every day—and that the Law is not "in heaven" but near to us, engraved in us (30:12–14). Through the mythology, Judaism too expresses the universal necessity of the moral law.

Kant of course sees the Jewish religious laws as a burden, a dry legalism with no ethical content. But what he fails to see is that law is the essence of morality, which is always framed as general rules. And he fails to see that the set of religious laws that comprise *halacha*, insofar as they express in concrete and particularist terms what are in fact the universal laws of morality, are not merely consistent with the universal rules of rationality but in fact beautifully express them.

Judaism is indeed a religion of reason.

Related Chapters

2 Philo, 7 Ibn Paquda, 13 Ibn Ezra, 42 Sforno, 45 Mendelssohn, 51 Holdheim, 57 Salanter, 62 Berdichevsky, 65 Cohen, 70 Kaplan, 72 Strauss, 73 Strauss, 74 Levinas, 76 Berkovits, 82 Wyschogrod, 83 Borowitz

65

Hermann Cohen (1842–1918)

At Home in the Exile

Judaism, as a religion of reason, should oppose political Zionism

Antisemitism as a political movement was in full force in Europe at the end of the nineteenth century. But while some Jews saw in antisemitism a motive for Jewish nationalism in the form of Zionism, Cohen, from within his Kantian system, has the opposite reaction.

For Judaism is not ultimately about the historical details, nor about the particularism of Jewish identity. In contrast to the "Science of Judaism" emphasis on the historical development of the Jews, what really matters is Judaism's *a*historical, eternal message of universal morality, which unfolds *through* history. Jewish Law should thus *not* be seen as the political constitution of a nation-state, as some claim, but as expressing the universal monotheism at the basis of universal morality. Indeed a non-Jewish person devoted to monotheism and morality would be a better Jew than a Jewish person who isn't!

Judaism's task, then, is to spread the light of monotheistic morality to the world. But to perform this task adequately at least two things are required.

First, the Jewish people must remain distinct from others, for were we to assimilate and disappear then the monotheism it is our privilege to bear would itself disappear. The continued observance of Jewish Law, whether fully or in part, whether daily or only on the Sabbath, helps maintain this necessary Jewish separation from the surrounding communities.

Second, the Jews must remain dispersed throughout the nations—for were we gathered into our own nation-state, in the Land of Israel, we would become just one more people among the many peoples. We would lose our particular vocation of disseminating monotheistic morality, and of thus ushering in the messianic future of a universal, common humanity. The Holy Land remains special to us as the land from which we derived our eternal heritage—but to return there is to sacrifice our future and our purpose to an ancient relic.

But what about Jewish suffering, and the increasing scourge of antisemitism? This suffering is not actually something to be avoided or overcome, but in fact is the price to pay for bearing witness to the truth of monotheism. Though this sounds strange, it makes sense. As the prophet Isaiah taught, the children of Israel suffered back then for the faults of the pagan worshippers (Isaiah 53); so too, now, to this day we suffer vicariously for the global faults and wrongs that obstruct the moral world of monotheism.

This becomes clearer when we analyze Yom Kippur, the Day of Atonement. The individual Jew on this day takes on moral responsibility for the entire community, in the liturgical acknowledgment that *we* have sinned, *we* have lied, and so on. You only truly grasp the force of universal morality, morality binding on all, when you internalize your responsibilities toward the other. You only come to *identify* with all, with universal humanity, when you internalize these responsibilities. In so doing, you acknowledge divine sovereignty (or the rational nature of that moral law), you instantiate and model the universal law. And just as the individual Jew does this for his community, so too the Jewish community as a whole does this for the world community. The Day of Atonement is really about the redemption of all humankind.

Jews preserving Judaism among the nation-states of the world—and suffering for it—is what preserves monotheistic morality for all. That is the world-historical mission of the Jewish people, and why Judaism, as a religion of reason, must oppose political Zionism. Zionists say we are in exile, but, to the contrary, our religion of reason is general, and universal, and thus perfectly at home in the Diaspora. It is all humanity that is in exile, and the real Zion is the messianic future of the prophets, when all nations and states shall dissolve into the universal kingdom of God.

Related Chapters

12 Halevi, 19 Nachmanides, 44 Spinoza, 48 Zunz, 50 Geiger, 51 Hold-heim, 52 Sofer, 58 Kalischer, 59 Pinsker, 60 Herzl, 61 Ahad Ha'am, 62 Berdichevsky, 64 Cohen, 66 Rosenzweig, 68 Bialik, 69 Kook, 72 Strauss, 73 Strauss, 78 Fackenheim, 79 Leibowitz

66

Franz Rosenzweig (1886–1929)

A People without (Need of) a Land

A people with a spiritual mission is not tied to a land, but at home everywhere

Jewish assimilation, and thus disappearance, was a real possibility toward the end of the nineteenth century in Germany. The philosopher G. W. F. Hegel (1770–1831) had taught that each distinct people has its particular spirit and historical role to play; the Jews had theirs in ancient times, so there wasn't much point in remaining a Jew now. Meanwhile Jewish thinker Hermann Cohen (1842–1918) argues that the essence of Judaism is its moral content, its general ethical truths. But then why bother with specifically Jewish practice and identity, you might ask, as long as you generally adhered to those moral principles? You could just as well convert to another religion, or adopt atheism, or throw yourself into socialism, as long as you were a good person.

Rosenzweig, to the contrary, rejects philosophies that justify assimilation—because Judaism cannot be reduced to something else (such as a "spirit") or essentialized in any way. What matters is not some set of ideas but the *people*; and not so much their religious beliefs but their religious *experiences*.

For Jews experience God not as some distant impersonal creator, but as a being deeply and continuously involved in the world. Divine revelation, one mode of involvement, is not a one-time or rare thing restricted to the past; God's creative power and love are experienced as an ongoing affair, alive in the present and pointing to the future in the form of redemption. But neither is redemption restricted to the distant future: it is something we can experience now, ourselves, through Jewish practices, through rituals and learning. In a similar way, the major events of Jewish history are not mere historical occurrences, now dead and buried; insofar as we identify with them we keep them alive with us to this moment—and so we experience eternity within finite forms.

In this sense we are outside history altogether. Our founding principles and experiences are, once formed, eternal, removed from the vicissitudes of time. This includes our ongoing spiritual mission too, which makes us unlike all other peoples. The long Talmudic period (after the Temple's destruction and our subsequent expulsion from Jerusalem) crystallized this mission by spiritualizing Jewish practices, by divorcing Judaism from physical land and territory. Other nations remained locked to their land, but we became a dispersed people, a diasporic people spread far and wide, bringing our religion with us while undergoing no national development. Exile is part of who we are, even as far back as Abraham in Mesopotamia: an essentially spiritual people estranged from land and from the bondage of worldly affairs. The Land of Israel may be the Holy Land, but it was merely a temporary spiritual center for our people, an item of nostalgia—not fitting now for an eternal, spiritual people.

We Jews are *not* like other peoples. This is the mistake of political Zionism, which aims to make us such. We should not return to a land in order to become something we are not. As a spiritual people we are at home not in one place but everywhere. But by the same token neither should we simply disappear into our surroundings. We must continue to nourish our spiritual identity—by increasing the opportunity for Jewish education, by increased learning, by more serious attention to *halacha* in order to investigate what in it remains (or can remain) living in us—in order to bring redemption now into the experience of more people.

What we need are not more Jewish books but more Jewish *people*.

Related Chapters

12 Halevi, 13 Ibn Ezra, 19 Nachmanides, 21 Ben Samuel, 40 Ebreo, 41 Almosnino, 44 Spinoza, 50 Geiger, 51 Holdheim, 52 Sofer, 54 Krochmal, 55 Hirsch, 58 Kalischer, 59 Pinsker, 61 Ahad Ha'am, 63 Schneersohn, 65 Cohen, 67 Buber, 68 Bialik, 69 Kook, 71 Soloveitchik, 78 Fackenheim, 79 Leibowitz, 85 Ross

67

Martin Buber (1878–1965)

The *Ménage à Trois*

God is to be found in the relationship between I and You

For many people "God" is an abstraction, something to be analyzed logically and debated philosophically, something we make arguments about and whose existence we try to prove. But to conceive of God as a problem to be solved, Buber thinks, is to misconceive Him. Religious belief should be grounded not in philosophy, but in some form of direct experience. In particular, it is in our most personal relationships with other human beings that we develop our most personal of relationships with God.

To be a human being is to be in relationships. But there are two different sorts of relationships, which we may designate by the phrases "I–You" and "I–It."

The I–You relationship is characterized by intimacy, mutuality, dialogue, exchange; it is a two-way relationship in which we treat the other as a genuine person with needs and interests to be explored and respected. We are thus directly engaged with that other person as those needs and interests are directly present to us. The I–It relationship, to the contrary, is one-way: the other is a mere object to us with no intrinsic ends of its own, something that we may simply use or exploit or dismiss as we see fit. There is no direct engagement here: we may think of the other any way we like, mediated by our own concepts and ideas, however it suits us. Our typical I–You relationships are with other persons, naturally, and I–It relationships are with "things," but they are not necessarily restricted in this way. We may also have I–You relationships with a pet or a tree or even with inanimate objects, and we may similarly have I–It relationships even with people—as we do, for example, when we think of others as mere objects to be used for our own ends.

There is nothing wrong with I–It relationships, at least when they involve mere objects. But we become fully human only through the I–You relationship with other human beings. When we treat other people as an object, as an "It," we lose something of our own humanity.

What does this have to do with God?

For many people "God" is an abstraction to be analyzed logically and debated philosophically. But to conceive God in this way is to conceive of Him as an object, an object of thought, and so to have an I–It relationship with Him. To the contrary we must aim for an I–You relationship with God: one where God is directly present to our experience and not mediated in any conceptual way.

And in fact that relationship is always present to us, to be found in every genuine I–You relationship we enjoy! God is not merely something "wholly other" but is also wholly present in *all* our I–You relationships. It is thus no accident that we speak of God as being a "person," since it is in our relationships with persons that we discover God—at least when we put aside our reasoning and language and concepts, our arguments and debates.

And so God is neither a principle nor an idea nor an object, nor is He the conclusion of some logical argument. Rather, God is something to be experienced within our proper relationships with other beings. We speak with God, in effect, whenever we speak with another genuine You.

Thus every particular You affords us a glimpse of the eternal You.

Related Chapters

21 Ben Samuel, 22 De Leon, 23 Abulafia, 36 Alemanno, 40 Ebreo, 43 Spinoza, 66 Rosenzweig, 71 Soloveitchik, 74 Levinas, 75 Heschel, 76 Berkovits, 82 Wyschogrod

68

Hayim Nahman Bialik (1873–1934)

Building a Modern University with Ancient Stones

On the inauguration of the Hebrew University, and of a renewed national life

For all the great Jewish centers we have created throughout the Western world, Bialik notes, they have never withstood the inevitable day of wrath. Under rampaging mobs they crumble, our people crushed in their ruins. The 1903 pogrom at Kishinev, that city of slaughter in which the Jews simply submitted to their destruction, tells us what we need to know about life in the Diaspora.

And now in 1925 we witness a modern miracle: the inauguration of the Hebrew University of Jerusalem, a Jewish university, in the Land of Israel. Tens of thousands of Jews, abroad and at home, surely sing in their hearts the traditional prayer to the Living God for preserving us and sustaining us to see this hour—when the Jewish people begins its rebirth, kindling the first candle of its intellectual and cultural renaissance.

But what form should this take?

Though we move forward, we must be grounded in our past; a literature, a culture, without tradition and continuity is incapable of development and self-renewal. We may no longer be traditionally religious, but we cannot deny that the children of Israel and the Torah are one. Torah is more than creed, more than ethics, commandments, and learning, but combines and transcends them all. Now that we are returning to our homeland to resume our full national life, our material and spiritual life, we must build upon this foundation. Diaspora Jewish culture was always absorbed into its alien surroundings, but now we can build our own culture, on our own foundations.

We should begin with a process of "canonization": working through our texts, ancient and recent, to compile those most worthy of preservation and development. This happened with the creation of the Bible, then of the Mishna, then of the Talmud, these literary ingatherings; we must repeat the process to determine those texts that best capture our past, reflect our national vision, and thus should guide us toward a future unified Hebrew literature. We might start, for example, with the most valuable *aggadah* from the Talmud, the stories, the legends that bring that text to life.

Not that we overlook the *halacha*, of course. *Halacha* has been the heart and soul of the Jewish people for millennia. Though the aesthetically oriented among us may cringe, here is what the halachist says: "If someone breaks off his study to say 'how lovely is this tree!' then scripture regards him as guilty of a deadly sin" (cf. *Pirke Avot* 3:9). But the sympathetic ear detects here the apprehension, the anxiety, of a wandering people who has nothing to call its own but a book, The Book, and for which any attachment of its soul to a land of temporary sojourn means mortal danger.

Ultimately *halacha* and *aggadah* are so intimately entwined as to be inseparable. Every *halacha* condenses entire histories of the Jewish way of life, while *aggadah* that doesn't produce *halacha*, that doesn't guide us toward concrete practices and norms, is useless, empty. We may no longer feel bound by *halacha* in this modern age, but it is up to our writers, our artists, to draw water from the rock of *halacha* and produce our *new* Hebrew norms, obligations, culture—our life.

During the long, dispersed exile our time, our space, even our minds were not fully our own. But here now in our land, as we construct our first modern university with the ancient stones of Jerusalem, we seek to establish our own duties and obligations, self-created, self-imposed, to mint our fluid and unformed will into solid coin that will endure.

Related Chapters

12 Halevi, 19 Nachmanides, 44 Spinoza, 50 Geiger, 51 Holdheim, 52 Sofer, 58 Kalischer, 59 Pinsker, 60 Herzl, 61 Ahad Ha'am, 62 Berdichevsky, 63 Schneersohn, 65 Cohen, 66 Rosenzweig, 69 Kook, 78 Fackenheim, 79 Leibowitz

69

Abraham Isaac Kook (1865–1935)

The Jew and the Land, as Spirit and Flesh

On the foundations of religious Zionism

Though many prior to him disagreed, for Kook, the Jewish religion itself doesn't merely endorse, but actively supports, political Zionism—even where the movement was led by anti-religious secularists.

First, the sources of religious prohibition against Zionism are being improperly interpreted. While the Talmud perhaps allows the individual not to pursue *aliyah* (return to the Land of Israel) if there are dangers to his life in so doing, in fact there is a *collective* commandment to settle and preserve the Land that remains binding even where there is such danger, where it is necessary to fight and risk life.

There is also the mystical element. The Land of Israel has holy qualities that resonate with similar qualities in the soul of a Jew. In the heart of every child of Israel burns the fire of the Land of Israel; the Land is part of the Jewish soul. Many Jews can only reach their spiritual potential while living in the Land, just as the Land can only fully realize its own powers when inhabited by Jews. Jewish life in exile has no real foundation, lives only on the spiritual fumes of our past. We see it disintegrating today at an alarming rate, and there is no hope for it unless it replants itself by the wellspring of its real life, in the Land of Israel.

Nor should we be put out by the fact that the pioneers settling the Land are secular, sometimes even anti-religious! Secular Jews are still Jews, part of the body of Jewry. They, too, like all elements of the cosmos, contain sparks of divine light, and our task is to collect those sparks into one blazing fire. There is even a kernel of truth in their atheism, for it comes from their commitment to critical thinking—a commitment we share, and can even learn from, even if they reach incorrect conclusions with it. Despite their misconception they are doing divine work in settling the Land, building it up; we are one with them, and our tasks aligned, whether they recognize it or not. The secular nature of the project so far is only temporary, we can be sure, laying the groundwork for the ultimate phase.

Which would be—perhaps—the messianic era?

Some of our coreligionists complain that we are attempting to "hasten the end," to actively bring the messiah. But nothing in our faith negates the idea that we can begin to shake off the dust of exile by our own efforts. We prepare for the messiah not merely by study and prayer, which is the way of the exile, but also by building up the Land—just as we must build up a healthy body in order for our spirit to flourish.

And who can doubt—in particular after the upheaval of the Great War—that the times are indeed changing, that, perhaps, the arrival of the messiah himself, of universal peace illuminated by the light of Israel, might be imminent?

Our people has recently founded the Hebrew University, to become a leading disseminator of learning and knowledge. As long as it also pays rigorous attention and serious respect to the development of the spirit of Israel, to the Bible, the Talmud, then the diverse sparks of our people may indeed be collected into one burning flame, and we may abide in peaceful dwellings and secure abodes to which all the nations of the world will stream to learn "Torah from Zion and the word of the Lord from Jerusalem" (Isaiah 2:3).

Related Chapters

12 Halevi, 19 Nachmanides, 22 De Leon, 23 Abulafia, 36 Alemanno, 44 Spinoza, 50 Geiger, 51 Holdheim, 52 Sofer, 58 Kalischer, 59 Pinsker, 60 Herzl, 61 Ahad Ha'am, 62 Berdichevsky, 63 Schneersohn, 65 Cohen, 66 Rosenzweig, 68 Bialik, 71 Soloveitchik, 78 Fackenheim, 79 Leibowitz, 86 Rosenberg

70

Mordecai Kaplan (1881–1983)

Not as Jews, nor as Americans, but as Jewish Americans

On reconstructing Judaism for the modern American Jew

American Jewish life in the early twentieth century is in crisis, according to Kaplan. Orthodoxy is out of line with modern thought. Reform Judaism attempts to have the Jewish religion without the thriving Jewish people who live it, yielding, in fact, a sharp break with Judaism that can only lead to its utter disappearance. And Conservative Judaism endorses the eternal *halacha* as delivered to Moses while simultaneously noting that many biblical laws are now obsolete!

What's necessary is neither to abolish Judaism nor to cling to its obsolete forms, but to *reconstruct* it.

This first requires recognizing that Judaism is more comprehensive than just religion, but includes that nexus of history, literature, language, social organization, and norms that form an entire civilization. For the Jewish people to thrive *as* a civilization, we must therefore strengthen our social organization. We thus shouldn't build synagogues that isolate worship but rather community centers that include not only a sanctuary but also recreational facilities, social halls, libraries, meeting rooms.

As for reconstructing the religion, we do not seek to reject the tradition and start anew, for we grant the kernel of truth in its quest for spiritual development. Rather, we maintain continuity with tradition in order to utilize its momentum and emotional force. Thus we preserve but we *reinterpret* the key ideas of tradition—God, commandment, chosenness, and so on—in terms accessible to the modern mind.

Clearly the God idea is a central one. Judaism cannot dispense with it, but neither can most modern Jews accept the traditional anthropomorphic, supernatural, even philosophical notions of God. We must now recognize that what matters is less the content of the God-idea than the way it moves us to act toward our highest goals. We may now understand by "God" the force that motivates us toward moral ends, toward improving ourselves and the world.

The traditional divine attributes may be reinterpreted the same way. Rather than construe God as a "person" who created the universe, we may identify God with the general creative principle of the cosmos, with all acts of creation, in which we may now participate. God as "redeemer" now means that we treat, *as* divine, all efforts to bring ourselves and our common humanity to their highest levels, such as efforts to create a world filled with peace and prosperity for all, free of slavery and war. In so doing we transition from an other-worldly orientation to a this-worldly one: the "world to come," then, now reflects our dream to bring about the better world for which we yearn.

As for "chosenness"? The modern mind, sensitive to humanity as a whole, can no longer embrace that notion as traditionally interpreted, particularly with its supernatural elements. Instead we must recognize that the Jews have not a special role to play but rather a special *calling*, a vocation, in our dedication to the God-idea. We are "God's people" not because God chose us but because we have chosen to dedicate ourselves to God.

The ancient founders of our religion might not recognize these reinterpretations. But the past cannot pass judgment on the present. Our knowledge of God is shaped by our knowledge of reality, and as the latter has grown and expanded so must the former. Only by reconstructing Judaism can the Jewish people continue to thrive with all their talents; and only by so thriving can we resist the assimilating forces of the American melting pot and, instead, manifest our dual identities and enjoy the best of both—not as Jews nor as Americans, but as Jewish Americans.

Related Chapters

11 Halevi, 13 Ibn Ezra, 24 Albalag, 37 Bivach, 38 Abravanel, 39 Del Medigo, 47 Ascher, 48 Zunz, 50 Geiger, 51 Holdheim, 52 Sofer, 53 Frankel,
54 Krochmal, 55 Hirsch, 56 Hirsch, 57 Salanter, 64 Cohen, 81 Plaskow,
82 Wyschogrod, 83 Borowitz, 84 Adler, 85 Ross

71

Joseph Soloveitchik (1903–93)

From Sinai to Moriah, a Tale of Three Adams

Halachic man partners with God in sanctifying the world

The first two chapters of Genesis contain different accounts of creation. But rather than see this as evidence for multiple authors of the Bible (as some scholars do), Soloveitchik sees an important insight into two distinct aspects of, or two distinct types of, human beings. It is not so much an apparent contradiction between two versions of the story but a real contradiction in the very nature of human beings.

"Adam" in the first chapter represents a cognitive or intellectual man. He aims to understand the world not for metaphysical speculation, but for technological mastery. He studies the world, extracts its laws, then bends it to his will. Adam the second, to the contrary, is a religious man, a spiritual man, who asks not "How does this work?" but "Why does this exist?" When Adam the first discovers a relevant law of nature his inquiry is finished, but for Adam the second it is just beginning. For him the very concept of lawfulness is itself among the deepest mysteries.

But in addition to these two Adams, now, there is a third: halachic man, as it were. Halachic man displays some features of cognitive man and some of religious man, while rejecting others. Halachic man is in effect torn between this-worldliness and other-worldliness.

To elaborate, recall the teaching of Immanuel Kant (1724–1804) that human beings bring various concepts to bear on our experiences as we "understand" the world. Scientists bring scientific concepts (such as "force" and "cause"), while halachic man brings halachic concepts. The scientist thus experiences (for example) the sunset as a process of planetary motion, while halachic man experiences it in terms of the various obligations that time of day brings: recitation of blessings and prayers, the counting of the Omer, and so on. In "understanding" in this way, halachic man is a bit like cognitive man—though his goal is not mere mastery of the world, nor does his inquiry end when he discovers a relevant equation.

For at the same time, halachic man shares with the religious man an attunement toward a realm beyond this world. But while religious man sees God as *entirely* beyond this world, hoping to connect with God by negating this world and himself with it, matters are quite different with halachic man.

The connection halachic man makes with the divine occurs in two stages. In the first, we might say that God, in His infinite being, contracts Himself within the system of halachic concepts, the laws and principles that halachic man studies. God who is incomprehensible allows Himself to be comprehended, within limits, in these halachic terms. In the second stage, which occurs when halachic man lives and practices the *halacha* that he studies, he brings about the lowering of the divine presence into the world—or, alternatively, elevates this world, sanctifies it, makes it sacred.

There is no abnegation of the self or the world here. Rather, in bringing the divine presence into this lower world, halachic man not only affirms this world, but also affirms the important place that humanity has in the world.

We received the Torah on Mount Sinai, then, not as mere, passive recipients, but in order to become (as it were) co-creators of the world. It is for this reason that Mount Sinai itself is today of no special significance—but Mount Moriah in Jerusalem, the site of our two holy Temples, the place where Abraham set out to sacrifice Isaac and thus where humankind actively partnered with God to fulfill His will, remains to this day the holiest site in Judaism.

Related Chapters

13 Ibn Ezra, 21 Ben Samuel, 22 De Leon, 23 Abulafia, 24 Albalag, 36 Alemanno, 41 Almosnino, 43 Spinoza, 66 Rosenzweig, 67 Buber, 69 Kook, 75 Heschel, 79 Leibowitz, 81 Plaskow, 84 Adler, 86 Rosenberg

72

Leo Strauss (1899–1973)

Reason versus Revelation and the Modern Predicament, Part I

Can either be the source of absolute truth, to resist the modern attack on meaning?

In various guises the "theological-political predicament" confronts every modern Jew. In one guise it is the dilemma of having to choose between political liberalism (which leads ultimately to assimilation and Jewish disappearance) or some form of Jewish nationalism (such as Zionism) that fiercely distinguishes the Jew from other people. In another guise it is the dilemma of choosing between the modern rational life (as exemplified by philosophy) or the traditional life (as exemplified by scripture). While some seek reconciliation between the respective poles of these dilemmas, Strauss emphasizes the gap between them and their irreconcilability. No happy synthesis can be found, in other words, that would actually be superior to either of the elements.

You must therefore make a choice in each case—but which should you choose?

In fact the modern crisis isn't restricted to Jews alone, though we feel it particularly sharply. It is precipitated by the wave of thought stemming from such thinkers as Friedrich Nietzsche (1844–1900) and Martin Heidegger (1889–1976), who promulgated doctrines like these: that the human will is superior to reason; that history and historical processes are not rational; that there is no such thing as a fixed human nature, so we can be and do anything we want; that human beings thus create their own meanings and values, and pursue them by means of will, not reason;

that there is no absolute truth but only exertions of power, and so on. To resist these—and the dangerous commitment to irrationalism they suggest—would require a return commitment to some form of absolute truth that goes beyond mere human will and power.

But there are only two possible sources of such truth: philosophy (or reason) and revelation (or religion).

The philosopher Hermann Cohen (1842–1918) tries to synthesize these, by attempting to construct a "religion of reason" out of Jewish sources. In reality he merely endorses an account of religion developed by Immanuel Kant (1724–1804)—as a set of moral principles derivable from reason, grounded in the assumption of monotheism—and finds some Jewish texts into which those ideas could be read. But even aside from doubts about Kant in general, this amounts not to a synthesis, but to a *surrender* of Jewish revelation to philosophy. Were Cohen's analysis correct there would be no reason to continue to be *Jewish*: you should just be a good, rational, morally upstanding philosopher.

In any case, the analysis is not correct. In fact it fails to adequately capture the essence of Jewish revelation, which holds both that we can have actual knowledge (not a mere "assumption") of God's existence and that moral laws derive from God's will (not our own reason). Cohen's effort to construct a Judaism that coheres with enlightened, liberal ideals, so that Jews themselves could neatly integrate into a state and society modeled on such ideals, simply fails—as the subsequent Nazi history made all too tragically clear.

Baruch Spinoza (1632–77), to the contrary, is considered not a synthesizer, but a figure for whom philosophy openly defeats revelation. And indeed Spinoza does mount a formidable attack on orthodox religion—not just Judaism but implicitly also Christianity—insofar as both orthodoxies are based on the Bible. For once the Bible is understood as a work composed by human beings (rather than from divine revelation), whose teachings are confused, unclear, ambiguous, self-contradictory—absurd—then all such orthodoxies have the foundation taken out from them.

But has Spinoza actually shown all this? Has Spinoza really demonstrated that reason defeats revelation?

Continued in part II (chapter 73 of this volume).

Related Chapters

15 Ibn Daud, 16 Maimonides, 17 Maimonides, 24 Albalag, 39 Del Medigo, 44 Spinoza, 45 Mendelssohn, 62 Berdichevsky, 64 Cohen, 65 Cohen, 73 Strauss, 83 Borowitz, 86 Rosenberg

73

Leo Strauss (1899–1973)

Reason versus Revelation and the Modern Predicament, Part II

The past can teach the moderns why we should remain Jews

Has Baruch Spinoza actually demonstrated that reason defeats revelation?

Spinoza does show that the biblical text presents many difficulties. But where the philosopher sees here powerful evidence against the reality of divine revelation, the believer sees deep teachings and divine mystery. For Spinoza to succeed in refuting religion he must disprove, philosophically, the very notion, the very possibility, of divine revelation. But how exactly could he do that?

In his famous work *The Ethics*, he attempts to provide a philosophically complete and clear account of the cosmos that proves both predeterminism and causal necessitarianism. The truth of these doctrines—that everything is predetermined in advance and that everything must happen exactly as it does—would indeed rule out the possibility of revelation. But now they only succeed in doing so if the system that entails them is itself both complete and clear. As anyone who has engaged with Spinoza's writings can attest, it is far from either. Ultimately, in fact, his work *presupposes* the falseness of revelation, and thus does not disprove it.

So modern philosophy, following Spinoza in its attack on revealed religion, fails to prove its own highest premises to be true! But then modern philosophy—that is, reason—cannot be said to possess or discover knowledge itself, nor to conclusively know what in fact is good for human beings. Hence the vicious attacks on reason led by Nietzsche and others, which then culminated in the horrors of the twentieth century.

What we need is to return to a time when there was greater clarity about the nature of, and relationship between, reason and revelation.

Maimonides, for example, stresses that the content of revelation is neither doctrine nor dogma—which would bring it into possible conflict with reason—but *Law*, and this divinely revealed Law has never been refuted by reason. It's a Law that aims toward perfecting the human soul, with adequate room for reason insofar as there is always work to do in clarifying the Law and room to raise questions and even doubts. This Law forms the basis of the Jewish community, obliges the Jew who wishes to be a part of that community to obey it, and in so doing helps nurture each Jew toward spiritual perfection. Also crucial here is the insight that it's good for individuals to be members of communities, of *distinguishable* communities—not just of the "universal human community" guided by "universal laws of reason," even if some laws also are universally binding on all.

There is plenty of room to philosophize here, within the context of the Law, or within the political community. Admittedly, philosophy can sometimes pose dangers to the Law, particularly in the hands either of those who are poorly suited to philosophy or of those not committed to the Law, either of whom might use philosophy to attack and undermine the Law. It is to minimize this danger that Maimonides himself writes esoterically, which suggests that his commitment to the Law is firmer than perhaps careful philosophizing alone would dictate. In any case, it is this commitment to the divine revelation, as something distinguishable from, but not contrary to, reason, that ultimately provides both the general response to the decay of modern philosophy and the particular response to the Jewish problem.

For, in short, it provides a defense of the viability and value of Judaism, of remaining Jewish, in the modern world.

The past indeed has something to teach the moderns in this regard.

Related Chapters

15 Ibn Daud, 16 Maimonides, 17 Maimonides, 24 Albalag, 39 Del Medigo, 44 Spinoza, 45 Mendelssohn, 62 Berdichevsky, 64 Cohen, 65 Cohen, 72 Strauss, 83 Borowitz

74

Emmanuel Levinas (1906–95)

Seeing God in the Face of the Other

We experience God's presence in experiencing our moral obligations to other persons

Famously, the Israelites at Mount Sinai, upon hearing of the commandments, answered, "We will do and we will understand" (Exodus 24:7). According to Levinas, this teaches the important principle that action precedes understanding; or, more generally, that ethics, the norms of acting, are more fundamental than the epistemology, the theory of knowledge, that has traditionally come first.

Indeed, consider the paradox of monotheism that confronts epistemology. It consists in the simultaneous truth of three claims: that God is perfect, that everything the perfect God creates is itself perfect, and that the world created by God is imperfect. None of these may be given up, yet their simultaneous truth obviously goes beyond reason, for it requires both that the created world should be perfect and that it is not. Resolving this paradox is central for religion; yet its suprarational nature means that religion must find another, non-epistemological, dimension in which to resolve it.

The answer may be found in "phenomenology," the study of how we experience the world, how it appears to us. Consider our awareness of the "Other," of other persons, the way others present themselves to us: we cannot but meet the gaze of another person without recognizing in them certain demands made on us, that we acknowledge their presence, their needs and interests. The fundamental experience of others teaches us immediately of our obligations to them—of the primacy of the *ethical*.

And insofar as there are potentially an infinite number of Others, we also become aware through this encounter, in our finite way, *of* the infinite. In this manner the transcendent infinite makes its appearance in the finite realm of the immanent. It is in our awareness of others and of our obligations to them—in our infinite moral relations, in other words—that we experience awareness of God. Through love of the Other we experience love of God; the respect we feel toward the stranger, toward the helpless, is our sanctification of the Eternal.

Monotheism, and Judaism in particular, are not metaphysical positions but *ethical structures*.

So construed, we may resolve the paradox of creation (above) by understanding it as an ongoing *process*, one constituted by the work of sanctification, of making holy, of striving after justice. What we do when we pursue these ends, when we as Jews pursue justice and morality, is God's own work. Our dedication to *tikkun olam* (repairing the world) just is our creating the world in partnership with God. As such, we participate in His work, the infinite being works in and with us finite beings, in the ongoing perfecting of the world. Thus God both transcends the world and is very much within it, as it strives toward perfection.

Jewish rituals and commandments are part of this process. They provide the necessary pause that allows us to take distance from our natural attitudes, to experience shame before the evil of which we are capable, to recognize our obligations toward the Other and fulfill them.

We are made in God's image, then, insofar as we are moral beings.

That is our covenant with God.

The State of Israel, then, does more than herald a new age of material security for the Jewish people. It offers a truly special opportunity: to carry out the social laws of Judaism and the ethical obligations we owe to each other, to pursue justice and morality, and so to fulfill the covenant, on the grandest scale—and in so doing bring us closer to the messianic era.

Related Chapters

2 Philo, 7 Ibn Paquda, 18 Maimonides, 42 Sforno, 51 Holdheim, 57 Salanter, 62 Berdichevsky, 64 Cohen, 67 Buber, 70 Kaplan, 75 Heschel, 76 Berkovits, 82 Wyschogrod, 83 Borowitz

75

Abraham Joshua Heschel (1907–72)

God in Search of Man

The experience of divine concern is at the heart of authentic religious practice

Authentic religious practice, for Heschel, ultimately relates to experience: Those who are so attuned distinctly experience the presence of something that is not of this world. This experience permeates the great Jewish texts and much of our religious past. And while the religion our predecessors created is indeed constituted by answers to the great questions—What kind of cosmos do we live in? What is the purpose of my life? How should I live?—those very questions, and our subsequent answers, are ultimately grounded in that religious experience. There is a holy dimension within and behind the world as we perceive it, and our chief task now is to retune ourselves so that we may be receptive to it.

Some blame secular science and the skepticism of modern philosophy for the decline of religion in our society. But religion itself shares some blame. It has declined not because it was refuted but because it became irrelevant, dull. When living faith is replaced by creed and doctrine, when worship is replaced by discipline, when love, by habit—in short, when faith becomes an heirloom rather than an active fountain, it dies. It is an answer to those great questions, but when religion no longer keeps those questions alive and pressing for us, it becomes irrelevant.

How may we retune ourselves?

There are three sources of that religious experience that leads to God. We may sense the divine presence either in the cosmos, in scripture, or in sacred deeds: that is, in learning, worship, or action.

As for the first, we do not begin with dogma or creed but instead must see the cosmos through the eyes of wonder, through amazement, a radical amazement that leads us not to ask merely "What laws of nature explain this?" but rather, "Why is there anything at all, *including* laws of nature?"

As for the second, we must also realize that scripture is not merely about ancient history or metaphysics but about how we may sanctify life. It is not our vision of God but God's vision of us. God did not reveal the eternal mysteries or His essence, but instead revealed what He asks of us, how we should live—His *will*.

And that in turn reveals that there are deeds we are to perform, the commandments. But rather than demand first a belief in God before we perform these actions we must see that performing these actions itself opens us up to the holy dimension of experience. The pious life allows us to experience the holy. The key issue is not how to continue our existence, then, but how to *exalt* it. Our concern isn't merely for some eternal life beyond the grave, but to make this life eternal in nature—by living it in contact with the divine.

What this experience makes immediately clear and present isn't God's existence or power, but His *concern* for us. Divine concern is the fundamental category, not being. Failure to grasp this is the key mistake dating all the way back to Aristotle's "unmoved mover," continuing through the medievals' insistence on the "perfect," "timeless," "unchanging" God, and so on. But that God is not the God of scripture. That God is not the God of lived experience. That God is not one concerned with the world, much less with human existence. That God is not the one who asks that we partner with Him in creation, to carry out His vision, to complete the world.

The God of concern is the God who *is* concerned—not indifferent to human beings, but in need of them.

Related Chapters

76

Eliezer Berkovits (1908–92)

Man in Search of God

The experience of divine concern is both the foundation and endpoint of Judaism

The core of theology, according to Berkovits, is the personal encounter with the divine: an experience that irresistibly reveals to you the divine presence. This encounter is there in the great revelation before the Israelites on Mount Sinai, it is there in the prophetic experiences throughout scripture, and it remains relevant today—even in the post-Holocaust world.

The encounter is profoundly paradoxical, but therein lies its foundational role. It transcends human comprehension yet demonstrates the key truth, that God cares about human beings. The latter it does on the basis of another paradox. On the one hand the encounter is experienced as deeply threatening. As scripture teaches, you cannot see God's face, nor even hear His voice, and live (Exodus 33:20, Deuteronomy 4:33), for God is a "consuming fire" (Deuteronomy 4:24)—not because He is angry with our sinful world but because the infinite potency of His being cannot be tolerated by any finite, created thing. The person experiencing the divine presence feels that crushing power, feels his own limited existence turning into *nothing*.

And yet at the same time he feels himself *sustained* by the very same God whose presence threatens him. During the encounter he feels God propping him up, preserving him, caring for him. In the very moment of his own nothingness he recognizes that this care is his being valued by God, his being "crowned with glory and honor" (Psalms 8:5) in an invitation to fellowship with God. God reveals Himself to him but must, to the degree that He cares for and sustains him—in *order* to sustain him as an independent being—also remain hidden.

That the encounter is rare is also necessary.

During the experience, while it is happening, you are incapable of refusing belief in God or commitment to God. It is irresistible, irrefutable, inescapable. But where there is compulsion, even if just the logical or experiential sort, there is no freedom; and where there is no freedom there cannot be *genuine* fellowship and relationship. For the sake of such, then, the time between encounters, stretching over generations, even centuries—divine hiddenness—is essential.

These points must also be kept in mind when we grapple with the horrors of the Holocaust, which understandably shakes the faith of many. Yes, God remained hidden throughout that dreadful ordeal. But if the human ability to perpetrate incomprehensible crimes testifies to God's nonexistence, as some assert, what about our equally incomprehensible ability for great kindness, for self-sacrificial heroism, for unquestioning faith even in the face of those horrors, instances of which there were many?

The question for the Jew is not to explain why God was silent while the crematoria consumed one third of the Jewish people. It is rather, first, to grasp that in order for God to allow our freedom of action at all, even to commit the most profound evil, He must remain hidden; and then to appreciate just how affirmations of faith may remain meaningful even despite the tragedy.

So divine hiddenness creates our greatest possibilities for us. It permits our survival during the encounter; our independence, as a separate being with our own nature; our freedom of choice and behavior. The miraculous affirmation of our faith, not merely in God but also in the values and meaning that God represents to us, is only made more significant before the incomprehensible horrors—and is perhaps necessary in order that we may yet again experience the divine encounter, which is both the foundation and ultimate endpoint of our religion.

Related Chapters

10 Halevi, 13 Ibn Ezra, 15 Ibn Daud, 25 Abner of Burgos, 26 Pollegar, 27 Ibn Kaspi, 29 Gersonides, 31 Ben Joshua, 32 Crescas, 34 Crescas, 35 Albo, 40 Ebreo, 41 Almosnino, 43 Spinoza, 49 Steinheim, 57 Salanter, 64 Cohen, 67 Buber, 71 Soloveitchik, 74 Levinas, 75 Heschel, 77 Arendt, 80 Jonas, 83 Borowitz

77

Hannah Arendt (1906–75)

The Banality of Evil

However evil the Holocaust was, Eichmann's own evil was not radical but merely banal

The traditional "problem of evil" is that the existence of so much evil in the world seems to refute the existence of God. Certainly no recent event raises that problem more powerfully than the murder of six million Jews during the Nazi-perpetrated Holocaust. When Nazi officer Adolf Eichmann was captured in 1960 and brought to the State of Israel to stand trial for his significant role in the Final Solution, Arendt's reporting on the trial generated some controversy, not least concerning her analysis of evil.

In her view the Jerusalem trial generates at least three problems: (1) that of impaired justice, since the Jewish people who were the victims were also serving as plaintiffs and judges; (2) a crime against humanity (not merely a "crime against the Jews") should be adjudicated in a more general venue; and (3) it fails to understand the criminal who had committed the crime. All are problematic, but we shall focus on the last.

Many see in the Nazis, and in Eichmann, the most profound evil; *radical* evil, even, to the core, consisting in evil intentions and deliberations. Indeed it was more this evil itself that was on trial than the individual himself, as so much testimony was about the Holocaust in general and the long history of Jew-hatred in Germany; it was more about what the Jews had suffered than about what Eichmann had actually done. But in reality Eichmann the individual cannot be said to be radically evil. One cannot extract any diabolical or demonic profundity from him. He was neither perverted nor sadistic. In fact he was a careerist, he was confused, he was a clown, one who spoke and thought in shallow clichés.

Perhaps we shouldn't even say he "thought" at all. His actions were not "intentional," if that means they were carefully thought out and chosen. He did not or could not take distance from what his surrounding context was demanding of him; he was simply obedient, not thinking of the implications of his actions. On the deepest of levels he did not understand what he was doing. His was not "radical evil."

It was simply banal.

True, he sometimes gave the appearance of the contrary. At one point he explained that his actions were governed by Kantian moral principles, as if he had studied the great philosopher Immanuel Kant (1724–1804)! But the claim was outrageous on the face of it. Kant's moral philosophy is closely bound with one's ability for intellectual judgment, which rules out simple blind obedience—which was all Eichmann actually meant by invoking Kant, that he was just doing his duty. Indeed a key element of Kant's moral philosophy is that you should act by principles that can be universalized, that everyone could act by. "Committing genocide" is not one such principle. On further questioning Eichmann admitted that the only principle he really followed was to act in such a way that the *Führer* would approve. Not exactly a universalizable principle!

That Eichmann's evil was not radical but merely banal does not mean that the verdict was unjust, or that he shouldn't hang. Insofar as he and his superiors wrongly claimed the right to determine who to share the earth with, no member of the human race can be expected to share the earth with *them*. While we must reject pure vengeance in the pursuit of justice, justice here does support the death sentence.

But it is a sentence for the actions committed, not for the evil they represented—banal as it was.

Related Chapters

78

Emil Fackenheim (1916–2003)

The 614th Commandment

The authentic Jew must not give Hitler a posthumous victory

The authentic Jew of today is forbidden to hand Hitler a posthumous victory, Fackenheim famously asserts. The Nazi leader attempted to destroy Judaism; we must not now cooperate in its destruction. This new imperative bears the same degree of obligation as the traditional 613 commandments it supplements, not merely for religious Jews but secular ones as well.

Formulating the idea as a new commandment reflects the fact that the Holocaust is a *novum*, an utterly new thing, without any precedent. The more psychologists or historians attempt to explain it, the more we grasp its ultimate inexplicability. The same goes for the philosophers, whose systems cannot accommodate it. It's new even in Jewish history, already no stranger to national catastrophe. It is so unique that the traditional invocation, that the names of evildoers should be wiped from history, cannot apply to Hitler's—for Auschwitz must be remembered.

Nor can we hope to find any meaning in the Holocaust, religious or secular, redemptive or other. The long tragic arc of Jewish history could often be interpreted in this way, but to connect storm troopers with any cause of humanity, let alone the will of God, is impossible—even blasphemous.

Auschwitz was a victory neither for God nor humanity, but only for Hitler.

But Hitler's war did not end with his death, regrettably. He sought to destroy not merely individuals Jews, but Jewishness. When, in the face of threat or hostility or even just discomfort, Jews abandon their Jewishness, apologize for it, hate it, slander it, they are doing Hitler's work for him. The temptation may well be powerful, but yielding to it rewards Hitler with his posthumous victory.

An authentic Jew will know he or she is obliged to resist this, as by a divine commandment.

This formulation is perhaps problematic. Only Orthodox Jews accept or observe all 613 commandments, but Jewish authenticity cannot be restricted to the Orthodox. Who would deny Jewish authenticity to those nonreligious Jews who gave scraps of food to others when starving themselves, or stole medicines to help those even sicker than they? And while calling this obligation a *commandment* may feel strange to these authentic Jews, who admit no divine commander, even they feel this obligation—as the commanding voice of Auschwitz.

What exactly is this obligation? It is, first of all, an obligation to confront the Holocaust, to grapple with it and to teach of it to our children, despite the burden on them of so doing. The religious may ask why God failed to save the Jewish people, while the secular may ask how human beings could behave in this way, but all must confront these questions. Further, we are obligated, somehow, not to go mad as we confront them, and to endure all the contradictions of our singled out condition.

And finally, we are obligated to carry on—*as Jews*.

That may mean many things, but among them we must include the important connection between the Holocaust and the State of Israel. Israel has quickly become the new center of Jewish civilization, both religious and secular. Though the state cannot be said to have messianic significance, as the messiah is supposed to redeem humanity from poverty and war, it surely seems to be an example of divine salvation, both in arising after the catastrophe and surviving the 1967 Arab-Israeli War. However we understand it, it seems the best place where Jews can assure that Hitler's project will finally fail. Every authentic response to the Holocaust, whether religious or secular, Jewish or not Jewish, is thus a commitment to the autonomy and security of the State of Israel.

Related Chapters

12 Halevi, 19 Nachmanides, 58 Kalischer, 59 Pinsker, 60 Herzl, 61 Ahad Ha'am, 62 Berdichevsky, 63 Schneersohn, 65 Cohen, 66 Rosenzweig, 68 Bialik, 69 Kook, 77 Arendt, 79 Leibowitz, 80 Jonas, 82 Wyschogrod, 83 Borowitz

79

Yeshayahu Leibowitz (1903–94)

Idolatry of the 1967 Lands

*One should serve God, for the sake
of God, and leave politics out of it*

"Anthropocentric religion" centers on the human being, aiming to fulfill his needs and aspirations, his "salvation"; here one judges a religion by what it can give to human beings. "Theocentric religion," to the contrary, centers on God, and the key question is not what it gives to human beings but what it *demands* of them. As the *Shulchan Aruch*, the great summary of Jewish Law, puts it, "One must collect strength and stand up in the morning to serve one's creator."

Too many see Judaism in anthropocentric terms. But no, Judaism is about Torah and *mitzvot*, about worshipping God, fearing and loving God. Ask not what God can do for us, but what we can do for God. That is the central message of the book of Job, for just one of many examples. Job only approaches satisfaction when he realizes that his initial conception of God—as a being whose job is to fulfill man—yields to a subtler and truer one: God's divinity is His essence, and neither He nor His cosmos is fundamentally about fulfilling human needs or goals. As Maimonides recognizes, to understand that fact, and dedicate yourself to God's worship, produces the true happiness that cannot be troubled even by misfortunes such as Job's.

This means the study of Torah, the performance of *mitzvot*, should be pursued not for your sake but for *their* sake. The Talmud is also clear on this: "Whoever occupies himself with the Torah for its own sake, his learning becomes an elixir of life to him. . . . But whoever occupies himself with the Torah not for its own sake, it becomes to him a deadly poison" (Talmud Tractate *Ta'anith* 7a).

Yet even so, many contemporary religious Jews turn the Torah toward external ends.

The situation in the State of Israel is one particularly troubling example.

While the Jewish state is a political and perhaps moral necessity, that is the legitimate limit of political Zionism. Too many individuals confuse their patriotism and nationalism with their religion. They see in the state, and particularly in the territories captured in 1967, the imminent arrival of the messianic age. They thus aim to settle this territory with Jews as part of their messianic vision.

But this fetish for the land, this idolatry of the land, is only about their own needs. Like other messianic movements they project their own political ambitions into scripture, thereby polluting the religion. This inevitably leads to disaster: the Shabbatai Zvi episode (for example) wasn't merely shameful but devastating,* and even the great Talmudic sage, Rabbi Akiva, who, thinking that messianic redemption was nigh, endorsed the revolt against Rome and fell prone to what Isaac Abravanel (1437–1508) described this way: "What often happens to the wise—that he will believe that for which his soul longs and yearns."

For Israel to retain those territories, to dominate another people, will corrupt its soul. More deeply, to the degree to which control over these lands is imbued with religious significance, it will harm the Jewish religion.

Torah and *mitzvot* are neither national nor moral nor social. They are about serving God, for the sake of God. That is between each individual and his or her creator. In the long exile, individual Jews could not exist except through immersion in the Jewish religious community. But now that we have reestablished our national collective in the State of Israel, we must reemphasize the personal aspect of our religion. You should serve God, for God's own sake, and leave your politics entirely out of it.

---

*Shabbatai Zvi (1626–76) was widely thought to be the messiah, in a career that ended dreadfully both for him and for the Jewish people.

Related Chapters

2 Philo, 12 Halevi, 13 Ibn Ezra, 18 Maimonides, 20 Nachmanides, 32 Crescas, 41 Almosnino, 58 Kalischer, 63 Schneersohn, 65 Cohen, 66 Rosenzweig, 68 Bialik, 69 Kook, 71 Soloveitchik, 77 Arendt, 78 Fackenheim, 83 Borowitz, 86 Rosenberg

80

Hans Jonas (1903–93)

God after Auschwitz

The existence of evil is ultimately due to God's revocation of His own power

Auschwitz took the ancient problem of evil to a new level of urgency—not merely for believers in general but for the Jewish people in particular, with whom God was understood to have made a special covenant. For centuries Jews had explained the evils inflicted upon them as divine punishment for failing to fulfill their side of that covenant, but Auschwitz destroys this explanation just as it destroyed infants and children. The enormity of the Holocaust cannot be justified by any infidelity. The question, Jonas insists, must be invoked anew: what God could allow Auschwitz?

We begin with a myth.

In the beginning, God, the ground of all being, chose for unknowable reasons to give Himself over to the chance and risk of becoming. And wholly so: entering into space and time, He held back nothing, nothing of Himself, nothing with which to direct the ongoing process of the cosmos. In order that the cosmos might be, and indeed be for itself, God renounced His own divine being. In doing so, no divine foreknowledge could remain. For Him to know what was to ensue in the world He had to wait and see. In time He observed human beings arise, with our consciousness and free will.

And then there was Auschwitz.

This myth reflects a God who may be said to suffer alongside and even because of His creatures. A God who is no longer eternally unchanging *being* but ongoing *becoming*, altered by the very temporal cosmos as He lives in continuous relationship to it. A caring God, not remote and impersonal as philosophers have tended to think. He cares, but He does not interfere: in allowing the cosmos to be, He leaves matters for others to do.

And most important, He is not an omnipotent—that is, all-powerful—God.

Indeed we could include both omnipotence and goodness in our conception of God only at the cost of unintelligibility, for it is surely unintelligible how an omnipotent and perfectly good God could allow Auschwitz. But the *Jewish* answer we seek cannot give up that intelligibility: the notion of a hidden or absurd God is profoundly un-Jewish, for the fundamental premise of Judaism is that God has revealed His commandments and Law to us, in the Torah. Nor may we dispense with God's goodness and still have a God worth worshipping.

In light of Auschwitz, therefore, we must understand God *not* to be omnipotent.

God was silent during the Holocaust not because He chose not to intervene, then, but because He could not intervene. In allowing the cosmos to be in the first place He divested Himself of the power to interfere, as our myth suggests.

While this may seem at odds with tradition, it actually has an important precedent in the ancient Jewish mystical texts known as the Kabbalah. There we find the idea of *tzimtzum*, that the unlimited being that is God had to contract Himself so that, vacated by Him, empty space could expand outside of Him and become the "Nothing" in or from which God then created the cosmos. As our myth now has it, God contracts so totally within Himself that He even cedes His power to the cosmos He creates.

The problem of evil is thus answered: evil exists ultimately due to God's revocation of His own power. Having given Himself whole to the becoming world, so that we mortals could be, God subsequently has no more to give. It is now ours to give back to Him, to redress the imbalance.

To repair the world.

Related Chapters

81

Judith Plaskow (b. 1947)

Made in Her Image

Feminist Judaism as a religion for all Jews

What might happen to the central categories of Jewish thought as women enter into the process of defining them? How might our understanding of, and approach to, Torah, the people of Israel, and God evolve as women appropriate them through the lens of their own experience? What might Jewish religiosity look like when it reflects *all* Jewish people—not just men?

These, according to Plaskow, are some of the questions of feminist Judaism.

Some see "feminism" as simply contradictory to traditional Judaism, given the latter's patriarchal history, legacy, and structure. Only men may initiate divorce, for example; women do not count in a *minyan* (quorum for public prayer); rabbinic history and its core texts (Talmud, midrash, etc.) have been dominated by men and their concerns and almost entirely exclude women, and so on. These differences in turn reflect a deeper metaphysical ideology. In *halacha*, for example, men define Jewish humanity. Men are the actors in religious and communal life because they are the normative Jews. Women are other than the norm, "the Other," less than fully human. This otherness of women resides in the heart of Jewish Law.

Consider even the starting point of the Jewish religion. Entering the covenant at Mount Sinai was and is Judaism's root experience. Yet in preparation for that event Moses warns, "Be ready for the third day; do not go near a woman" (Exodus 19:15). Although a seminal emission renders both a man and his female partner ritually unfit to approach the sacred, Moses does not say, "Men and women, do not go near each other." He addresses only the men. At this profoundest of moments women are invisible, a mere source of impurity. Whether they even stood at the mountain experiencing the great revelation we do not even know. The chronicler of that moment was not interested in their experience.

To change this deeply patriarchal system will require a revolution as great as the earlier transition from biblical to rabbinic Judaism, precipitated by the destruction of the Second Temple (70 CE). It will require more than merely obtaining equal rights for women within established Jewish institutions and practices, as important as that is. We must transform Judaism *itself* into a religion that women participate in shaping.

This will involve uncovering and making visible Jewish women's history and cultures, to be sure. But it will also require expanding the notion of Torah beyond the Bible and the rabbis, to include women's words, teachings, actions. We must develop feminist *midrash* (commentary and interpretation) and liturgy that reshape Jewish memory and Jewish vision. We might (for example) rework the ancient *midrash* about Adam's two wives (the traditional Eve and the rebel outcast, "Lilith") to expand and develop feminist themes. Perhaps *halacha* itself may be developed in a less distinctively masculine form, less a matter of rigid rulemaking than a shared communal process.

And of course we must also revamp and revitalize our theological discourse. We must reimagine what has been imagined as exclusively masculine throughout. When God is portrayed as a father, human fathers are understood as God-like; when God is a dominating male, human institutions will likely be male dominated. Many feminists are currently exploring the use of feminine language with respect to God. Some have even rewritten traditional liturgy describing God as a woman. There are many possibilities here and the work has just begun, but the necessity of taking this pluralistic approach to divine imagery, in order to transform centuries of masculine and hierarchy-oriented theology, is clear.

Judaism must become a religion for *all* Jews.

Related Chapters

17 Maimonides, 70 Kaplan, 71 Soloveitchik, 80 Jonas, 84 Adler, 85 Ross

82

Michael Wyschogrod (1928–2015)

The Body and the Blood

It is through God's preferential love of the Jewish people that He is able to love all humanity

We must free Judaism from its external philosophical influences, suggests Wyschogrod, such as Aristotle and Kant—*and* Maimonides. For it was the latter who, in reconciling Judaism with Aristotle, went overboard in rejecting divine anthropomorphism. In so doing Maimonides turned Judaism into a philosophical doctrine rather than what the Bible actually teaches: the story of God's unique, preferential love for the patriarch Abraham and his descendants. God fell in love with Abraham and founded a family with him; and so continues to dwell within and among the Jewish people.

Later thinkers, with similar external motivations, saw Israel's "chosenness" as symbolic of God's equal love for all humanity and Judaism as having a universalistic mission, to teach all humanity how to behave morally. Judaism to them was basically an early Christianity, which teaches the same universalism.

Right, but wrong. For what Christianity really teaches is (1) that the divine may be incarnated into human form, and (2) that God's love of all humanity is mediated through His special love for one particular individual—but both ideas are from the Hebrew Bible. God dwells within the body of the Jewish people, and His love of all humanity is mediated through His special love for that one particular people.

That sounds hard on the ears of many, but it should not. For a general or universal love, for "all humanity," is no true love at all. *Genuine* love is love of the individual, in his or her specificity. Undifferentiated love, dispensed equally to all, does *not* meet the individual in his individuality but at most sees him as a member of some group or class. A child whose parent loves her with only the undifferentiated love of all humanity could legitimately claim that *she* has not truly been loved.

But if genuine love requires specificity and preference, then a being who cannot love individuals in their specificity is incapable of loving anybody at all. Thus *everyone* has an interest in God's loving some people more than He loves others, for that just is the basis for God's being able to have a genuine relationship with *anybody* at all.

In any case, anybody can surely earn God's love, either by following the moral laws, by recognizing that all human beings are made in God's image and respecting them accordingly, or, if they feel envy about Israel's election, by converting and becoming a member of the Jewish people.

Maimonides's arch opposition to anthropomorphism obviously sits poorly with all this, but so much the worse for Maimonides. And anyway, the Jewish faith could hardly survive without the genuinely personal relationship between the Jew and God described above, a relationship that simply is not possible with Aristotle's (and therefore Maimonides's) "Unmoved Mover."

Nor should one make anything else somehow central to Judaism. Thinkers like Fackenheim wrongly grant the Holocaust a major role in motivating Jewish belief and practice, as if without Hitler there were no such motivation. Others, like Cohen, Buber, and Levinas, reduce Judaism to a universal ethics. But this move, which soon leads to the demise of Judaism at the hands of secular ethics, overlooks the truly essential, particularistic nature of Judaism and of God's special relationship with the Jewish people, as depicted in the Bible.

For the message is clear: "I will bless those who bless you, and curse him that curses you; in you shall all the families of the earth be blessed" (Genesis 12:3). In other words, it is through God's privileged love of the children of Israel that He comes to love all others.

Related Chapters

10 Halevi, 11 Halevi, 17 Maimonides, 32 Crescas, 38 Abravanel, 64 Cohen, 67 Buber, 70 Kaplan, 74 Levinas, 78 Fackenheim

83

Eugene Borowitz (1924–2016)

A Covenant Theology

On being committed to personal autonomy and God, Israel, and Torah

The modern American Jew has a dilemma, according to Borowitz: how can she be committed both to the individual autonomy of modern times and to the Jewish tradition? Or put somewhat differently: what should impel someone not committed to Orthodoxy to observe anything particular, other than the universal moral law?

Two major social ideologies fail to answer this problem. Zionism simply does not tempt American Jews in significant numbers into immigrating to Israel, and Kaplan's Reconstructionism fails to construct a persuasive account of Jewish moral obligation. Once you substitute sociology for God, after all, why should the fact that past Jews behaved a certain way impart any obligations on today's Jews?

The general "death of God" movement so conspicuous during the twentieth century has also failed. Some claim that the Holocaust makes it impossible to believe any longer in the ancient God. But what really died there was the belief in *human* morality. And as the decades accumulated into the 1960s and 1970s, the "individual freedom" era soon revealed itself as the scourge it was, creating problems with drugs, violence, sexual license, economic injustice, social malaise. After the Holocaust, and after this, our exalted view of ourselves and our moral capabilities is no longer sustainable.

What we now need is a way to endow our Jewish communal observances with the right measure of independent, individual authority and autonomy—which cannot be done without bringing God back into the equation.

It is time for a human *tzimtzum*, contraction, to make room for God again—as the ultimate ground of our values, in a non-Orthodox but still compelling fashion. Now that we American Jews have demonstrated that we fit into a pluralistic, universalistic society, we can embrace our particularity again. And once we realize that we are not always smarter than our forebears, that individualism has its limits and our community might yet have much to teach us, the idea of our original communal covenant can again become alive. The covenant was made, after all, between God and the entire House of Israel. The individual Jew shares in her people's relationship with God as a matter of birth, but when she actively chooses to, may also share in it as a matter of will. In so doing she acknowledges that our values are not merely our preferences, or our community's preferences, but are rooted in something outside ourselves.

Postmodern philosophy may be useful in formulating the renewed covenant in accordance with our contemporary times. Postmodernism tolerates a balance between that which is relatively fixed in thought and that which remains open to fresh imagination or insight. Most of all it insists that particularity precedes universality. It teaches that we can no longer think as if we transcend time, place, class, race, folk, culture, gender.

But with this dignity of particularity we can now embrace our membership in our community, the children of Israel—we can affirm that we participate in its historicity, that we relate to God as mediated through our community, that we are guided by the community in determining our Jewish duty—but not in a way that sacrifices individual autonomy or personal conscience. By seeing Judaism as the covenant faith, the Jew will regard it not as a private religion but as one he shares with his people. His autonomous right to decide what is Torah-for-him, which might lead to anarchy, will thus be expanded to what is Torah-for-him-as-a-member-of-the-covenant-folk.

From the point of view of "covenant theology," then, what binds us Jews together is far more important than what separates us.

Related Chapters

11 Halevi, 13 Ibn Ezra, 16 Maimonides, 37 Bivach, 38 Abravanel, 47 Ascher, 48 Zunz, 50 Geiger, 51 Holdheim, 52 Sofer, 53 Frankel, 54 Krochmal, 55 Hirsch, 56 Hirsch, 57 Salanter, 64 Cohen, 70 Kaplan, 72 Strauss, 73 Strauss, 74 Levinas, 75 Heschel, 76 Berkovits, 77 Arendt, 78 Fackenheim, 79 Leibowitz, 80 Jonas, 86 Rosenberg

84

Rachel Adler (b. 1943)

A Covenant for Lovers

Building on the halachic past a foundation for a more egalitarian Jewish future

In Orthodoxy, and even in much of the liberal Jewish movement until the middle of the twentieth century, Adler writes, being a woman was like being Alice at the Hatter's tea party: they weren't there at the beginning of the party and they did not make any of the rules. At best, women were made a focus of the sacred, rather than being active participants in its processes. And while she once understood such Jewish notions as "purity" and "impurity" as a cycle through which all members of society pass, male and female, further study convinces her that in fact "impurity" and "purity" define a class system within Judaism—in which the impure are mostly women.

Women, halachically, are on the periphery. Their spirituality as the "Other" is based on not-doing and not-being, while the masculine serves as the norm, to do and to be.

As *halacha* has systematically excluded the voices of women, some now urge rejecting it outright and constructing new, modern Judaisms. Plaskow, though not quite advocating that route, is ambivalent about *halacha*, emphasizing the reformation of theology while questioning whether any system based on law could be harmonized with a feminist emphasis on relationship. But law is too central to Judaism, too embedded in the Jewish narrative, to abandon it. As important as a feminist theology is, an authentic Jewish theology must accommodate the norms and praxis of Judaism; and the language for articulating these norms is necessarily halachic.

We must not reject *halacha*, then, so much as reclaim it, transform it; forge a new framework that breaks the tradition's monopoly on the rules, categories, and authorities.

But how?

As legal scholar Robert Cover (1943–86) argues, law functions in two modes. The "imperialistic" mode is characterized by authority and the enforcement of rules, which has been the norm for Jewish Law. But law can also function in a "jurisgenerative" mode—that is, one where law is seen as embodying the community's highest ideals, including its master narrative, which naturally evolve over time. On this view there may be competing groups within a society developing and defending different norms and moral visions, aiming to persuade others; these groups build on what has been but aim to create richer worlds that *could* be. This mode is a better model for what we seek—not to reject the past but to build a bridge from it, from Jewish tradition, text, and Law, to the more ideal world.

One excellent place to start is with Jewish marriage.

Classical *halacha* conceives marriage as an act of *kinyan*, acquisition, in which the husband "acquires" the wife like a piece of property. Not only is this offensive but it also fails to express the reciprocity and concern that should characterize the bond between two persons who wish to sanctify their relationship as permanent partners. Rather than base marriage in property law, then, we might invoke other traditional sources and reconceive it (for example) in terms of the laws governing *partnerships*. To this end we may rewrite the traditional *ketubah* (marriage contract) and replace it with a *B'rit Ahuvim*, a Covenant for Lovers, specifying the terms of partnership that ought to constitute a marriage.

In this way we grant a ritual expression to the theological ideals we are endeavoring to realize, but do so on the basis of traditional Jewish Law and texts, reconfigured in improved ways.

We don't reject the halachic past, in other words, but build upon its foundation the better future we seek.

Related Chapters

85

Tamar Ross (b. 1938)

Expanding the Palace of Torah

An Orthodox approach to feminism

One must appreciate Adler's revised *ketubah*, Ross acknowledges, for showing how to make use of traditional resources in modern and helpful ways. But while Adler, in the Reform movement, wants to break the traditional male monopoly on interpretive authority and "create anew," for feminist ideas to gain any traction within Orthodoxy itself, they must be developed by means of accepted procedures and conventions. Adler speaks of building a bridge to a new future from the past, but overlooks the fact that the past, its norms and rules, must shape the nature of the bridge to be formed.

Any changes within Orthodoxy must be grounded in the established, classical legal tradition—and plausibly be understood as the continued unfolding of the same divine revelation that began at Sinai.

To be sure there is some overlap between the motivations and goals of non-Orthodox and Orthodox feminists. Both are influenced by trends in the broader feminist movement. Both aim to overcome women's subordination and achieve equality within their communities. Both are concerned to introduce feminine ways of thinking into their respective practices—such as, in the Orthodox community, the rise of women's prayer groups, new forms of *divrei Torah* (Torah commentary), novel, women-oriented lifecycle rituals, and so on. And both are firmly committed to Maimonides's famous statement, "The gates of interpretation are never sealed": we may start with that single text, the Bible, but precisely what we take that text to teach us is never finished.

And that is the key, for the Orthodox—for we understand that divine revelation is ongoing and cumulative; and that rather than restrict or reject the tradition we can, to borrow an idea from Rav Kook, *expand* the palace of Torah.

When we do this we find that feminism is not actually external to the Torah but *internal* to it. In fact there are three basic Jewish principles that may allow us to reorient the pervasive male bias in scripture without creating untenable conceptions of either God or of divine methods of communication. First is the idea just noted, that Torah is a cumulative process. Second is the idea that God's word is heard both through interpretation of texts and through history, itself a form of ongoing revelation. And third, finally, is this essential Orthodox idea: that throughout all these processes the original eternal message is never replaced.

But even that original message clearly acknowledges the active input of Moses in transmitting the word of God; acknowledges, that is, the impossibility of avoiding human standpoints. So Orthodox Judaism itself teaches that we always interpret God's word through human categories, perspectives, and culture. That does of course create a great burden on us, and the great risk of simply getting it all wrong. Only with awe and apprehension, with fear and trembling—and the corresponding humility—can we approach the text and attempt to discern God's word in it, to get at the objective meanings through our always fallible, subjective lenses.

But by the same token, this means we need not follow the "liberal" thinkers who, in order to upgrade the status of women within the Jewish religion and community, minimize or directly reject the divine nature and religious validity of the ancient texts and traditions. For the authentic Orthodox tradition can accommodate the fact that God Himself, through His texts and through ongoing revelation, continues to teach us how to behave, even in new and modern ways—though we can only hope that we get it right, and have the humility to recognize it when we get it wrong.

Related Chapters

53 Frankel, 66 Rosenzweig, 70 Kaplan, 81 Plaskow, 84 Adler

86

Shimon Gershon Rosenberg (Shagar) (1949–2007)

Postmodern Times

The need to reconcile Judaism with modernity has become obsolete

Since the late eighteenth century, Jewish thinkers have been fixated on the problem of reconciling traditional Judaism with "modernity." But they need do so no more, according to Rosenberg, for the problem is now obsolete: reconciling Judaism with modernity has become less compelling because modernity itself has waned. What's necessary, instead, is for traditional Judaism to grapple with *post*-modernity, or postmodernism.

"Modernity" meant several things. It saw change as positive and necessary. It distrusted tradition, and so rewarded the individual with responsibility for himself and his life. With the individual so placed at the center, it stressed personal initiative, the creation of one's own values. Its individualism, skepticism, and pluralism were very much secular values, thus putting it in conflict with traditional Judaism, which stressed tradition, conservatism, and community.

Many great thinkers attempted solutions to this conflict. Hirsch tried to make Jews citizens of both cultures. Kook aspired to sanctify the material world, to find holiness within the secular, to harmonize the two worlds. Leibowitz sharply compartmentalized them, separating the material world of science from the religious world of norms and values. And in arguing that obeying *halacha* draws the divine presence into the world, Soloveitchik offered a compromise between Kook and Leibowitz.

But the very problem to which they are responding is driven by another modern idea: that truth is singular and absolute, so if two systems offer different accounts of the truth they cannot both be correct.

In postmodernism, that idea *itself* is obsolete.

We may distinguish between a "hard" and a "soft" postmodernism. Both start with the realization that there are no epistemic or moral foundations and precepts, no absolute ideals and truths, no "grand narrative" of the cosmos. For hard postmodernism the conclusion is immediately nihilism: everything is random and pointless and meaningless.

But soft postmodernism resists that dark consequence. There may be neither absolute truth nor goodness, but there still is truth and goodness—as human-made, social constructs. While the dangers of relativism are present here, this viewpoint offers many advantages to the religious believer. It can foster a humility and tolerance capable of greatly enriching the religious worldview. It strengthens the value placed on faith insofar as it imbues *all* human constructs with value and validity and sees religion as no less valid an option than others. And indeed it is better for faith than the earlier modernism was, because that period, with its clash of competing truths, amounted to a two-century onslaught against religion and faith.

With postmodernism, the challenge for believers is no longer to defend religion against the claims of science or atheism. It is instead to show how choosing religion, from among the multiple competing worldviews, is a valuable choice for one to make.

So the religious Jew need no longer defend himself or herself against the "Other," the Jew of other denominations, the secular Jew, the non-Jew. For it is now possible for you to live in multiple worlds, including the worlds of science and of faith, without defending one against the other or reconciling the one to the other. It is now possible for you to believe both in the teachings of science and in the things some claim are inconsistent with science: divine providence, the immortality of the soul, the value and efficacy of prayer, and so on.

The challenge is merely to show how immensely valuable it is to be rooted in the community, in tradition, in belonging—and that argument speaks for itself.

Related Chapters

55 Hirsch, 56 Hirsch, 69 Kook, 71 Soloveitchik, 72 Strauss, 79 Leibowitz, 83 Borowitz

87

Samuel Lebens (b. 1983)

Living the Dream

A twenty-first-century solution to the medieval problem of divine unity

New tools can sometimes help with old problems. In this case we may make progress on a medieval problem, according to Lebens, by using ideas from eighteenth-century Hassidism filtered through twenty-first-century philosophy of fiction.

The old problem is that of the mysterious Kabbalistic *sefirot*. Some conceive the ten *sefirot* as different emanations from God; some, as different descriptions of God; some, as different aspects of God; and so on. But these are all problematic in various ways—in particular, the last one, for it seems to posit a multiplicity within the Jewish God whose absolute unity is proclaimed daily.

Skip ahead several centuries now, to the great Hassidic rabbi Schneur Zalman (1745–1813). Zalman grappled with another problem: understanding the Kabbalistic doctrine of *tzimtzum*, or contraction, by means of which God "made room" for other beings to exist beside Himself. Taking a cue from the Bible—"In the heavens above and on the earth below there is nothing else [besides God]" (Deuteronomy 4:39)—Zalman argues that while all created beings, even the physical earth and we ourselves, appear to be real from our perspective, in relation to God they actually are not. It's as if God is dreaming a dream. According to that dream, within that dream, many beings exist in the cosmos. But from outside the dream, from God's waking perspective so to speak, it is all just an illusion. Call this doctrine "Hassidic idealism": all that exists is God and the things He invents or dreams in His mind, that is, the fictions He creates.

Now skip ahead several more centuries. In his novel *Breakfast of Champions* (1973), Kurt Vonnegut Jr. inventively inserts himself as a character into the story. He even has himself interacting with the other characters, going so far as to reveal to one of them that he (the character) is fictional. Philosophical work now explores the idea that certain sentences concerning fictions legitimately count as true, once properly qualified. The case is made, for example, that given the fictional world created by Arthur Conan Doyle, "Sherlock Holmes is a detective" should count as true even if Sherlock Holmes never actually existed. In light of this idea, and of the analogy between a work of fiction and the cosmos as dreamed by God, a case can equally be made that most of the things you believe about the "cosmos"—including that you are made of flesh and blood (for example)— still legitimately count as true, even if qualified by "relative to the fiction."

And the *sefirot*?

Well, if Vonnegut can insert himself as a character into his novel, he can also insert himself as *more* than one character. He could have written himself into his story in two different versions, or even more. Perhaps the different versions of himself could even get into an argument in the novel, for example, about what should happen to the other characters! He could do all this even while remaining, outside the story, the one person he is.

But now the same can be said of God. If God can be a character in the story that is our cosmos, then He can be more than one character. He can appear in two different manners, in two different forms. For example, He could manifest Himself as mercy, but also as justice, to invoke two traditional attributes. Or He could manifest Himself as several characters, as ten characters, even. Each divine aspect, each description, each emanation can ultimately refer back to the same single God who, outside the story, is one.

And that is the story of the *sefirot*.

Related Chapters

22 De Leon, 23 Abulafia, 36 Alemanno, 80 Jonas

Afterword

Jewish Philosophy:
Past, Present, and Future?
By Samuel Lebens

This book opens with Philo. It is a good place to start. Philo can certainly lay a claim to being the first committed Jew, well versed in Western philosophy, to attempt a systematic articulation of his Jewish commitments in the language of that philosophy. And yet, there's a sense in which this book *could* have begun, right at the beginning, with Abraham.

According to the standard Jewish narrative, Abraham was born among idolaters, and came to have faith in monotheism. A famous midrash (*Genesis Rabbah* 38:13) reports that Abraham was left, one day, in charge of his father's idol shop. He took the opportunity to destroy all the idols, leaving only one intact. When his father returned, Abraham protested his innocence, and claimed that the remaining statue was the one that had destroyed the others. His father was unimpressed. Statues can't move! Abraham felt he had proved his point. And thus, the text sets Abraham up, quite literally, as the first iconoclast.

Indeed, whatever the actual facts of his life, Abraham has become a symbol: the founder of monotheism. Perhaps this renders him a philosopher. Maimonides certainly thought so. He paints the following picture:

Abraham was forty years old when he recognized his Creator. When he recognized and knew, he began to reply to [the questions of] the inhabitants of Ur Kasdim and engage in discussion with them, telling them that the path they were following was not the path of truth. . . . When the people would gather around him and ask him about his words, he would explain [his ideas] to each one of them according to their understanding, until he had turned them to the path of truth. Ultimately, tens of thousands gathered around him. These are the "men of the house of Abraham" [alluded to in scripture]. He planted in their hearts this great fundamental principle, composed texts about it, and taught it to Isaac, his son. (*Mishne Torah, Hilkhot Avodat Kochavim* 1:3)

Abraham here is not merely an iconoclast. He also debates. He teaches. He writes books. He sounds like a philosopher.

Abraham's "fundamental principle" wasn't an intellectual sideshow. The great philosopher and historiographer R. G. Collingwood (1889–1943) argues—convincingly—that monotheism was a pivotal step forward for human inquiry (*An Essay on Metaphysics* [Oxford: Clarendon Press, 2002]). Collingwood distinguishes been polymorphic and monomorphic sciences. A polymorphic science posits discrete sets of scientific laws to govern over discrete phenomena. For example, a polymorphic science might think that the laws of water and the laws of fire are completely unrelated. To be an expert in one set of laws would offer us no insights into the other. Monomorphic science, by contrast, suggests that all of the local laws of nature—the laws that govern water on earth, say, and the laws that govern fire on earth—are merely local variations of a single set of general rules that apply in all places and times, throughout the entire universe. The aspiration to find that grand "theory of everything" still plays a role in motivating theoretical physicists today.

Collingwood argues that monotheism was a key step in the rise of monomorphic science. When polytheism captured the human imagination, the idea that water had its own god, and that fire had a *different* god, made the search for unifying principles seem futile. But once we came to believe that all of the distinct phenomena of the cosmos are governed by one single God, scientific inquiry could move forward. Ever since, scientists have been bringing diverse phenomena together under overarching theoretical explanations. The theories that explain the motion of billiard balls on earth can also explain the birth of stars in distant galaxies.

One shouldn't exaggerate the point. Clearly, plenty of scientists are not theists. And religious authorities have an ignoble history of sometimes stifling free inquiry and the progress of the sciences. Notwithstanding these facts, Abraham's monotheism did, likely, play a key role in creating the scientific method to begin with.

If Abraham were alive today, what would he think of the state of contemporary Jewish philosophy? What would Saadia Ben Joseph Gaon think? Or, the fathers of Hassidism?

Such questions may be perilous. There is no way of truly *knowing* what they might think were they to (say) return to life. Moreover, intellectual schools that survive for generations are allowed to shift their views. Plato wouldn't recognize or agree with much of what philosophers would today call Platonism. That doesn't stop it from being Platonism. The Talmud itself imagines Moses not recognizing the teachings attributed to him by Rabbi Akiva (Talmud Tractate *Menachot* 29b). The Talmud doesn't mean to say that Rabbi Akiva wasn't teaching the Torah of Moses. Intellectual schools evolve. As Professor Tamar Ross would put it, Torah is an *expanding palace*.

And yet, despite these reservations, I ask these questions about Abraham and the others because I think that there were (at least) two constant threads that linked every stage of Jewish thought—threads that are essential to the identity of Jewish thought—and in light of some contemporary trends I worry about their future.

The first thread, I could call "encounter." Rabbi Eliezer Berkovits made the notion of *encounter* a central part of his philosophy, founded on the notion that the Jewish people *encountered* God at Sinai. The revelation wasn't merely the communication of text, laws, or scripture. The revelation was a human-divine encounter in which we became aware that God cares for us. Martin Buber made the encounter of an *I* and a *Thou* central to *his* philosophy, and Emmanuel Levinas gave a foundational place to the notion of a face-to-face encounter. According to all of these thinkers, Judaism is supposed to be living and animated rather than formulaic and dry. But more often than not, in today's intellectual climate, Jewish thought is taught, in Jewish studies departments, not as a living phenomenon but as *history*. Intellectual history is important and valuable, but it is no substitute for philosophy.

One of my teachers talks about museum-exhibit philosophy. It occurs when you wheel a lifeless statue of a philosopher into the view of your students, so that you can discuss what motivated this thinker, what led him to think his thoughts, and what influence he had on others, before wheeling him out again. Museum-exhibit philosophy isn't philosophy at all. It's intellectual history (which has its place), but it isn't an *encounter*.

Rabbi Joseph Soloveitchik writes,

> When I sit down to learn Torah, I find myself immediately in the company of the sages of the [tradition]. The relations between us are personal. The Rambam [Maimonides] is at my right, Rabbenu Tam is at my left, Rashi sits up front and interprets, Rabbenu Tam disputes him; the Rambam issues a ruling, and the Rabad objects. They are all in my little room, sitting around my table. They look at me affectionately, enjoying arguing and studying the Talmud with me, encourage and support me the way a father does. Torah study is not merely a formal, technical matter embodied in the discovery and exchange of facts. It is a powerful experience of being friends with many generations of Torah scholars, the joining of one spirit with another, the union of souls . . . . When I solve a problem in the Rambam's and Rabbenu Tam's writings, I see their glowing faces . . . . I always feel as if the Rambam and Rabbenu Tam are kissing me on the forehead and shaking my hand. (Joseph Soloveitchik, *And From There You Shall Seek* [New York: Ktav Publishing House, 2008], 145)

He describes an *encounter*. *The Jewish God Question* hasn't been a trip through a museum. It's been about engaging with arguments, and *encountering* their proponents. I worry that Jewish thought, as an academic discipline, is too rarely about this sort of an *encounter*. It takes human thinkers from Jewish history, and turns them into lifeless museum statues; the very thing that Abraham set out to break with his hammer.

In rabbinical seminaries, the notion of encounter is alive, but much more emphasis is put on learning the Talmud than on learning Jewish philosophy per se. Talmudic study tends to emphasize the legal side of the Jewish intellectual tradition. We are not raising a generation of philosopher-theologians, neither in the universities nor in the seminaries. Abraham would be dismayed by the proliferation of statues.

The second constant thread of the Jewish tradition, which I fear for, is the belief in *objective* and *ultimate* truth. It's true that rabbinic legalism allows for a surprising degree of pluralism, but pluralism about *legal* facts is one thing: pluralism about *brute* facts is another. When it comes to the brute fact of God's existence and of His commanding us, Jewish thought has not traditionally made room for much dissent. Biblical critics and scholars of the ancient Near East may complicate the story, but I will say this: rabbinic Judaism (whether it's historically accurate or not) doesn't recognize anything other than monotheism from Abraham onward.

Monotheism played a central role in undergirding the rise of mono-morphic sciences, with its bold claim that there *are* fundamental truths; that all of the disparate perspectives, experiences, and phenomena of this world bottom out into one fundamental purpose, governed by one funda-mental law, and animated by one fundamental will. But today, the notion of absolute truth is under attack.

We see this on both sides of the political spectrum. The populist right has developed an antipathy toward experts, science, and data, which they associate with the liberal elites, from whom they feel alienated. And the far left has been so concerned to promote safe spaces for the persecuted that freedom of speech is regularly brought under attack, in a phenomenon that has been described as the "closing of the American mind." If ever there was a message that unites all of the great movements of Jewish philosophy, however, it was that there *are* (at least some) non-negotiable rights and wrongs, that there *are* facts and true grand narra-tives, and that with patient study and discipline, these could help us to explain the world around us.

Immersed in a "post-truth" climate, even Jewish thinkers have be-gun to experiment with intellectual traditions that question the notion of objective truth: postmodernism, poststructuralism, postcolonialism, and others. They do this, often, for the best of reasons. They worry that there is no way to reconcile the teachings of Judaism with the knowledge that we have today: How can we reconcile the Jewish tradition with the respect that we now recognize is due to *other* religious outlooks, and to people of different communities? How can we reconcile the Jewish tradi-tion with our newfound perspective on gender and sexuality? How can we salvage traditional Jewish life without giving up on personal autonomy? And how can we make sense of continued Jewish commitment in the face of empirical evidence (from the natural sciences, to biblical studies and archaeology) that seem to undermine it? These questions are serious and pressing. Postmodernism can seem like an attractive option. There are *no* hard and fast truths. Each person can have her own truth. Conflict here is an illusion generated by taking the notion of objective truth too seriously.

And yet, however well motivated this turn may have been, I find it deeply troubling. In a recent essay describing the work of Rabbi Shagar (Shimon Gershon Rosenberg), who borrowed heavily from postmodernist thinkers, one scholar wrote: "'Logical' or 'rational' modes of dialogue hold no superior qualities to other interpretative motifs but rather are pretentious 'meta-narratives' only applicable to some people and in particular contexts." But if logical modes of dialogue hold no superior qualities to other motifs, how am I even supposed to scrutinize the rationality of the claim that "'logical' or 'rational' modes of dialogue hold no superior quali-ties"? Am I supposed to scrutinize it *illogically*? I worry that I am sound-ing pretentious now, but *really*, can it be pretentious to want to scrutinize thoughts in accord with logic and reason? And if we don't, then doesn't anything go? Aren't all bets off?

What is more: postmodernism will only ever, in truth, appeal to a vanishing elitist minority. Despite the popular disregard for the so-called "fake news," and for experts, and the liberal elite, very few people are truly able to disregard the notion of *truth*. Postmodernism doesn't fly in sci-ence departments, or in the workplace—in places where facts still matter. A Conservative rabbi recently wrote that religious affiliation is like brand loyalty. "There are many ways to God," his position amounts to assert-ing. "You just happen to like this one because you grew up with it!" (See Nathan Guttman, "Have We Got a Girl for You!" [*Haaretz*, October 1, 2004]). In truth, I doubt that this is a message that will engender long-term commitment from his congregants and the generation of children that they will raise in a market of many competing brands. Abraham's strident defense of objective truth is beginning to wither.

What does the future of Jewish philosophy hold if it loses the central notions of *encounter* and *objective truth*? Can these strands be saved?

One of the last vanguards in the humanities against the postmodern attack on truth has been in the philosophy departments where (especially in English-speaking countries) the last century has seen the rise of a new school of philosophy: *analytic philosophy*.

What is analytic philosophy? In its first flush of youth, in the days of G. E. Moore (1873–1958) and Bertrand Russell (1872–1970), analytic philosophy could be characterized in terms of certain specific doctrines. But over time what has emerged, far more essentially, and what really unites analytic philosophers into a single tradition, is (as Professor Michael

Rea has pointed out) a style of philosophizing and a shared intellectual history. That characteristic style includes the following features: writing that expresses philosophical positions in sentences that can be formalized and logically manipulated; writing that prioritizes precision, clarity, and logical coherence; writing that avoids non-decorative use of metaphor and other rhetorical flourishes; and working with well-understood, primitive concepts and defining very clearly new terms and concepts. If there's no single shared doctrine, one can still sense the values underlying this tradition: logic, reason, and clarity, the very values that postmodernism derides as a "pretentious meta-narrative."

When an analytical philosopher looks to the philosophers of the past, she doesn't engage merely in intellectual history—though she has to do some of that in order to understand their words. Primarily, she is interested in *engaging* with the philosophers of the past. Can she improve upon their arguments? Can she find new ways of articulating their insights? Can she find new counter-arguments? Can she defend them against later critics? She engages in a live *encounter* with the past. And she does so with an appreciation of the value of *truth*. *The Jewish God Question* has attempted to do just this, by presenting its thinkers as speaking directly to you, as if contemporaneous, aiming to engage you in a conversation.

I contend that if this generation is to produce any Jewish philosopher-theologians to carry the tradition forward, it will have to happen in the world of academic philosophy. But the challenges are gargantuan. Jewish philosophy, whatever its ideological coloring (be it Spinozistic, Reform, Conservative, Orthodox, Zionist, or anti-Zionist), can only truly be considered *Jewish* to the extent that it engages with the evolving canon of Jewish literature, and brings the discussion forward. The requisite degree of Jewish literacy is hard to come by. But in order to be truly rigorous and to be comfortable with the philosophical vernacular of this age (just as Philo and Maimonides worked in the philosophical vernacular of their age), practitioners will also have to be well trained in the rigors of analytic philosophy.

I can count on one hand (two at a stretch) the number of well-trained academic philosophers with a serious degree of Jewish literacy. Most are struggling to find secure work in academia, and some have already left to pursue other careers because they can't support their families as academic philosophers—especially if they dedicate too much time to the subfield of constructive Jewish philosophy.

Jewish culture and identity have shown tremendous tenacity over the millennia. I have no doubt that a new generation of Jewish philosopher-theologians will emerge: philosophers who commit themselves to an honest encounter with the Jewish philosophers of old (and with God); who commit themselves equally to the values of intellectual honesty, objectivity, logic, and reason; who speak the intellectual language of their age, just as Abraham communicated in the vernacular of the residents of Ur Kasdim. But for this to happen, the Jewish community must take it upon itself to support the endeavor. The Jewish community has generously supported departments of Jewish studies (where intellectual history takes place), and it has supported rabbinical seminaries (where legal scholarship takes place, and religious leaders are trained). But now Jewish philosophy, our ancient tradition, is in need of similar support—to continue the legacy of Abraham.

Glossary of Hebrew Terms

aggadah: nonlegal portions of the Talmud, often consisting of stories and legends of the great rabbinic sages

aliyah: "ascent"; used as a general term for immigrating from exile to the Land of Israel

B'rit Ahuvim: "Covenant for Lovers," Rachel Adler's revised version of a traditional religious marriage contract

divrei Torah: "words of Torah"; more generally, interpretation of or commentary on Torah, Talmud, and so on

halacha, halachot (plural): Jewish Law (or individual laws)

Hashem: "the Name"; used instead of the four-letter name of God

Kabbalah: the tradition of Jewish mysticism

Karaism: a Jewish sect, tracing as far back as the second century BCE, that recognizes the Hebrew Bible alone as a source of *halacha* and rejects the rabbinic, oral tradition (as reflected in the Talmud)

ketubah: traditional, religious marriage contract

kinyan: an act of acquisition in *halacha*, rules for which also inform the *ketubah*

matzah: the unleavened bread eaten by Jews over Passover, in commemoration of the exodus from Egypt

midrash: commentary on scripture

minyan: a quorum for prayer

Mishna: collection of oral laws finally transcribed into writing in the second century CE

mitzvah, mitzvot (plural): divine commandment(s)

mussar: "reproach" or "reproof"; used more generally for the practice of moral instruction and improvement

Noachide Laws: a set of seven laws that, according to the Talmud, were given by God after the famous flood and held to be binding on all human beings

Omer: a unit of measure in ancient Temple times; "counting the Omer" is a ritual performed between the festivals of Passover and Shavuot

Pirke Avot: "Chapters of the Fathers"; a famous collection of aphorisms from the Mishna

sefirot: "revelations" or "emanations" or aspects of God according to Kabbalah

Shechina: "dwelling"; used to refer to the divine presence of God, often conceived to have a feminine aspect

Shulchan Aruch: "The Set Table"; title of a compilation of *halacha* by Rabbi Joseph Karo in 1563

shuva: "return," as in the return of the Jewish people from exile to the Land of Israel

Talmud: vast compilation of the Mishna plus commentary from the oral tradition, committed to writing by the end of the sixth century CE

teshuva: "repentance"

tikkun olam: "repairing the world"

Tisha B'Av: the ninth day of the month of Av in the Hebrew calendar, traditionally a day of mourning (commemorating the destruction of both Temples and other Jewish tragedies)

tzimtzum: "contraction"; a Kabbalistic notion explaining how God "made space" in order to create the cosmos

yeshiva: institution of religious Jewish learning

Zohar: "Splendor"; the title of the foundational text for Kabbalah

Sources

Abbreviations

AK = Adam Kirsch. *The People and the Books: 18 Classics of Jewish Literature.* New York: W. W. Norton, 2016.

AL = Alan T. Levenson. *An Introduction to Modern Jewish Thinkers: From Spinoza to Soloveitchik.* 2nd ed. Lanham, MD: Rowman & Littlefield, 2006.

C-S 1996 = Dan Cohn-Sherbok. *Medieval Jewish Philosophy.* Surrey, UK: Curzon, 1996.

C-S 2007 = Dan Cohn-Sherbok. *Fifty Key Jewish Thinkers.* 2nd ed., 1997. Reprint, New York: Routledge, 2007.

FL 1997 = Daniel Frank and Oliver Leaman, eds. *Routledge History of Jewish Philosophy.* London: Routledge, 1997.

FL 2003 = Daniel Frank and Oliver Leaman, eds. *The Cambridge Companion to Medieval Jewish Philosophy.* Cambridge: Cambridge University Press, 2003.

FLM = Daniel Frank, Oliver Leaman, and Charles Manekin, eds. *The Jewish Philosophy Reader.* London: Routledge, 2000.

IH = Isaac Husik. *A History of Medieval Jewish Philosophy.* New York: Macmillan, 1918.

LAH = Hans Lewy, Alexander Altmann, and Isaak Heinemann, eds. *Three Jewish Philosophers: Philo, Saadya Gaon, Yehudah Halevi.* 3rd ed. New Milford, CT: Toby Press, 2006.

LB = Leora Batnitzky. *How Judaism Became a Religion: An Introduction to Modern Jewish Thought.* Princeton, NJ: Princeton University Press, 2011.

MFR = Paul Mendes-Flohr and Jehuda Reinharz, eds. *The Jew in the Modern World: A Documentary History*. 3rd ed., 1980. Reprint, Oxford: Oxford University Press, 2011.

MG = Michael L. Morgan and Peter Eli Gordon. *The Cambridge Companion to Modern Jewish Philosophy*. Cambridge: Cambridge University Press, 2007.

Chapter 1: Philo

Primary

FLM: "On the Creation of the World," 11–23

LAH: "Philo: Selections"

Yonge: *The Works of Philo: New Updated Edition*: "On the Creation," 1–12, 53–71; "The Special Laws, I," 32–52; "On the Life of Moses, I," 210–12

Philo online: http://www.earlyjewishwritings.com/philo.html

Secondary

AK: Chapter 3, "Reading against the Grain"

C-S 2007: "Philo"

LAH: "Introduction to Philo"

Chapter 2: Philo

Primary

FLM: "On the Creation of the World," 11–23

LAH: "Philo: Selections"

Yonge: *The Works of Philo: New Updated Edition*: "Allegorical Interpretation, I," 1–76; "On the Creation," 134–35; "On the Migration of Abraham," 2, 47; "The Decalogue," 33–35; "The Special Laws, II," 163–67

Philo online: http://www.earlyjewishwritings.com/philo.html

Secondary

AK: Chapter 3, "Reading against the Grain"

C-S 2007: "Philo"

LAH: "Introduction to Philo"

Chapter 3: Saadia Ben Joseph Gaon

Primary

Hyman and Walsh: *Philosophy in the Middle Ages*: Saadia: *Book of Doctrines and Beliefs*

LAH: "Saadya Gaon: *Book of Doctrines and Beliefs*"

Secondary
C-S 2007: "Saadiah Ben Joseph Gaon"
LAH: "Introduction to Saadya"

Chapter 4: Saadia Ben Joseph Gaon

Primary
Hyman and Walsh: *Philosophy in the Middle Ages*: Saadia: *Book of Doctrines and Beliefs*
LAH: "Saadya Gaon: *Book of Doctrines and Beliefs*"

Secondary
C-S 2007: "Saadiah Ben Joseph Gaon"
LAH: "Introduction to Saadya"

Chapter 5: Isaac Israeli

Primary
FLM: "The Book of Definitions," "The Mantua Text," and "The Book on Spirit and Soul"

Secondary
FL 1997: Tamar Rudavsky, "Medieval Jewish Neoplatonism," 151–56
IH: Chapter 1, "Isaac Israeli"
Levin and Walker: "Isaac Israeli"

Chapter 6: Solomon Ibn Gabirol

Primary
FLM: "The Fountain of Life"
Manekin: *Medieval Jewish Philosophical Writings*: "The Fountain of Life"

Secondary
C-S 2007: "Solomon Ibn Gabirol"
FL 1997: Tamar Rudavsky, "Medieval Jewish Neoplatonism," 156–59
IH: Chapter 5, "Solomon Ibn Gabirol"
S. Pessin: "Solomon Ibn Gabirol"

Chapter 7: Bachya Ibn Paquda

Primary
FLM: *The Book of Direction to the Duties of the Heart*
Mansoor: *The Book of Direction to the Duties of the Heart*

Secondary
C-S 2007: "Bahya Ibn Pakuda"
FL 1997: Tamar Rudavsky, "Medieval Jewish Neoplatonism," 159–62
IH: Chapter 6, "Bahya Ibn Pakuda"

Chapter 8: Abraham Bar Chiyya

Primary
Wigoder: *Meditation of the Sad Soul*

Secondary
FL 1997: Tamar Rudavsky, "Medieval Jewish Neoplatonism," 164–67
IH: Chapter 8, "Abraham bar Hiyya"

Chapter 9: Joseph Ibn Tzaddik

Primary
Horovitz: *Joseph Ibn Saddiq: The Microcosm*

Secondary
FL 1997: Tamar Rudavsky, "Medieval Jewish Neoplatonism," 167–71
IH: Chapter 9, "Joseph Ibn Zaddik"

Chapter 10: Judah Halevi

Primary
FLM: *The Kuzari*
Halevi: *The Kuzari: An Argument for the Faith of Israel*
LAH: *Kuzari* and "Songs"

Secondary
AK: Chapter 6, "The Scandal of Chosenness"
C-S 2007: "Judah Halevi"

FL 2003: Barry Kogan, "Judah Halevi and His Use of Philosophy in the *Kuzari*"
IH: Chapter 10, "Judah Halevi"

Chapter 11: Judah Halevi

Primary
FLM: *The Kuzari*
Halevi: *The Kuzari: An Argument for the Faith of Israel*
LAH: *Kuzari* and "Songs"

Secondary
AK: Chapter 6, "The Scandal of Chosenness"
C-S 2007: "Judah Halevi"
FL 2003: Barry Kogan, "Judah Halevi and His Use of Philosophy in the *Kuzari*"
IH: Chapter 10, "Judah Halevi"

Chapter 12: Judah Halevi

Primary
FLM: *The Kuzari*
Halevi: *The Kuzari: An Argument for the Faith of Israel*
LAH: *Kuzari* and "Songs"

Secondary
AK: Chapter 6, "The Scandal of Chosenness"
C-S 2007: "Judah Halevi"
FL 2003: Barry Kogan, "Judah Halevi and His Use of Philosophy in the *Kuzari*"
IH: Chapter 10, "Judah Halevi"

Chapter 13: Abraham Ibn Ezra

Primary
FLM: *Long Commentary on Exodus*

Secondary
FL 1997: Tamar Rudavsky, "Medieval Jewish Neoplatonism," 171–73
IH: Chapter 11, "Moses and Abraham Ibn Ezra"

Nadler and Rudavsky 2009: Gad Freudenthal, "Cosmology: The Heavenly Bodies," 333–38

Chapter 14: Abraham Ibn Daud (Rabad)

Primary
Weiss: *The Exalted Faith*

Secondary
C-S 2007: "Abraham Ibn Daud"
Encyclopedia Judaica, s.v. "Abraham Ben David Halevi Ibn Daud," http://www
.jewishvirtuallibrary.org/ibn-daud-abraham-ben-david-halevi (accessed December 5, 2017)
Fontaine: "Abraham Ibn Daud"
IH: Chapter 12, "Abraham Ibn Daud"

Chapter 15: Abraham Ibn Daud (Rabad)

Primary
Weiss: *The Exalted Faith*

Secondary
C-S 2007: "Abraham Ibn Daud"
Encyclopedia Judaica, s.v. "Abraham Ben David Halevi Ibn Daud," http://www
.jewishvirtuallibrary.org/ibn-daud-abraham-ben-david-halevi (accessed December 5, 2017)
Fontaine: "Abraham Ibn Daud"
IH: Chapter 12, "Abraham Ibn Daud"

Chapter 16: Maimonides

Primary
Maimonides: *The Guide for the Perplexed*, esp. Part I, Chapters 31–36

Secondary
C-S 2007: "Maimonides"
FL 1997: Howard Kreisel, "Moses Maimonides"
Goodman: *Maimonides and the Book That Changed Judaism*
IH: Chapter 13, "Moses Maimonides"

Chapter 17: Maimonides

Primary
Maimonides: *The Guide for the Perplexed*, esp. Part I

Secondary
C-S 2007: "Maimonides"
FL 1997: Howard Kreisel, "Moses Maimonides"
Goodman: *Maimonides and the Book That Changed Judaism*
IH: Chapter 13, "Moses Maimonides"

Chapter 18: Maimonides

Primary
Maimonides: *The Guide for the Perplexed*, esp. Part III, Chapters 10–12

Secondary
C-S 2007: "Maimonides"
FL 1997: Howard Kreisel, "Moses Maimonides"
Goodman: *Maimonides and the Book That Changed Judaism*
IH: Chapter 13, "Moses Maimonides"

Chapter 19: Moses Ben Nachman (Nachmanides, Ramban)

Primary
Nachmanides: *Writings of the Ramban/Nachmanides*
Nachmanides: "Addenda to Maimonides's *Sefer Hamitzvot*"

Secondary
Newman, "The Centrality of Eretz Yisrael in Nachmanides"

Chapter 20: Moses Ben Nachman (Nachmanides, Ramban)

Primary
Nachmanides: *Writings of the Ramban/Nachmanides*: vol. 2, "The Disputation of Barcelona"

SOURCES

Secondary
Jewish Virtual Library: "Encyclopedia Judaica: Disputation of Barcelona"
Roth: "The Disputation of Barcelona (1263)"

Chapter 21: Hillel Ben Samuel

Primary
Ben Samuel: "The Rewards of the Soul" (*Sefer Tagmulei ha-Nefesh*) S. Halber-
stamm, 1874

Secondary
IH: Chapter 14, "Hillel Ben Samuel"
Jewish Virtual Library, "Hillel Ben Samuel"

Chapter 22: Moses De Leon

Primary
Berg: *The Essential Zohar*
Scholem: *Zohar: The Book of Splendor: Basic Readings from the Kabbalah*

Secondary
AK: Chapter 8, "The Secret Life of God"
Berg: *The Essential Zohar*
FL 2003: Hava Tirosh-Samuelson, "Philosophy and Kabbalah: 1200–1600"

Chapter 23: Abraham Abulafia

Primary
Abulafia: *Ohr Ha-Sechel: Light of the Intellect*
Solomon: *Abraham Abulafia: Meditations on the Divine Name*

Secondary
Idel: *The Mystical Experience in Abraham Abulafia*

Chapter 24: Isaac Albalag

Primary
FLM: *The Emendation of the "Opinions"*
Manekin: "Isaac Albalag: From *The Emendation of the 'Opinions'*"

Secondary

C-S 1996: "Isaac Albalag," 108–12

FLM: "Jewish Aristotelianism in Spain and Provence," 245

Guttmann: *Philosophies of Judaism: A History of Jewish Philosophy from Biblical Times to Franz Rosenzweig*, 227–32

Chapter 25: Abner of Burgos

Primary

Hecht: "The Polemical Exchange between Isaac Pollegar and Abner of Burgos/ Alfonso of Valladolid"

Secondary

C-S 1996: "Abner of Burgos," 134–37

FL 1997: Charles Manekin, "Hebrew Philosophy in the Fourteenth and Fifteenth Centuries," 366–69

FL 2003: T. M. Rudavsky, "The Impact of Scholasticism upon Jewish Philosophy in the Fourteenth and Fifteenth Centuries," 350–55

Chapter 26: Isaac Pollegar

Primary

Pollegar: *Sepher Ezer Ha-Dat: The Support of the Faith*

Secondary

C-S 1996: "Isaac Pollegar," 141–45

FL 1996: Charles Manekin, "Hebrew Philosophy in the Fourteenth and Fifteenth Centuries," 366–69

FL 2003: T. M. Rudavsky, "The Impact of Scholasticism upon Jewish Philosophy in the Fourteenth and Fifteenth Centuries," 350–55

Chapter 27: Joseph Ibn Kaspi

Primary

FLM: "A Refining Pot for Silver"

Neusner and Avery-Peck: "On Education and Philosophy"

Secondary

C-S 1996: "Joseph Caspi," 145–47

FL 1997: Idit Dobbs-Weinstein, "The Maimonidean Controversy," 343–45

FLM: "Jewish Aristotelianism in Spain and Provence: Introduction," 245–46

Chapter 28: Levi Ben Gerson (Gersonides)

Primary
Gersonides: *The Wars of the Lord*, vol. 2
FLM: "The Wars of the Lord"
Manekin: "Levi Gersonides: From *The Wars of the Lord*"

Secondary
C-S 2007: "Gersonides"
Gersonides: *The Wars of the Lord*, vol. 2: Feldman, "Synopses"
Feldman: *Gersonides: Judaism within the Limits of Reason*
IH: Chapter 15, "Levi Ben Gerson"

Chapter 29: Levi Ben Gerson (Gersonides)

Primary
Gersonides: *The Wars of the Lord*, vol. 2: Feldman, "Synopses"
FLM: "The Wars of the Lord"
Manekin: "Levi Gersonides: From *The Wars of the Lord*"

Secondary
C-S 2007: "Gersonides"
Gersonides: *The Wars of the Lord*, vol. 2: Feldman, "Synopses"
Feldman: *Gersonides: Judaism within the Limits of Reason*
IH: Chapter 15, "Levi Ben Gerson"

Chapter 30: Aaron Ben Elijah of Nicomedia

Secondary
IH: Chapter 16, "Aaron Ben Elijah of Nicomedia"
Kohler: "Aaron Ben Elijah, the Younger, of Nicomedia"

Chapter 31: Moses Ben Joshua of Narbonne (Narboni)

Primary
FLM: "The Treatise on Choice"
Manekin: "Moses of Narbonne (Narboni): *The Treatise on Choice*"

Secondary
C-S 1996: "Moses Ben Joshua Narboni," 149–51
FL 1997: Charles Manekin, "Hebrew Philosophy in the Fourteenth and Fifteenth Centuries: An Overview," 367–72
FL 2003: Hava Tirosh-Samuelson, "Philosophy and Kabbalah: 1200–1600," 238–39
FLM: "Introduction," 244–47

Chapter 32: Chasdai Ben Judah Crescas

Primary
Manekin: "Hasdai Cresdas: from *The Light of the Lord*"
FLM: "The Light of the Lord"

Secondary
C-S 2007: "Hasdai Crescas"
FL 1997: Daniel J. Lasker, "Chasdai Crescas"
IH: Chapter 17, "Hasdai Ben Abraham Crescas"

Chapter 33: Chasdai Ben Judah Crescas

Primary
Manekin: "Hasdai Cresdas: from *The Light of the Lord*"
FLM: "The Light of the Lord"

Secondary
C-S 2007: "Hasdai Crescas"
FL 1997: Daniel J. Lasker, "Chasdai Crescas"
IH: Chapter 17, "Hasdai Ben Abraham Crescas"

Chapter 34: Chasdai Ben Judah Crescas

Primary
Manekin: "Hasdai Cresdas: from *The Light of the Lord*"
FLM: "The Light of the Lord"

Secondary
C-S 2007: "Hasdai Crescas"
FL 1997: Daniel J. Lasker, "Chasdai Crescas"
IH: Chapter 17, "Hasdai Ben Abraham Crescas"

Chapter 35: Joseph Albo

Primary
Manekin: *The Book of Principles*

Secondary
C-S 2007: "Joseph Albo"
IH: Chapter 18, "Joseph Albo"
Manekin: "Introduction," 29–31

Chapter 36: Yochanan Alemanno

Secondary
FL 1997: Hava Tirosh-Rothschild, "Jewish Philosophy on the Eve of Modernity," 526–27
FL 2003: Hava Tirosh-Samuelson, "Philosophy and Kabbalah: 1200–1600," 240–45

Chapter 37: Abraham Bivach (Bibago)

Primary
FLM: "The Way of Faith"

Secondary
C-S 1996: "Abraham Ben Shem Tov Bibago," 172–75
FL 1997: Charles Manekin, "Hebrew Philosophy in the Fourteenth and Fifteenth Centuries: An Overview," 353–58

Chapter 38: Isaac Abravanel

Primary
FLM: "Commentary on Joshua," "The Works of God," "Principles of Faith"

Secondary

C-S 2007: "Isaac Abrabanel"

FL 1997: Hava Tirosh-Rothschild, "Jewish Philosophy on the Eve of Modernity," 508–11

FL 2003: Seymour Feldman, "The End and Aftereffects of Medieval Jewish Philosophy," 420–24

Chapter 39: Elijah Del Medigo

Primary

FLM: "The Examination of the True Religion"

Secondary

C-S 1996: "Elijah Ben Moses Abba Delmedigo," 180–82

FL 2003: Seymour Feldman, "The End and Aftereffects of Medieval Jewish Philosophy," 416–20

Ross: "Elijah Delmedigo"

Chapter 40: Leone Ebreo (Judah Abravanel)

Primary

FLM: "Dialogues on Love"

Secondary

C-S 1996: "Judah Ben Isaac Abrabanel," 182–83

FL 1997: Hava Tirosh-Rothschild, "Jewish Philosophy on the Eve of Modernity," 522–25

Chapter 41: Moses Ben Baruch Almosnino

Primary

Borovaya: "The Chronicles of Ottoman Kings"

Secondary

Borovaya: *The Beginnings of Ladino Literature: Moses Almosnino and His Readers*

FL 1997: Hava Tirosh-Rothschild, "Jewish Philosophy on the Eve of Modernity," 531–45

Chapter 42: Obadiah Sforno

Primary
FLM: "Light of the Peoples"
Sforno: *Commentary on the Torah*

Secondary
FL 1997: Hava Tirosh-Rothschild, "Jewish Philosophy on the Eve of Modernity," 518
FLM: "Introduction," 283–84

Chapter 43: Baruch Spinoza

Primary
Spinoza: *Ethics*
Spinoza: *Short Treatise on God, Man, and His Well-Being*

Secondary
FL 1997: Seymour Feldman, "Spinoza"
Nadler: "Baruch Spinoza"

Chapter 44: Baruch Spinoza

Primary
FLM: "Theological-Political Treatise"
Yaffe: *Spinoza's Theologico-Political Treatise*

Secondary
FL 1997: Seymour Feldman, "Spinoza"
FL 1997: Ze'ev Levy, "Jewish Nationalism"
Nadler: "Baruch Spinoza"

Chapter 45: Moses Mendelssohn

Primary
FLM: "Jerusalem"
MFR: "The Right to Be Different," "On the Need for a German Translation of Scripture," "On the Curtailment of Jewish Juridical Autonomy," "Judaism Is the Cornerstone of Christianity," "Judaism as Revealed Legislation"

Secondary
AL: "Moses Mendelssohn's Defense of Judaism: Between Reason and Revelation"
C-S 2007: "Moses Mendelssohn"
FL 1997: Michael L. Morgan, "Mendelssohn"

Chapter 46: Solomon Maimon

Primary
Maimon: *An Autobiography*
MFR: "The New Hasidim," "My Emergence from Talmudic Darkness"

Secondary
LB: "Maimon: Looking for Enlightenment in an Unenlightened World," 116–21
C-S 2007: "Solomon Maimon"
MG: Paul W. Franks, "Jewish Philosophy after Kant: The Legacy of Salomon Maimon"

Chapter 47: Saul Ascher

Primary
FLM: "Leviathan"
MFR: "Leviathan"

Secondary
Meyer: *Response to Modernity: A History of the Reform Movement*: 21–23, 51–52
Hiscott: "Haskalah Protagonists: Saul Ascher—Biography"

Chapter 48: Leopold Zunz

Primary
MFR: "On Rabbinic Literature," "Scholarship and Emancipation," "Features of the Jews to Be Corrected"

Secondary
FL 1997: David N. Myers, "The Ideology of *Wissenschaft des Judentums*"
Singer and Hirsch: "Leopold Zunz"

Chapter 49: Solomon Steinheim

Primary
FLM: "On the Perennial and the Ephemeral in Judaism"

Secondary
FLM: "History and Tradition in Nineteenth-Century Jewish Thought," 368–69
Meyer: *Response to Modernity: A History of the Reform Movement*: "New Conceptions of Judaism," 67–74

Chapter 50: Abraham Geiger

Primary
FLM: "Letter to J. Derenbourg," "Judaism and Its History"
Geiger: *Judaism and Its History*
MFR: "Jewish Scholarship and Religious Reform"

Secondary
AL: "Abraham Geiger's Defense of Judaism: Continuity and Change"
C-S 2007: "Abraham Geiger"
LB: "Abraham Geiger and the Reform Movement," 36–40

Chapter 51: Samuel Holdheim

Primary
FLM: "The Ceremonial Law in the Messianic Era," "This Is Our Task"

Secondary
Ellenson: *After Emancipation: Jewish Religious Responses to Modernity*: "Samuel Holdheim and Zacharias Frankel on the Legal Character of Jewish Marriage," 139–53
FL 1997: David Ellenson, "Traditional Reactions to the Modern Jewish Reform: The Paradigm of German Orthodoxy," 742–43
Meyer: *Response to Modernity: A History of the Reform Movement*: "The Poles of Modernization: Samson Raphael Hirsch and Samuel Holdheim," 77–84

Chapter 52: Moses Sofer (Hatam Sofer)

Primary
LB: "Conclusion," 183–86
MFR: "A Reply concerning the Question of Reform," "Last Will and Testament"

Secondary
Orthodox Union Staff: "Rabbi Moshe Sofer"
Shapiro: *Changing the Immutable: How Orthodox Judaism Rewrites Its History*

Chapter 53: Zacharias Frankel

Primary
FLM: "The Symptoms of the Time"
MFR: "Hebrew as the Language of Jewish Prayer," "On Changes in Judaism"

Secondary
Ellenson: *After Emancipation: Jewish Religious Responses to Modernity*: "Samuel
  Holdheim and Zacharias Frankel on the Legal Character of Jewish Marriage,"
  139–53
Gottlieb: "Orthodox Judaism and the Impossibility of Biblical Criticism"
LB: "History and Politics: The Positive-Historical School and Its Aftermath,"
  43–48
Meyer: *Response to Modernity: A History of the Reform Movement*: "A Historical
  Judaism: Zacharias Frankel and Abraham Geiger," 84–89

Chapter 54: Nachman Krochmal

Primary
FLM: "The Guide of the Perplexed of the Time"
Harris: *Nachman Krochmal: Guiding the Perplexed of the Modern Age*

Secondary
Jacobs: "Nachman Krochmal: A Guide for the Perplexed of His Era"
LB: "Chapter Two Conclusion," 48–49

Chapter 55: Samson Raphael Hirsch

Primary
Hirsch: *The Nineteen Letters on Judaism*
MFR: "Religion Allied to Progress," "The Secession of the Orthodox," "A Ser-
  mon on the Science of Judaism"

Secondary
AL: "Samson Raphael Hirsch's Defense of Judaism: The Reconciliation of Modernity and the *Mitzvot*"

C-S 2007: "Samuel Hirsch"
FL 1997: Harry Lesser, "Samson Raphael Hirsch"
LB: "Against History: Samson Raphael Hirsch and the Invention of Orthodoxy,"
 40–43

Chapter 56: Samson Raphael Hirsch

Primary
Hirsch: *The Nineteen Letters on Judaism*
MFR: "Religion Allied to Progress," "The Secession of the Orthodox," "A Sermon on the Science of Judaism"

Secondary
AL: "Samson Raphael Hirsch's Defense of Judaism: The Reconciliation of Modernity and the *Mitzvot*"
C-S 2007: "Samuel Hirsch"
FL 1997: Harry Lesser, "Samson Raphael Hirsch"
Gottlieb: "Orthodox Judaism and the Impossibility of Biblical Criticism"

Chapter 57: Israel Salanter

Primary
AL: "Epistle of Musar"

Secondary
AL: "Israel Salanter: Restoring 'Fear of Heaven' to Human Behavior"
LB: "The Reinvention of Tradition," 122–27

Chapter 58: Zvi Hirsch Kalischer

Primary
Hertzberg: "Seeking Zion"

Secondary
C-S 2007: "Zevi Hirsch Kalischer"
Goldwater: *Pioneers of Religious Zionism*: "Rabbi Zvi Hirsch Kalischer," 37–62
Ravitzky: *Messianism, Zionism, and Jewish Religious Radicalism*: "Messianism and Activism," 26–32

Chapter 59: Leon Pinsker

Primary

Hertzberg: Moses Hess, "Rome and Jerusalem"; Leo Pinsker, "Auto-Emancipation: An Appeal to His People by a Russian Jew"

Secondary

C-S 2007: "Moses Hess," "Leon Pinsker"
LB: "The Advent of the Zionist Movement," 148–51

Chapter 60: Theodor Herzl

Primary

Herzl: *The Jewish State*
Herzl: "Texts concerning Zionism: 'Altneuland' [Old New Land]"

Secondary

AL: "Theodor Herzl: A Jewish Modernist from Western Europe"
C-S 2007: "Theodor Herzl"
LB: "Herzl and the Jewish State," 152–55

Chapter 61: Ahad Ha'am (Asher Ginsberg)

Primary

MFR: "The First Zionist Congress"
Simon: "Slavery in Freedom," "Flesh and Spirit," "Priest and Prophet"

Secondary

AL: "Ahad Ha'am: A Jewish Modernist from Eastern Europe"
C-S 2007: "Ahad Ha-am"
LB: "Ahad Ha'am and Cultural Zionism," 155–60

Chapter 62: Micah Joseph Berdichevsky

Primary

Hertzberg: "Wrecking and Building," "In Two Directions," "The Question of Culture," "The Question of Our Past," "On Sanctity"

SOURCES

Secondary
LB: "Chapter Eight Conclusion," 161–62
Shapira: "Herzl, Ahad Ha'Am, and Berdichevsky: Comments on Their Nationalist Concepts"

Chapter 63: Shalom Dov Baer Schneersohn

Primary
Ravitzky: *Messianism, Zionism, and Jewish Religious Radicalism*

Secondary
Rabinowitz: "The Zionists Are Not Our Saviors"
Ravitzky: *Messianism, Zionism, and Jewish Religious Radicalism*: "Forcing the End," 14–19

Chapter 64: Hermann Cohen

Primary
Cohen: *Religion of Reason Out of the Sources of Judaism*
FLM: "Hermann Cohen, *Religion of Reason Out of the Sources of Judaism*"

Secondary
C-S 2007: "Hermann Cohen"
FL 1997: Kenneth Seeskin, "Jewish Neo-Kantianism: Hermann Cohen"
MG: Andrea Poma, "Hermann Cohen: Judaism and Critical Idealism"

Chapter 65: Hermann Cohen

Primary
Cohen: *Reason and Hope: Selections from the Jewish Writings of Hermann Cohen*: "Religion and Zionism"
FLM: "Hermann Cohen, *Religion of Reason Out of the Sources of Judaism*"
MFR: "A Debate on Zionism and Messianism"

Secondary
C-S 2007: "Hermann Cohen"
FL 1997: Kenneth Seeskin, "Jewish Neo-Kantianism: Hermann Cohen"
LB: "Cohen and Religion's Share in Reason," "Ethics and Atonement," 53–59
MG: Andrea Poma, "Hermann Cohen: Judaism and Critical Idealism"

Chapter 66: Franz Rosenzweig

Primary
Rosenzweig: *The Star of Redemption*
AL: "The Star of Redemption"
FLM: "Franz Rosenzweig, *The Star of Redemption*," "Letters to Eugen Rosenstock-Huessy"

Secondary
AL: "Franz Rosenzweig: From Alienated Existentialist to *Ba'al Teshuvah*"
C-S 2007: "Franz Rosenzweig"
FL 1997: Oliver Leaman, "Jewish Existentialism: Rosenzweig, Buber, and Soloveitchik"
MG: Peter Eli Gordon, "Franz Rosenzweig and the Philosophy of Jewish Existence"

Chapter 67: Martin Buber

Primary
Buber: *I and Thou*

Secondary
C-S 2007: "Martin Buber"
FL 1997: Oliver Leaman, "Jewish Existentialism: Rosenzweig, Buber, and Soloveitchik"
MG: Tamra Wright, "Self, Other, Text, God: The Dialogical Thought of Martin Buber"

Chapter 68: Hayim Nahman Bialik

Primary
Bialik: *Revealment and Concealment*: "Halacha and Aggadah"
MFR: "The City of Slaughter," "The Hebrew Book"

Secondary
Jewish Virtual Library: "Hayyim Nahman Bialik"
LB: "Ahad Ha'am and Cultural Zionism," 159–60
Plen: "Hayim Nahman Bialik: The Jewish National Poet"

Chapter 69: Abraham Isaac Kook

Primary

FLM: "The Lights of Penitence," "Fragments of Light: A View as to the Reasons for the Commandments"

Hertzberg: "The Land of Israel," "The War," "The Rebirth of Israel," "Lights for Rebirth"

Secondary

AL: "Abraham Isaac Kook: Mysticism and Nationalism"

Goldwater: *Pioneers of Religious Zionism*: "Rabbi Abraham Isaac Hacohen Kook"

Mirsky: *Rav Kook: Mystic in a Time of Revolution*

Polonsky: *Religious Zionism of Rav Kook*

Chapter 70: Mordecai Kaplan

Primary

AL: "From *Judaism as a Civilization*"

Kaplan: *Judaism as a Civilization: Toward a Reconstruction of American-Jewish Life*

MFR: "The Reconstruction of Judaism"

Secondary

C-S 2007: "Mordecai Kaplan"

LB: "Kaplan: From Religion to Civilization," 169–73

Samuelson: *An Introduction to Modern Jewish Philosophy*: "Mordecai Kaplan"

Chapter 71: Joseph Soloveitchik

Primary

FLM: "The Community"

Soloveitchik: *Halakhic Man*

Soloveitchik: *The Lonely Man of Faith*

Secondary

AL: "Joseph Soloveitchik: *Halachah* and Existentialism"

LB: "Soloveitchik and *The Lonely Man of Faith*," 59–64

MG: Lawrence J. Kaplan, "Joseph Soloveitchik and Halakhic Man"

Chapter 72: Leo Strauss

Primary
FLM: "The Mutual Influence of Theology and Philosophy"
Strauss: "Why We Remain Jews: Can Jewish Faith and History Still Speak to Us?"

Secondary
FL 1997: Kenneth Hart Green, "Leo Strauss"
LB: "Strauss and the Theologico-Political Predicament of Modernity," 173–78
MG: Steven B. Smith, "Leo Strauss and Modern Jewish Thought"
Portnoff: *Reason and Revelation before Historicism*: Part 2, "Strauss's Formulation of the Relationship between Reason and Revelation in Modern Thought"

Chapter 73: Leo Strauss

Primary
FLM: "The Mutual Influence of Theology and Philosophy"
Strauss: "Why We Remain Jews: Can Jewish Faith and History Still Speak to Us?"

Secondary
FL 1997: Kenneth Hart Green, "Leo Strauss"
LB: "Strauss and the Theologico-Political Predicament of Modernity," 173–78
MG: Steven B. Smith, "Leo Strauss and Modern Jewish Thought"
Portnoff: *Reason and Revelation before Historicism*: Part 2, "Strauss's Formulation of the Relationship between Reason and Revelation in Modern Thought"

Chapter 74: Emmanuel Levinas

Primary
FLM: "Hear Israel"
Levinas: *Difficult Freedom: Essays on Judaism*: "The State of Israel and the Religion of Israel"
Levinas: *Nine Talmudic Readings*

Secondary
C-S 2007: "Immanuel Levinas"
LB: "French Philosophy and Postliberalism," 100–104
MG: Richard A. Cohen, "Emmanuel Levinas: Judaism and the Primacy of the Ethical"

Chapter 75: Abraham Joshua Heschel

Primary
AL: "Depth Theology"
FLM: "On Prayer"
Heschel: *Man Is Not Alone: A Philosophy of Religion*
Heschel: *God in Search of Man*

Secondary
AL: "Abraham Joshua Heschel: Universal Hasidism"
C-S 2007: "Abraham Joshua Heschel"
MG: Leora Batnitzky, "Revelation, Language, and Commentary: From Buber to Derrida," 307–8

Chapter 76: Eliezer Berkovits

Primary
Berkovits: *God, Man, and History: A Jewish Interpretation*: "The Paradox of the Encounter," "Faith, Reason, and the Encounter," and "The God of the Encounter"
Berkovits: *Faith after the Holocaust*: "God and the Holocaust"
Berkovits: *Essential Essays on Judaism*: "The Encounter with the Divine," "Faith after the Holocaust"

Secondary
Berkovitz: *Essential Essays on Judaism*: David Hazony, "Introduction"
Jewish Virtual Library: "Eliezer Berkovitz"
MG: Berel Lang, "Evil, Suffering, and the Holocaust," 282–85

Chapter 77: Hannah Arendt

Primary
Arendt: *Eichmann in Jerusalem: A Report on the Banality of Evil*
Arendt: *The Jew as Pariah: Jewish Identity and Politics in the Modern Age*: "'Eichmann in Jerusalem': An Exchange of Letters between Gershom Scholem and Hannah Arendt," 240–51

Secondary
C-S 2007: "Hannah Arendt"
Passerin d'Entreves: "Hannah Arendt"

Chapter 78: Emil Fackenheim

Primary

Fackenheim: *God's Presence in History: Jewish Affirmations and Philosophical Reflections*

FLM: "Emil Fackenheim: The Jewish Bible after the Holocaust: A Re-Reading"

Secondary

LB: "The Challenge of Post-Holocaust Jewish Thought," 92–95

MG: Michael L. Morgan, "Emil Fackenheim, the Holocaust, and Philosophy"

Portnoff: *Reason and Revelation before Historicism*: Part 3, "Fackenheim's Formulation of the Relationship between Philosophy and Revelatory Theology"

Samuelson: *An Introduction to Modern Jewish Philosophy*: "Emil Fackenheim and Contemporary Jewish Philosophy"

Chapter 79: Yeshayahu Leibowitz

Primary

FLM: "Fear of God in the Book of Job"

Leibowitz: *Judaism, Human Values, and the Jewish State*

Neusner and Avery-Peck: "On Science and Jewish Religion"

Shulchan Aruch, "Laws of Early Rising," *Halacha* 1

The Abravanel quote is given in Leibowitz, "*Lishmah* and Not-*Lishmah*," in *Judaism, Human Values, and the Jewish State*, 72

Secondary

LB: "Leibowitz: Jewish Religion and the Jewish State," 64–68

Rynhold: "Yeshayahu Leibowitz"

Chapter 80: Hans Jonas

Primary

Jonas: *Mortality and Morality: A Search for the Good after Auschwitz*: "The Concept of God after Auschwitz"

Secondary

Tirosh-Samuelson and Wiese: *The Legacy of Hans Jonas: Judaism and the Phenomenon of Life*

Wiese: *The Life and Thought of Hans Jonas: Jewish Dimensions*

Chapter 81: Judith Plaskow

Primary

Plaskow: *Standing Again at Sinai: Judaism from a Feminist Perspective*

Secondary

Adler: "Judith Plaskow"

Frankenberry: "Feminist Philosophy of Religion"

Tirosh-Samuelson: *Women and Gender in Jewish Philosophy*

Chapter 82: Michael Wyschogrod

Primary

Wyschogrod: *The Body of Faith: God in the People Israel*

Secondary

LB: "Michael Wyschogrod and the Challenge of God's Scandalous Love"

Soloveichik: "God's First Love: The Theology of Michael Wyschogrod."

Chapter 83: Eugene Borowitz

Primary

Borowitz: *Renewing the Covenant: A Theology for the Postmodern Jew*

Borowitz: "Crisis Theology and the Jewish Community"

Borowitz: *A Life of Jewish Learning: In Search of a Theology of Judaism*

FLM: "The Autonomous Jewish Self"

Secondary

Jewish Virtual Library: "Eugene B. Borowitz"

Ochs: *Reviewing the Covenant: Eugene B. Borowitz and the Postmodern Renewal of Jewish Theology*

Chapter 84: Rachel Adler

Primary

Adler: *Engendering Judaism: An Inclusive Theology and Ethics*

Adler: "The Jew Who Wasn't There: *Halacha* and the Jewish Woman"

Secondary

Ellenson: *After Emancipation: Jewish Religious Responses to Modernity*: "To Re-shape the World: Interpretation, Renewal, and Feminist Approaches to Jewish Law and Legal Ruling in America and Israel"

Frankenberry: "Feminist Philosophy of Religion"
Tirosh-Samuelson: *Women and Gender in Jewish Philosophy*

Chapter 85: Tamar Ross

Primary
Ross: *Expanding the Palace of Torah: Orthodoxy and Feminism*
Ross: "Orthodoxy and the Challenge of Biblical Criticism: Reflections on the Importance of Asking the Right Question"
Maimonides's quote comes from *The Guide for the Perplexed*, II.25

Secondary
Ellenson: *After Emancipation: Jewish Religious Responses to Modernity*: "To Reshape the World: Interpretation, Renewal, and Feminist Approaches to Jewish Law and Legal Ruling in America and Israel"
Frankenberry: "Feminist Philosophy of Religion"
Tirosh-Samuelson: *Women and Gender in Jewish Philosophy*

Chapter 86: Shimon Gershon Rosenberg (Shagar)

Primary
Rosenberg: *Faith Shattered and Restored: Judaism in the Postmodern Age*

Secondary
Jotkowitz: "'And Now the Child Will Ask': The Post-Modern Theology of Rav Shagar"
Rosenberg: *Faith Shattered and Restored: Judaism in the Postmodern Age*: Zohar Maor, "Introduction"

Chapter 87: Samuel Lebens

Primary
Lebens: "Hassidic Idealism: Kurt Vonnegut and the Creator of the Universe"

Bibliography

Abulafia, Abraham. *Ohr Ha-Sechel: Light of the Intellect.* Providence University, 2008.

Adler, Rachel. *Engendering Judaism: An Inclusive Theology and Ethics.* Philadelphia, PA: Jewish Publication Society, 1998.

———. "The Jew Who Wasn't There: *Halacha* and the Jewish Woman." *Response: A Contemporary Jewish Review* (Summer 1973). https://jwa.org/sites/jwa.org/files/jwa001c.pdf (accessed December 12, 2017).

———. "Judith Plaskow." Jewish Women's Archive. https://jwa.org/encyclopedia/article/plaskow-judith (accessed December 11, 2017).

Arendt, Hannah. *Eichmann in Jerusalem: A Report on the Banality of Evil.* New York: Schocken Books, 1963.

———. *The Jew as Pariah: Jewish Identity and Politics in the Modern Age.* Edited by Ron Feldman. New York: Grove Press, 1978.

Batnitzky, Leora. *How Judaism Became a Religion: An Introduction to Modern Jewish Thought.* Princeton, NJ: Princeton University Press, 2011.

———. "Michael Wyschogrod and the Challenge of God's Scandalous Love." *Jewish Review of Books* (Spring 2016). https://jewishreviewofbooks.com/articles/2003/michael-wyschogrod-and-the-challenge-of-gods-scandalous-love (accessed December 12, 2017).

Ben Samuel, Hillel. "The Rewards of the Soul." Edited by J. B. Sermoneta. Jerusalem, 1981.

Berg, Rabbi Michael, ed. *The Zohar.* Commentary by Yehuda Ashlag. 23 vols. 2nd ed. Los Angeles: Kabbalah Centre International, 2003.

Berg, Rav P. S. *The Essential Zohar: The Source of Kabbalistic Wisdom*. New York: Three Rivers Press, 2002.

Berkovits, Eliezer. *Essential Essays on Judaism*. Edited by David Hazony. Jerusalem: Shalem Press, 2002.

———. *Faith after the Holocaust*. New York: Ktav, 1973.

———. *God, Man, and History: A Jewish Interpretation*. New York: Jonathan David, 1959.

Bialik, Hayim Nachman. *Revealment and Concealment*. Jerusalem: Ibis Editions, 2000.

Borovaya, Olga. *The Beginnings of Ladino Literature: Moses Almosnino and His Readers*. Indianapolis: Indiana University Press, 2017.

Borowitz, Eugene B. "Crisis Theology and the Jewish Community." *Commentary* (July 1, 1961). https://www.commentarymagazine.com/articles/crisis-theology-the-jewish-community (accessed December 12, 2017).

———. *A Life of Jewish Learning: In Search of a Theology of Judaism*. New York: Hunter College of the City University of New York, 2000.

———. *Renewing the Covenant: A Theology for the Postmodern Jew*. Philadelphia, PA: Jewish Publication Society, 1991.

Buber, Martin. *I and Thou*. Translated by Walter Kaufmann. 1923. Reprint, New York: Charles Scribner's Sons, 1970.

Cohen, Hermann. *Reason and Hope: Selections from the Jewish Writings of Hermann Cohen*. Translated by Eva Jospe. New York: W. W. Norton, 1971.

———. *Religion of Reason: Out of the Sources of Judaism*. Translated by Simon Kaplan. 1919. Reprint, New York: Frederick Ungar Publishing, 1972.

Cohn-Sherbok, Dan. *Fifty Key Jewish Thinkers*. 2nd ed., 1997. Reprint, New York: Routledge, 2007.

———. *Medieval Jewish Philosophy*. Surrey, UK: Curzon, 1996.

Ellenson, David. *After Emancipation: Jewish Religious Responses to Modernity*. Cincinnati, OH: Hebrew Union College Press, 2004.

———. "To Reshape the World: Interpretation, Renewal, and Feminist Approaches to Jewish Law and Legal Ruling in America and Israel." *Journal of Jewish Ethics* 2, no. 2 (2016): 38–63.

Fackenheim, Emil L. *God's Presence in History: Jewish Affirmations and Philosophical Reflections*. 1970. Reprint, Northvale, NJ: Jason Aronson, 1997.

Feldman, Seymour. *Gersonides: Judaism within the Limits of Reason*. Oxford: The Littman Library of Jewish Civilization, 2010.

Fontaine, Resianne. "Abraham Ibn Daud." *Stanford Encyclopedia of Philosophy* (Spring 2015 edition), edited by Edward N. Zalta. https://plato.stanford.edu/entries/abraham-daud (accessed December 5, 2017).

Frank, Daniel, and Oliver Leaman, eds. *The Cambridge Companion to Medieval Jewish Philosophy*. Cambridge: Cambridge University Press, 2003.

———. *Routledge History of Jewish Philosophy*. London: Routledge, 1997.

Frank, Daniel, Oliver Leaman, and Charles Manekin, eds. *The Jewish Philosophy Reader*. London: Routledge, 2000.

Frankel, Zecharias. *The Ways of the Mishna (Darchei Ha-Mishna)*. Leipzig, 1859.

Frankenberry, Nancy. "Feminist Philosophy of Religion." *Stanford Encyclopedia of Philosophy* (Winter 2011 edition), edited by Edward N. Zalta. https://plato.stanford.edu/entries/feminist-religion (accessed December 11, 2017).

Geiger, Abraham. *Judaism and Its History: In Two Parts*. 1871. Reprint, Lanham, MD: University Press of America, 1985.

Gersonides (Levi Ben Gerson). *The Wars of the Lord*. Translated by Seymour Feldman. 3 vols. Philadelphia, PA: Jewish Publication Society, 1999.

Goldwater, Raymond. *Pioneers of Religious Zionism*. Brooklyn: Lambda Publishers, 2009.

Goodman, Micah. *Maimonides and the Book That Changed Judaism: Secrets of "The Guide for the Perplexed."* Translated by Y. Sinclair. 2010. Reprint, Philadelphia, PA: Jewish Publication Society, 2015.

Gottlieb, Michah. "Orthodox Judaism and the Impossibility of Biblical Criticism." *Lehrhaus* (August 10, 2017). http://www.thelehrhaus.com/commentary-short-articles/2017/8/7/orthodox-judaism-and-the-impossibility-of-biblical-criticism (accessed December 10, 2017).

Graetz, Heinrich. *History of the Jews (Geschichte der Juden)*. 11 vols. Leipzig, 1853–70.

Guttmann, Julius. *Philosophies of Judaism: A History of Jewish Philosophy from Biblical Times to Franz Rosenzweig*. 1964. Reprint, New York: Schocken Books, 1973.

Halevi, Judah. *The Kuzari: An Argument for the Faith of Israel*. Edited by Henry Slonimsky. Translated by Hartwig Hirschfeld. New York: Schocken Books, 1964.

Harris, Jay M. *Nachman Krochmal: Guiding the Perplexed of the Modern Age*. 1851. Reprint, New York: New York University Press, 1993.

Hecht, Jonathan, ed. and trans. "The Polemical Exchange between Isaac Pollegar and Abner of Burgos/Alfonso of Valladolid according to Parma MS 2440 'Iggeret Teshuvat Apikoros' and 'Teshuvot la-Meharef.'" PhD diss., New York University, 1993.

Hertzberg, Arthur. *The Zionist Idea: A Historical Analysis and Reader*. Philadelphia, PA: Jewish Publication Society, 1997.

Herzl, Theodor. *The Jewish State*. 1896. Reprint, Mineola, NY: Dover Publications, 1988.

———. "Texts concerning Zionism: 'Altneuland' [Old New Land]." 1902. Translated by D. S. Blondheim. Jewish Virtual Library. http://www.jewishvir tuallibrary.org/quot-altneuland-quot-theodor-herzl (accessed December 11, 2017).

Heschel, Abraham Joshua. *God in Search of Man*. New York: Farrar, Straus & Giroux, 1955.

———. *Man Is Not Alone: A Philosophy of Religion*. New York: Farrar, Straus & Giroux, 1951.

Hess, Moses. *Rome and Jerusalem: The Last National Question*. Leipzig, 1862.

Hirsch, Samson Raphael. *The Nineteen Letters on Judaism*. Translated by Bernard Drachman. 1836. Reprint, New York: Philipp Feldheim, 1960.

Hiscott, William. "Haskalah Protagonists: Saul Ascher—Biography." Haskala. http://www.haskala.net/en/haskala-protagonists/saul-ascher/biography.html (accessed December 10, 2017).

Horovitz, Saul, ed. *Joseph Ibn Saddiq: The Microcosm*. Translated by Jacob Haberman. Madison, NJ: Fairleigh Dickinson University Press, 2003.

Husik, Isaac. *A History of Medieval Jewish Philosophy*. New York: Macmillan, 1918.

Hyman, Arthur, and James Walsh, eds. *Philosophy in the Middle Ages*. 2nd ed. Indianapolis: Hackett, 1984.

Idel, Moshe. *The Mystical Experience in Abraham Abulafia*. Translated by Jonathan Chipman. Albany: State University of New York Press, 1988.

Jacobs, Louis. "Nachman Krochmal: A Guide for the Perplexed of His Era." *My Jewish Learning*. https://www.myjewishlearning.com/article/nachman-kroch mal-a-guide-for-the-perplexed-of-his-era (accessed December 10, 2017).

Jewish Virtual Library. "Eliezer Berkovitz." http://www.jewishvirtuallibrary.org/eliezer-berkovitz (accessed December 11, 2017).

———. "Encyclopedia Judaica: Disputation of Barcelona." http://www.jewishvir tuallibrary.org/disputation-of-barcelona (accessed December 11, 2017).

———. "Eugene B. Borowitz." http://www.jewishvirtuallibrary.org/eugene-b -borowitz (accessed December 12, 2017).

———. "Hayyim Nahman Bialik." http://www.jewishvirtuallibrary.org/hayyim -nahman-bialik (accessed December 11, 2017).

———. "Hillel Ben Samuel." http://www.jewishvirtuallibrary.org/hillel-ben -samuel (accessed December 10, 2017).

Jonas, Hans. *Mortality and Morality: A Search for the Good after Auschwitz*. Edited by Lawrence Vogel. Evanston, IL: Northwestern University Press, 1996.

Jotkowitz, Alan. "'And Now the Child Will Ask': The Post-Modern Theology of Rav Shagar." *Tradition: A Journal of Orthodox Jewish Thought* 45, no. 2 (Summer 2012): 49–66.

Kaplan, Mordecai. *Judaism as a Civilization: Toward a Reconstruction of American-Jewish Life.* 1934. Reprint, Philadelphia, PA: Jewish Publication Society, 2010.

Kirsch, Adam. *The People and the Books: 18 Classics of Jewish Literature.* New York: W. W. Norton, 2016.

Kohler, Kaufmann. "Aaron Ben Elijah, the Younger, of Nicomedia." *Jewish Encyclopedia* (1906). http://www.jewishencyclopedia.com/articles/33-aaron-ben -elijah-the-younger-of-nicomedia (accessed December 8, 2017).

Lebens, Samuel. "Hassidic Idealism: Kurt Vonnegut and the Creator of the Universe." In *Idealism: New Essays in Metaphysics,* edited by T. Goldschmidt and K. L. Pearce, 158–77. Oxford: Oxford University Press, 2018.

Leibowitz, Yeshayahu. *Judaism, Human Values, and the Jewish State.* Edited by Eliezer Goldman. Cambridge, MA: Harvard University Press, 1992.

Levenson, Alan T. *An Introduction to Modern Jewish Thinkers: From Spinoza to Soloveitchik.* 2nd ed. Lanham, MD: Rowman & Littlefield, 2006.

Levin, Leonard, and R. David Walker. "Isaac Israeli." *Stanford Encyclopedia of Philosophy* (Spring 2013 edition), edited by Edward N. Zalta. https://plato .stanford.edu/entries/israeli (accessed December 5, 2017).

Levinas, Emmanuel. *Difficult Freedom: Essays on Judaism.* Translated by Sean Hand. 1963. Reprint, Baltimore, MD: Johns Hopkins University Press, 1990.

———. *Nine Talmudic Readings.* Translated by Annette Aronowicz. 1968. Reprint, Bloomington: Indiana University Press, 1990.

Lewy, Hans, Alexander Altmann, and Isaak Heinemann, eds. *Three Jewish Philosophers: Philo, Saadya Gaon, Yehudah Halevi.* 3rd ed. New Milford, CT: Toby Press, 2006.

Maimon, Solomon. *An Autobiography.* Translated by J. Clark Murray. Champaign: University of Illinois Press, 2001.

Maimonides, Moses. *The Guide for the Perplexed.* 2nd ed. Translated by M. Friedländer. 1904. Reprint, New York: Dover Publications, 1956.

Manekin, Charles, ed. *Medieval Jewish Philosophical Writings.* Cambridge: Cambridge University Press, 2007.

Mansoor, Menahem, ed. and trans. *Bahya Ibn Pakuda: The Book of Direction to the Duties of the Heart.* Liverpool, UK: Littman Library of Jewish Civilization, 1973.

Mendes-Flohr, Paul, and Jehuda Reinharz, eds. *The Jew in the Modern World: A Documentary History.* 3rd ed. 1980. Reprint, Oxford, UK: Oxford University Press, 2011.

Meyer, Michael A. *Response to Modernity: A History of the Reform Movement.* Detroit, MI: Wayne State University Press, 1988.

Mirsky, Yehudah. *Rav Kook: Mystic in a Time of Revolution.* New Haven, CT: Yale University Press, 2014.

Morgan, Michael L., and Peter Eli Gordon. *The Cambridge Companion to Modern Jewish Philosophy.* Cambridge: Cambridge University Press, 2007.

Nachmanides (Ramban). *Writings of the Ramban/Nachmanides.* Translated and annotated by Charles B. Chavel. New York: Judaica Press, 2010.

Nadler, Steven. "Baruch Spinoza." *Stanford Encyclopedia of Philosophy* (Fall 2016 edition), edited by Edward N. Zalta. https://plato.stanford.edu/entries/spinoza (accessed December 10, 2017).

Nadler, Steven, and Tamar Rudavsky, eds. *The Cambridge History of Jewish Philosophy: From Antiquity through the Seventeenth Century.* Cambridge: Cambridge University Press, 2009.

Neusner, Jacob, and Alan J. Avery-Peck. *The Blackwell Reader in Judaism.* Oxford: Blackwell Publishers, 2001.

Newman, Aryeh. "The Centrality of Eretz Yisrael in Nachmanides." *Tradition* 10, no. 1 (1968): 21–30.

Ochs, Peter, ed. *Reviewing the Covenant: Eugene B. Borowitz and the Postmodern Renewal of Jewish Theology.* Albany: State University of New York Press, 2000.

Orthodox Union Staff. "Rabbi Moshe Sofer." Orthodox Union. June 14, 2006. https://www.ou.org/judaism-101/bios/leaders-in-the-diaspora/rabbi-moshe -sofer-the-chasam-sofer (accessed December 10, 2017).

Passerin d'Entreves, Maurizio. "Hannah Arendt." *Stanford Encyclopedia of Philosophy* (Winter 2016 edition), edited by Edward N. Zalta. https://plato .stanford.edu/entries/arendt (accessed December 11, 2017).

Pessin, Sarah. "Solomon Ibn Gabirol." *Stanford Encyclopedia of Philosophy* (Winter 2016 edition), edited by Edward N. Zalta. https://plato.stanford.edu/ entries/ibn-gabirol (accessed December 5, 2017).

Plaskow, Judith. *Standing Again at Sinai: Judaism from a Feminist Perspective.* San Francisco: HarperCollins, 1990.

Plen, Matt. "Hayim Nahman Bialik: The Jewish National Poet." *My Jewish Learning.* https://www.myjewishlearning.com/article/hayim-nahman-bialik (accessed December 11, 2017).

Pollegar, Isaac. *Sepher Ezer Ha-Dat: The Support of the Faith.* Andesite Press, 2015.

Polonsky, Pinchas. *Religious Zionism of Rav Kook.* Translated by Lise Brody. Newton, MA: Machanaim USA, 2009.

Portnoff, Sharon. *Reason and Revelation before Historicism.* Toronto: University of Toronto Press, 2011.

Rabinowitz, Zadok Hacohen. "The Zionists Are Not Our Saviors" (c. 1900). Reprinted in Mendes-Flohr and Reinharz, *The Jew in the Modern World,* 608–10.

Ravitzky, Aviezer. *Messianism, Zionism, and Jewish Religious Radicalism.* Translated by Michael Swirsky and Jonathan Chipman. Chicago, 1993. Reprint, University of Chicago Press, 1996.

Rosenberg, Shimon Gershon. *Faith Shattered and Restored: Judaism in the Post-modern Age*. Edited by Zohar Maor. Translated by Elie Leshem. Jerusalem: Koren Publishers, 2017.

Rosenzweig, Franz. *The Star of Redemption*. Translated by William W. Hallo. 1921. Reprint, Notre Dame, IN: Notre Dame Press, 1985.

Ross, Jacob. "Elijah Delmedigo." *Stanford Encyclopedia of Philosophy* (Summer 2016 edition), edited by Edward N. Zalta. https://plato.stanford.edu/entries/delmedigo/#4 (accessed December 10, 2017).

Ross, Tamar. *Expanding the Palace of Torah: Orthodoxy and Feminism*. Waltham, MA: Brandeis University Press, 2004.

———. "Orthodoxy and the Challenge of Biblical Criticism: Reflections on the Importance of Asking the Right Question." *The Torah: A Historical and Contextual Approach*. 2014. http://thetorah.com/the-challenge-of-biblical -criticism (accessed December 12, 2017).

Roth, Cecil. "The Disputation of Barcelona (1263)." *Harvard Theological Review* 43, no. 2 (April 1950): 117–44.

Rynhold, Daniel. "Yeshayahu Leibowitz." *Stanford Encyclopedia of Philosophy* (Summer 2011 edition), edited by Edward N. Zalta. https://plato.stanford .edu/entries/leibowitz-yeshayahu (accessed December 11, 2017).

Samuelson, Norbert M. *An Introduction to Modern Jewish Philosophy*. Albany: State University of New York Press, 1989.

Scholem, Gershom, ed. *Zohar: The Book of Splendor: Basic Readings from the Kabbalah*. New York: Schocken Books, 1949/1977.

Sforno, Obadiah. *Commentary on the Torah*. Translated and edited by Raphael Pelcovitz. Brooklyn: Mesorah Publications, 1997.

Shapira, Anita. "Herzl, Ahad Ha'Am, and Berdichevsky: Comments on Their Nationalist Concepts." *Jewish History* 4, no. 2 (Fall 1990): 59–69.

Shapiro, Marc B. *Changing the Immutable: How Orthodox Judaism Rewrites Its History*. Portland, OR: Littman Library of Jewish Civilization, 2015.

Shulchan Aruch. "Laws of Early Rising." *Halacha* 1. https://en.wikisource.org/wiki/Translation:Likutei_Halakhot/Orach_Chayim (accessed April 9, 2018).

Simon, Leon, ed. and trans. *Selected Essays of Ahad Ha-'Am*. 1912. Reprint, New York: Atheneum, 1981.

Singer, Isidore, and Emil G. Hirsch. "Leopold Zunz." *Jewish Encyclopedia* (1906). http://www.jewishencyclopedia.com/articles/15299-zunz-leopold (accessed December 10, 2017).

Solomon, Avi, trans. *Abraham Abulafia: Meditations on the Divine Name*. Amazon Digital Services. 2012. https://www.amazon.com/Abraham-Abulafia-Meditations-Divine-Name-ebook/dp/B003YUCR1S/ref=sr_1_2?ie=UTF8&qid=1512590297&sr=8-2&keywords=abulafia (accessed December 5, 2017).

Soloveitchik, Joseph B. *The Lonely Man of Faith*. 1965. Reprint, New York: Doubleday, 1992.

———. *Halakhic Man*. Translated by Lawrence Kaplan. Philadelphia, PA: Jewish Publication Society of America, 1983.

Soloveichik, Meir Y. "God's First Love: The Theology of Michael Wyschogrod." *First Things*. November, 2009. https://www.firstthings.com/article/2009/11/gods-first-love-the-theology-of-michael-wyschogrod (accessed December 12, 2017).

Spinoza, Baruch. *Ethics*. Parts I and II. Translated by G. H. R. Parkinson. Oxford: Oxford University Press, 2000.

———. *Short Treatise on God, Man, and His Well-Being*. Translated by A. Wolf. London: Adam and Charles Black, 1910.

Strauss, Leo. "Why We Remain Jews: Can Jewish Faith and History Still Speak to Us?" (1962). In *Jewish Philosophy and the Crisis of Modernity: Essays and Lectures in Modern Jewish Thought*, ed. Kenneth Hart Green. Albany: State University of New York Press, 1997.

Tirosh-Samuelson, Hava, ed. *Women and Gender in Jewish Philosophy*. Bloomington: Indiana University Press, 2004.

Tirosh-Samuelson, Hava and Christian Wiese, eds. *The Legacy of Hans Jonas: Judaism and the Phenomenon of Life*. Leiden, Netherlands: Brill, 2008.

Wiese, Christian. *The Life and Thought of Hans Jonas: Jewish Dimensions*. Waltham, MA: Brandeis University Press, 2010.

Weiss, Gershon, ed. *Abraham Ibn Daud: The Exalted Faith*. Translated by Norbert M. Samuelson and Gershon Weiss. Madison, NJ: Fairleigh Dickinson University Press, 1987.

Wigoder, Geoffrey, ed. and trans. *Abraham Bar-Hayya: Meditation of the Sad Soul*. London: Routledge & Kegan-Paul, Littman Library of Jewish Civilization, 1969.

Wyschogrod, Michael. *The Body of Faith: God in the People Israel*. 1983. Reprint, Lanham, MD: Rowman & Littlefield, 1996.

Yaffe, Martin D., trans. *Spinoza's Theologico-Political Treatise*. Newburyport, MA: Focus Publishing, 2004.

Yonge, C. D., trans. *The Works of Philo: New Updated Edition*. Peabody, MA: Hendrickson Publishers, 1993.

Index